Understanding Competitive Advantage

Fredrik Nilsson · Birger Rapp

Understanding Competitive Advantage

The Importance of Strategic Congruence
and Integrated Control

With 44 Figures

 Springer

Professor Dr. Fredrik Nilsson
Professor Dr. Birger Rapp
EIS/IDA
Linköping University
581 83 Linköping
Sweden
freni@ida.liu.se
birra@ida.liu.se

ISBN 3-540-40872-X Springer Berlin Heidelberg New York

Cataloging-in-Publication Data
Library of Congress Control Number: 2004110171

Springer is a part of Springer Science+Business Media

springeronline.com

© Springer Berlin · Heidelberg 2005
Printed in Germany

Hardcover-Design: Erich Kirchner, Heidelberg

SPIN 10956892   42/3130-5 4 3 2 1 0 - Printed on acid-free paper

Preface

The link between strategies and control systems – and how it ultimately affects the competitiveness of firms – is an area that is attracting the attention of practitioners and scholars. There is a need to discuss which combinations of strategies and control systems can be assumed to contribute to competitive strength. In this book we have chosen to highlight the role of management control and manufacturing control in this respect. For a long time these two types of control systems were regarded as more or less separate subjects of research and study. However, the differences between management control and manufacturing control are diminishing, a tendency that we support. The book is written in this spirit of approval.

The models and hypotheses advanced in the book were developed over a long period of time. They are based on research and have been published and otherwise presented in a variety of different circumstances (see, for example, Jansson et al., 2000; Kald et al., 2000; Nilsson, 1994, 1997, 2002; Rapp et al., 2000). Our colleagues have stimulated our thinking and have contributed to further refinement of the thoughts presented in the book. We would like to thank Professor Leif Appelgren, Professor Thomas Falk, Professor Nils-Göran Olve, Professor Rolf Rundfelt, Professor Bengt Savén, Associate professor Vivian Vimarlund and Assistant professor Alf Westelius for their valuable comments and inspiration.

Our interaction with graduate students at our department has also helped to make this a better book. Many thanks to Petter Ahlström, Linda Askenäs, Fredrika Berglund, Åse Bäckström, Magnus Kald, Andreas Käll, Carl-Johan Petri and Stefan Svarén. We would also like to thank Associate Professor Jan Lindvall and the graduate students in the "Modern Management Control Systems" course, who critically read an earlier draft of the manuscript. A previous draft has also been used as course literature at the University of Gotland. We would like to thank these students for all their comments, which have contributed to the clarity of the message in this book. Finally, we wish to express our gratitude to Dr. Werner A. Mueller at Springer-Verlag GmbH & Co. KG for publishing the book. Åsa Ericson has done an impressive job in the final preparation for publication. Richard Wathen deserves a special word of thanks for his prompt and efficient language review of several manuscripts.

Our ambition is continue to develop the models and hypotheses presented in the book. We would highly appreciate your recommendations and thoughts about it. Your views on the content would be welcome, as would your calling our attention to any specific error or omission. If you have any comments, please contact Professor Fredrik Nilsson or Professor Birger Rapp at Economic Information Systems, Department of Computer and Information Science, Linköping University, SE-581 83 Linköping, Sweden. E-mail: freni@ida.liu.se or birra@ida.liu.se.

Linköping, Sweden

May 2004

Fredrik Nilsson
Birger Rapp

Contents

Prologue

Today's firms face the challenge of designing and using new strategies and control systems to maintain existing competitive advantages and to create new ones. In this book, a framework for addressing this challenge is developed from theories, as well as practical experience, in the fields of strategy, management control and manufacturing control.

1 Introduction

This book provides an analysis of ways for the individual firm to create competitive advantage on its own market. Our theoretical starting-point is that the alignment of strategies and control systems affects the firm's chances of successfully positioning itself in its chosen arena of competition. The firm is in a better position to concentrate on activities that create value for the customer if its strategies and control systems are mutually consistent and adapted to expected external demands. This book is thus a contribution to the literature that treats competitive advantage on the basis of the match between the environment and internal resources. Our ambition has been to provide additional knowledge in the area through a comprehensive discussion on co-ordination and integration of strategies and control systems. This chapter is intended to introduce the reader to the theories and basic concepts considered in the book.

The Importance of Strategies and Control Systems

To understand how competitive advantage is created is critical to the development of a firm. In the long run, inadequate knowledge of the factors affecting business competitiveness can have repercussions on the economy of entire countries. An example is provided by Hayes and Abernathy in their paper for the *Harvard Business Review* entitled "Managing our Way to Economic Decline" (Hayes and Abernathy, 1980). The authors discuss extensively the reasons why American industry lost its competitive advantage during the 1970's. From their own experience as researchers and consultants, one of their conclusions was that American firms at that time were deficient in strategic planning and follow-up. The explanation was that senior executives, who often had backgrounds in finance and accounting, lacked adequate knowledge of their business at the operational level. Consequently, strategic planning was far too general and probably failed to consider the complex relationships between different organizational levels. Follow-up, or the evaluation of performance in relation to strategies, tended to have a similar focus. According to the authors, there was heavy dependence on short-term financial measures like return on investment (ROI). Although long-range planning was abandoned at many companies in the early 1970's, the formulation of strategies remained largely an activity for top management. Thus, the link between high-level strategy and tactical and operational decision-making was tenuous.[1]

In many respects, the article by Hayes and Abernathy is still relevant today. An ever-larger number of Western firms are now finding it increasingly difficult to maintain their competitive strength. With globalization, firms are confronted with new arenas of competition, as well as new demands: a broader product range, higher quality, more reliable delivery, and lower prices (Cooper, 1996). To improve their responsiveness to these kinds of requirements, many firms have tried to make their organizations more flexible and adaptable. Seeking to come closer to their markets and customers, they have resorted to management by objectives and highly decentralized decision-making (Dent, 1996). By comparison with the situation described by Hayes and Abernathy, there was a shift in the 1980's and 1990's from more "detached" strategic planning to greater emphasis on the tactical and operational levels (cf. Johnson, 1992).

In cases where the focus on tactical and operational planning and follow-up has been carried too far, however, there is a danger that corporate activities will be inadequately co-ordinated. This shortcoming is often evidenced by ill-considered changes in corporate, business, and manufacturing strategies. For example, many well-known companies have been forced to make abrupt adjustments like drastically downsizing money-losing units within their core businesses. These firms are often characterized by far-reaching decentralization and a very large number of fairly small business units. In such circumstances, it is very difficult to achieve consistency among strategies and control systems and to assure that they are adapted to expected external demands.[2] One major challenge is thus to grant business units sufficient freedom in tactical and operational decision-making while maintaining well-functioning overall co-ordination of different corporate activities.

Bridging Economic Theory and Management Practice

One perspective on the creation of competitive advantage is found in research based on economic theory. Studies of this type are frequently devoted to explaining the effect of declining competitiveness on the development of national economies. Here, interest-rate levels, and the government budget balance are examples of conditions considered to determine a country's competitive strength. The success of a country in a specific industry is explained in terms of production factors like labor and natural resources (Porter, 1996, p. 155 ff). However, some economists maintain that these theories are not sufficiently sophisticated to explain clearly how competitiveness develops over time. One of these scholars is Porter (ibid, p. 161), who has contended that instead of focusing on the economy as a whole, we must analyze and understand industries and their different segments. From his perspective, upgrading national productivity results from the efforts of thousands of firms to achieve competitive advantage in their industry. In this context, and according to Porter's reasoning , it is especially important to analyze the rivalry among existing firms, the threat of new entrants, the threat of substitute products and services, the bargaining power of suppliers, and the bargaining power of purchasers. This five-force framework, introduced by Porter in the 1980's (Porter, 1980, p. 4 ff), was intended to help managers to analyze different industries in terms of competition level and profit potential. For corporate management it is especially important to understand how the forces in the framework affect each and every business unit, in order to formulate a strategy that successfully positions the products on the markets chosen.[3]

However, to comprehend adequately what determines the competitiveness of the individual firm, one needs an even broader frame of reference. Porter (1985, p. 33 ff) argues that it is also necessary to examine the internal structures[4] of the firm and to eliminate activities that do not create value. For the configuration of the firm's value chain determines what opportunities will be available to the firm in positioning its services and products[5] on the market. Thus, if a firm is seeking a low-cost position (i.e. a cost-leadership strategy), quite different activities are brought into focus than if it is trying to establish its products as unique (i.e. a differentiation strategy). According to Porter (ibid, p. 11), management must therefore choose a clear – and preferably unique – strategy and then ensure that this strategy is reflected in the configuration of the value chain. If management proceeds in this fashion, they should be able to create a position which will enable the firm to achieve a good return even when the industry structure is not favorable (ibid, p. 3). By not limiting the discussion to the effects of industry structure on competitiveness, but also examining ways for an individual firm to compete successfully by adapting its strategies and structures, Porter has succeeded in bridging the gap between economic theory and management practice (cf. Rumelt et al., 1994). One of his contributions in this regard is highlighting the importance for a firm of establishing and maintaining a match between external variables (the environment) and internal variables (the structure) (Venkatraman and Camillus, 1984; Nath and Suharshan, 1994).

Matching Environment and Internal Structures

One central assumption in this book is that firms affect, and are affected by, their environment (cf. Venkatraman and Camillus, 1984).[6] In discussing the matching of environment and internal structures, we have been influenced by so-called contingency theory. Basically, this theory holds that "there is no one best way of organizing. The appropriate form depends on the kind of task or environment with which one is dealing" (Morgan, 1986, p. 49). For example, a form of organization based on centralized decision-making is not very appropriate in a turbulent environment with rapidly shifting demand.[7] The internal structures of the firm – organization, control systems and processes – must therefore be adapted to the external conditions under which the firm operates (Chandler, 1962).[8] We have assumed that the firm's environment affects the design and use of its internal structures; however, that influence is not exerted directly, but through the strategy formulated by management (Archer and Otley, 1991). This assumption is based on our view of strategy as the result of a deliberate choice, in which management seeks to match the environment to the internal structures of the firm (cf. Venkatraman and Camillus, 1984; Nath and Sudharshan, 1994). In many earlier contingency-theory studies, by contrast, the environment was considered to have a direct effect on the internal structures of the firm (see, for example, Burns and Stalker, 1961; Lawrence and Lorsch, 1967). According to Chapman (1997), the reason for this assumption was that strategy was difficult to describe since accepted typologies were lacking.

The prevailing view among many researchers in the field of strategy is that management is in a position to make strategic choices. It does not necessarily follow, however, that all strategies are solely a result of management intentions. Mintzberg and Waters (1985, p. 257) distinguish: "deliberate strategies – realized as intended – from emergent strategies – patterns of consistencies realized despite, or in the absence of, intentions." Thus, according to Mintzberg and Waters, a change of strategy may be planned, but it may also be the result of an emergent strategy. In almost all cases, a realized strategy is probably a combination of the two, i. e., of deliberate and emergent strategies. We therefore assume that management, at least to some extent, can influence whether the firm will operate in a turbulent or a stable environment. This standpoint, however, does not exclude the existence of situations where strategies can be imposed upon the firm. In their article, Mintzberg and Waters discuss this type of situation, where the firm is virtually forced by its environment to undertake a number of activities that in combination have major strategic significance. According to Mintzberg and Waters (1985), the clearest case is one in which a firm is compelled by an influential outside individual or group to follow a particular strategy. In one example, taken from Mintzberg's and Waters' article, a Canadian government minister gave Air Canada little choice but to buy a certain type of aircraft. The authors seem to view this type of strong direct influence as relatively rare; more often, the business environment may limit what the firm and its management can actually accomplish.

The extent of the strategic changes that management can bring about is also dependent on the time frame selected. The assumption in this book is that a firm's fundamental strategy is stable in the short run.[9] The reason is that the alignment of the environment, strategy, and internal structures requires comprehensive and relatively time-consuming co-ordination (Galbraith and Nathanson, 1978). This co-ordination is essential if the chosen strategy is to be successfully implemented. With constant changes in strategy, there is a danger that the firm will lose its bearings and that employees at all levels will find it hard to determine the activities on which to focus. It then becomes more difficult to configure the value chain, and thus to co-ordinate important functions like purchasing, production, and sales. However, the matching of external demands and internal resources must never be an end in itself, and the firm must regularly review its strategic position. According to some scholars, this review takes place successively as strategy – continually and little by little – is adapted to the firm's environment (Miles and Snow, 1978). Others hold that in the long run almost all firms are forced to implement radical strategic changes in order to remain competitive (Porter, 1980). We agree with the latter view.

In regard to the firm's internal structures and the manner of their adaptation to strategy, we have chosen to focus on the firm's control systems. As far back as 1965, Anthony advanced the view that management control is the principal tool of management for successfully implementing a chosen strategy (Anthony, 1965). Also highlighted early on was the importance of adapting manufacturing control to strategy (Skinner, 1969). Since the publication of these normative studies, substantial interest has been devoted to empirical study of the way in which a firm's strategy is reflected in the design and use of its control systems. In the area of management control, the matching of strategy and control, as well as its effect on competitive advantage, and ultimately performance,[10] has in most cases been tested in large-sample surveys. Although the findings have not always been clear-cut, it has often been possible to show a significant correlation between the variables studied (Langfield-Smith, 1997). The contribution of such surveys has been to provide a reasonably good explanation, for example, of the effect of a cost-leadership strategy (standardized, low-price products) on the management-control system at the business unit level.

One weakness of these studies is that comparisons of results are difficult owing to different definitions of the concepts of strategy and management control (Kald et al., 2000).[11] Another weakness is the lack of consideration given to the existence of strategies at several organizational levels and to the differences in management-control systems at different levels. According to Langfield-Smith (1997), many of the studies focus solely on the senior management level. Ittner and Larcker (2001), based on their review of the literature, note that the studies of management control at the operational level "typically ignore the higher-level strategic choices made by the firm, even though all of these choices are expected to influence accounting and control system design and organizational performance" (ibid, p. 364). Similar conclusions were drawn by Luft and Shields (2003) in their overview of 275 articles published in six leading management-accounting journals. Their review covers diverse streams of research and thus has a broad focus that is not limited to the relationship between strategy and control. The authors note that in the area of management accounting there are few, if any, cross-level studies, for example covering both the organization and organizational subunits.

On the basis of these reviews of the literature, it is reasonable to conclude that the alignment between strategy and control is often studied only in a selected and limited part of the company. We may assume that the interrelationship of strategy, control systems, and competitiveness is much more complex than suggested by the findings of these survey-based studies (*cf.* Mills et al., 1995; Luft and Shields, 2003). Thus, there is a need for detailed discussion of this interrelationship, and particularly of the ways in which large, complex organizations co-ordinate their strategies, and of the role of control systems in this regard. The present book is intended to provide a contribution to this discussion.

Strategic Congruence and Integrated Control

In the remainder of this presentation, we shall focus on two distinguishing features of strategy and control systems: strategic congruence and integrated control. Our discussion will start with two in-depth case studies of large and complex firms (Goold et al., 1994; Nilsson, 2002). The study by Goold et al. (1994) indicates that strategic congruence, defined as a consistency among different strategic levels, is a feature of many competitive companies. At such firms, acquisitions and divestitures are typically made for the purpose of focusing operations on what is considered the core business.[12] With a clearly defined core business, it should be easier to coordinate corporate, business, and functional strategies and thus to configure the value-creating activities of the firm (Skinner, 1974; Wheelwright, 1984; Porter, 1987).[13] For example, a company with a business strategy of being the low-cost producer in its industry will have to emphasize large-scale manufacturing of standardized products. It may also have to coordinate activities in the value chains of several business units in order to exploit economies of scale and thereby reduce the unit costs of company products (Porter, 1985, p. 326 ff).

Another possible conclusion from the case studies is that coherence in strategic planning and follow-up can help to facilitate the creation of competitive advantage (Nilsson, 2002).[14] Such a system of integrated control is intended to simplify the processes of formulation and implementation of corporate, business, and functional strategies. Particularly firms that are sometimes referred to as "world-class manufacturers" have shown an interest in integrated control systems (Nanni et al., 1992; Cooper, 1996). At these firms, manufacturing control, for example, has in some cases been integrated with the overall systems of planning and control (Yoshikawa et al., 1994). This integration provides a common frame of reference that facilitates communication both between corporate and business-unit management and between management and employees of business units. Uniform terminology and similar principles of control contribute to transparency in the processes of planning and follow-up, thus helping to interlink corporate, business, and functional goals and strategies. This leads to a better understanding of the effects of various activities in the value chain, separately and in combination, on the competitiveness and performance of the firm (cf. Argyris, 1977; Nilsson and Rapp, 1999).

Despite research results suggesting that the competitive advantage of a firm is affected by strategic congruence and integrated control, there are few studies, as far as the authors are aware, in which these two areas are discussed in conjunction. For example, in the field of strategy, the treatment of control systems appears relatively often to be at a general level. Our impression is that in these contexts control systems are not infrequently regarded as tools for applications in such areas as implementation of strategy and responsibility accounting. Researchers in the area of manufacturing have concentrated on strategies and control systems designed for the functional and business unit level, while relationship to the corporate level has been less frequently considered (see, for example, Kotha and Orne, 1989; Hill, 2000). Similarly, research in the field of management control has focused on the effects of strategies on traditional instruments of control like procedures for budgeting and capital expenditure. Especially in earlier studies, control of manufacturing has often been defined as operational control and has thus been considered to be of limited interest to researchers in management accounting (Anthony et al., 1989; Otley, 1994, 1999). In light of the above, we have decided to focus on the manufacturing function and the co-ordination and integration of its strategies and control systems with the rest of the firm. This means that planning and follow-up of other primary and secondary activities will be discussed only at a general level.

Purpose of the Book

As indicated in the Introduction, the creation of competitive advantage is a subject of considerable academic and practical interest. At the macro level, the focus is on the competitive strength of entire countries or regions. At the micro level, by contrast, the emphasis is on ways for the individual firm to create competitive advantage on its own market. This book focuses primarily on the micro level. Its purpose is to provide a comprehensive analysis of the creation of competitive advantage within the individual firm. The analysis is based on the premise that the alignment of strategies and control systems affects the possibilities of positioning the firm successfully in its chosen arena of competition. Two concepts that will receive special attention in this connection are strategic congruence and integrated control. By analyzing in detail how strategies are co-ordinated and how control systems facilitate this process, we can apply interesting perspectives on the ways in which a firm creates competitive advantage.

The two concepts chosen originate in established fields of research where a variety of theoretical perspectives have been claimed capable of explaining the competitiveness of firms. According to the overview by Fiegenbaum et al. (1996) of the literature on this subject, many of these perspectives focus either on external conditions or on internal organization.[15] Examples of theories in the first category are industrial economics, resource-dependence theory and institutional theory. In the second category, two examples from the review by Fiegenbaum et al. are motivation theory and resource-based theory. As previously indicated, our analysis has been strongly influenced by contingency theory, whose adherents have long emphasized the importance of a fit between the business environment, the strategy, and the internal structures (organization, systems and processes) of the firm. However, this choice has not ruled out using studies with other theoretical approaches to expand on our contribution and to position it.

What this Book Contributes

This book provides a contribution both within our academic field and beyond its bounds. One contribution within our field will be to provide additional knowledge on the creation of competitive advantage through strategic congruence and integrated control. We believe that further elaboration on the meaning of these two well-established concepts, and especially of their interrelationship, is very important for explaining a firm's competitiveness. The development of a tentative model is facilitated by the "knowledge synergies" created through integration of selected portions of research in strategy, management control, and manufacturing control. These areas have been large, well-established fields of research for a long time. Of course, we make no claim whatever that our review of them is exhaustive. Our ambition, rather, has been to highlight a number of central studies in each area and to show how in combination they can extend our knowledge and understanding of the influence of strategic congruence and integrated control on creating competitive strength. There are also a number of contributions in each of the three research areas covered in the book:

1. Strategy: Strategic congruence, strategic coherence, and similar terms were introduced long ago (Skinner, 1969; Hofer and Schendel, 1978). Since then many studies have devoted attention to this phenomenon (see for example, Nath and Sudharshan, 1994). Our review of different strategic typologies and their characteristics should contribute to more thorough discussion and analysis of the question which corporate, business and functional strategies may be assumed congruent.

2. Management control: How management control should be used in formulating and implementing strategies is a classic problem (*cf.* Anthony, 1965), but there is still disagreement on the way in which it should be resolved. One reason is the focus in earlier studies on tactical decision-making; here the role of management control in strategic planning and operational control was often neglected (Otley, 1994, 1999). Another reason is that research tends not to consider the interrelationship and

mutual influence of control systems at different organizational levels (Ittner and Larcker, 2001; Luft and Shields, 2003). If the scope of research in management control is extended to several levels of decision-making and organization, valuable insights can be gained.

3. Manufacturing control: In the area of manufacturing control, the focus in earlier research was on operational control and the functional level. Questions of overall strategy – especially corporate strategy – were often treated superficially (Kotha and Orne, 1989). Consequently, there is a need for research to concentrate much more than before on the link between manufacturing strategies, on the one hand, and business and corporate strategies, on the other (Hill, 2000, p. 28).

As for the contribution outside the scholarly field directly concerned, this book provides guidance on a question that has received considerable attention in public debate: what strategies create value, and why? Unfortunately, the discussion thus far has been overly concentrated on ways for firms to expand their operations – frequently through acquisitions. Surprisingly, there is seldom discussion on the fit between the strategies and control systems of the acquirer and those of the acquired firm. Nilsson (2002) contends that such matching can be advantageous. It should be noted, however, that Nilsson discusses the matching of management control between different organizational levels; he does not analyze in any detail manufacturing control and the link between it and financial planning and follow-up. Furthermore, his principal focus is on the matching of control systems; strategic congruence is touched upon more implicitly. A more thorough analysis of the effects of strategic congruence and integrated control on a firm's competitiveness would help management to determine what business the firm should be in and to find appropriate ways to influence the two relationships. Such an analysis would enhance the possibilities of creating value for owners, customers, and employees.

Target Readership

The academic debate on the creation of competitive advantage has been based largely on classic economic theory and industry analyses. We believe that it is time for students and scholars to recognize the importance of strategic congruence and integrated control, and especially the relationship between these two concepts, to the creation of competitive advantage. The book should be of interest to the following readers:

1. Advanced undergraduate students wishing to acquire a broader understanding of the ways in which competitive advantage is created. Particularly students interested in the interaction between business environment, strategies, and control systems, on the one hand, and the competitiveness and performance of the firm, on the other, should profit from this book. With its overall view of strategy, management control, and manufacturing control, the book is also an appropriate complement to the more specialized literature in each area.

2. Graduate students seeking to develop theories of managerial action as well as guidelines for designing and using internal structures to create competitive advantage. Since the tentative model presented broadens the base for further research in the field, the book should be of interest to more experienced scholars as well.

Organization of the Book

The subsequent presentation is divided into five chapters in addition to this one. Chapter 2 presents empirical research on the relationship between business environment, strategy, structure, competitive advantage, and performance. This review starts with the early classical studies leading to the breakthrough of strategy as a field in the early 1960's. Thereafter, we discuss the results of studies in which the authors have sought to find those combinations of strategy and structure that enable a firm to be efficient and competitive. The latest studies in this area, most of them published toward the end of the 1990's, share a strong focus on one particular structure: the control system. The chapter concludes by linking together the central concepts identified to provide a clear theoretical starting point and structure for the remainder of the book.

Chapter 3 begins by defining the concept of strategic congruence and relating it to other important concepts in the research area of strategy. It continues with a detailed discussion of three principal levels of strategy: corporate strategy, business strategy, and functional strategy. Since both researchers and practitioners have attached their own meaning to each of these levels, a large number of strategic typologies have been developed. We have therefore chosen to limit ourselves to well-recognized, established typologies and to comment upon them thoroughly with regard to archetypes, features, and contributions within and outside the scholarly field directly concerned. Another limitation is that we discuss functional strategies as they relate to the formulation and implementation of manufacturing strategies. On the basis of this review, we have chosen a strategic typology for each strategic level; these typologies are used later on in the discussion of the tentative model in Chapter 5.

Chapter 4 starts by defining the concept of integrated control and relating it to other central concepts in the research areas of management control and manufacturing control. Special interest is devoted to the extension of research to more organizational levels and more decision levels than before. After this background review, we discuss management control and manufacturing control on the basis of procedures for strategic planning and follow-up. The purpose of this discussion is to identify and describe a number of central dimensions in the design and use of control systems. These dimensions are important as a starting point for the description of the tentative model in Chapter 5 and for identifying the conditions that must be fulfilled if integrated control is to be achieved.

In Chapter 5 the concepts developed in the preceding three chapters are integrated in a tentative model. On the basis of the firm's business strategy and manufacturing strategy, we identify four distinct positions and one intermediate position. For each position, the requirements for creating strategic congruence and integrated control are discussed in detail. In the second section of the chapter, this discussion is enlarged to include two distinct strategic positions at the corporate level.

Chapter 6 begins with a summary of some of the principal assumptions introduced in previous chapters. The summary serves as a basis for conclusions regarding the combinations of strategies and control systems that should facilitate the creation of competitive advantage. We also discuss the dynamics of fit and their probable effect on strategic congruence and integrated control. Finally, two kinds of implications are suggested: practical business implications and implications for future research.

Notes

1. In an article entitled "Japan – Where Operations Really Are Strategic," Wheelwright compares US and Japanese industry in regard to the formulation and implementation of strategies (Wheelwright, 1981). The conclusion is that Japanese firms have been more successful than their US counterparts in linking overall strategic planning to operational decision-making. According to Wheelwright (p. 69), "In Japan, the integrity of production system and strategic purpose comes first. But Japanese manufacturers also realize that decisions at the level of operations can, if handled in a wise and consistent manner, have a useful cumulative effect at the level of strategy. Experience has taught the Japanese the value of placing even short-term manufacturing decisions at the service of long-term strategy – a lesson that American companies have learned only imperfectly." How Japanese companies go about breaking down overall goals and strategies to the lowest organizational level has also been discussed by other writers, among them Bromwich and Bhimani (1994) and Yoshikawa et al. (1994).

2. Lindvall (2001, p. 97) contends that far-reaching decentralization of profit responsibility is becoming less common in Swedish business. The reason is that the freedom accompanying profit responsibility can also lead to major difficulties in co-ordinating corporate businesses, with problems of suboptimization as a result. As an illustration, Lindvall quotes an interview with former Ericsson CEO Lars Ramqvist in the Swedish newspaper *Dagens Industri*: "Far too many corporate units were given profit responsibility and immediately started to build up their own functions that cost enormous sums. Tendencies like these are clear, and we are dealing with them now" (Dagens industri, 1999).

3. In developing the five-force framework, Porter (1980) used concepts taken from industrial-organization (IO) economics. For further discussion, see, for example, Rumelt et al. (1994).

4. The concept of internal structures has been given several different definitions (see for example, Galbraith and Nathanson, 1978). In the present book we have chosen to define internal structures as consisting of organization, control systems, and processes.

5. For the purpose of simplifying the discussion and avoiding unnecessary repetition, the concept of "product" rather than "product or services" will be used from now on in this presentation.

6. There is no obvious answer to the question how to draw the line between a firm and its business environment. With a network approach the difficulties of defining the environment are clear (Castells, 1996). In Chapter 2 this discussion is further developed.

7. In an empirical study, Lawrence and Lorsch (1967) have shown how the uncertainty resulting from a turbulent sub-environment can be managed through a flexible and decentralized organization. By analogy, more centralized decision-making is appropriate when the environment is stable. Among other researchers presenting similar findings is Morgan (1986, p. 34), who maintains that centralized bureaucratic machinery is a superior form of organization for mass production in a stable environment.

8. One important mission for research in the field of contingency theory is to identify which factors are most relevant for explaining successful organizational solutions. In this connection, the business environment is usually held out as one major so-called contingency factor. Another significant factor is strategy, but as a variable intermediate between the environment and the internal structures of the firm. Examples of still other contingency factors are technology, industry, and size (Morgan, 1986, p. 48 ff).

9. What is to be considered short-run and long-run depends, for instance, on the type of business that the firm is in. IT consulting is an example of a business in which even a single year is hard to foresee. Quite a different example would be a company involved in oil drilling; such a company might use a time frame of several decades in its planning. Based on our own consulting experience, a common planning horizon is about three years, with planning horizon defined as the length of time for which the basic strategy of the firm is assumed to be stable.

10. In this book we have chosen to define performance on the basis of the degree to which value is created for employees, customers, and shareholders. Performance is further discussed in Chapter 2.

11. In Kald et al. (2000), the authors discuss in detail the possible conse-quences of superficial analyses that compare the findings of studies in which the variable of strategy has been operationalized in different ways. According to the authors, an analysis of the strategy variables used shows that they capture different dimensions of a firm's strategy. Therefore, ambiguous findings can be explained only through detailed efforts to relate strategy variables to one another.

12. "Heartland business" is a concept introduced by Goold et al. (1994, p. 278 ff) to denote the type of business where a firm can create high lev-els of net value. According to the authors, there should be a clear business logic for all corporate businesses included in a heartland. This logic may take the form of common critical success factors, though it need not be limited to a particular industry. Thus, and as shown in the case studies by Goold et al. (1994), even a conglomerate – that is, a corporate group with different businesses and therefore limited syner-gies – can create a distinct heartland. For a more detailed discussion, see Goold and Campbell (1987a) and Goold et al. (1994).

13. In three recent articles, Goold and Campbell (2002a, 2003a, 2003b) discuss the difficulties of balancing hierarchy, control and process. While clearly advocating decentralization, the authors also recognize that processes for co-ordination are often necessary. Especially in complex, interdependent corporate structures, according to Goold and Campbell (2002b, p. 222), the "parent" (broadly defined as the corpo-rate center) "may play an active role in creating an integrated strategy that will be accepted throughout the company and may establish the policics and constraints that regulate the decisions of all the units." At the same time, they note that in such extremely complex structures the differences between the "parent" and the "operating units" may be-come fuzzy. According to the authors (ibid, p. 240), the reason is that the parenting responsibilities are delegated to several different organ-izational units.

14. Nilsson (2002) also considers how situations of misfit could be han-dled. In such a situation it is important to find a balance between integrated control and control based totally on the needs of the busi-ness unit. Thus, creating competitive advantage and achieving good performance are not ruled out in situations where a high degree of stra-tegic congruence and integrated control is difficult to attain. However, special procedures will then be needed to manage any differences be-tween the respective control systems of the acquiring and acquired

companies. Such procedures are discussed extensively in Nilsson's doctoral dissertation (Nilsson, 1997). One example is the use of alternative integration mechanisms which reduce the need for co-ordination through the management control system. With the aid of co-ordination groups and various kinds of joint projects, for example, it is possible to achieve a relatively high degree of business integration without far-reaching co-ordination of control systems.

15. A third perspective identified by Fiegenbaum et al. (1996) is time.

2 Theoretical Foundations

This book is about competitive advantage and how it is created at the company level. It focuses on the role of strategies and control systems rather than on competition at the national and industry level. This chapter is devoted to empirical research on strategic management from a contingency-theory standpoint. Our review begins with the early studies that contributed to the development of contingency theory and the field of strategic management. It then presents the research elucidating the interrelationships between business environment, strategy, structure, competitive advantage, and performance. The purpose of this chapter is to identify central concepts in the tentative theoretical framework developed in subsequent chapters. There you will also find a discussion on operationalizing some of the concepts.

Contingency Theory

The view of the firm as an open system has for a long time been an important theoretical starting-point in the area of strategic management (Rumelt et al., 1994). As early as 1960's, scholars presented the idea that the firm is affected by its environment. Burns and Stalker (1961) were the first to publish findings that showed the impact of environmental uncertainty on the internal structures of the firm. Their work – *The Management of Innovation* – is based on a study of UK firms (most of which were investing in electronics development). On the basis of this empirical material, Burns and Stalker identified two different types of divergent systems of management practice: "mechanistic" and "organic." A mechanistic structure[1] was particularly appropriate for firms operating in stable conditions. This stability made it possible to break down and co-ordinate activities through centralized decision-making with a vertical flow of information. Examples of other characteristics were a formal organization with well-defined technical methods, functional roles, and a distinct "command hierarchy" (ibid, p. 5, p. 119 ff). By contrast, firms with an organic structure[2] were operating in a dynamic environment with unstable conditions. To permit the firm to adapt quickly to changes in the environment, decision-making was decentralized, and the information flow was lateral rather than vertical, "resembling consultation rather than command" (ibid, p. 121). The organization was less formalized than with a mechanistic structure; one consequence was that jobs became more difficult to define in a formal way (ibid, p. 6).

The theories of Burns and Stalker were further developed by Lawrence and Lorsch (1967) in *Organization and Environment*. The authors (ibid, p. 20) studied six organizations in the business of developing, marketing and producing plastics material, two in the consumer food industry, and two in the container industry. The plastics organizations were in a dynamic and diverse environment, the container organizations were in a stable environment, and the food organizations were in an environment with some turbulence (ibid, p. 155). The findings showed that high-performing organizations adapted their integration devices to the environment and its characteristics (ibid, p. 157). Another important finding was that within a company different styles of organization could be present. According to Lawrence and Lorsch, these differences in the design of internal structures were explainable by the nature of that phase of the environment with which each unit was dealing. For example, the R&D departments of the firms studied operated in turbulent sub-environments. Compared to the manufacturing departments, the R&D departments were less formally structured, with fewer levels in the managerial hierarchy (ibid, p. 30 ff).

Still another significant contribution to the literature treating the influence of the environment on firm organization is *Organizations in Action*, by Thompson (1967). Unlike the two works previously mentioned, Thompson's approach was primarily deductive. Even in the introduction to the book, he argues that companies are open systems which are affected by uncertainty related to technologies and the environment (ibid, p. 13). It is also very important, according to Thompson (ibid, p. 11), to ensure that the so-called "technical core" – comprising activities of high strategic significance – is not disturbed by environmental uncertainty. To protect the core, the firm must create some sort of "buffers." For example, at a manufacturing company it is essential that the manufacturing process not be disrupted by an uneven flow of materials. Nor is it desirable that short-term changes in demand affect the volume of production, since both personnel and equipment would then be utilized inefficiently, with high production costs as a consequence (ibid, p. 20). One very important conclusion is that the need for buffers increases in a more turbulent environment.

In these three works, Burns and Stalker (1961), Lawrence and Lorsch (1967), and Thompson (1967) laid the foundation for what would later emerge as a new school of organizational theory. This so-called contingency theory is based on the fundamental assumption that every organization is different. Thus, suitable internal structures can only be chosen by thoroughly investigating the environment in which the organization operates (cf. Morgan, 1986, p. 48 ff; Perrow, 1986, p. 178).[3, 4] This means, for example, that the business environment may be assumed to have pivotal significance for the design of the control systems at a particular company. For the control systems, as well as the organization and business processes, must be designed to permit management of the uncertainty created by the environment in the form of unpredictability (cf. Thompson, 1967, p. 159).

Strategic Management

As the contingency theory was emerging, there was a breakthrough in the field of strategic management. According to the overview by Rumelt et al. (1994, p. 16), three works considered to have had a special impact on early developments in the field are Chandler's *Strategy and Structure* (1962), the Harvard textbook *Business Policy: Text and Cases* (Learned et al., 1965), and Ansoff's *Corporate Strategy* (1965). Chandler's book describes how large US companies expanded their operations through diversification and how this strategy affected the internal structures of firms.[5] Four corporations – General Motors, Sears, Standard Oil of New Jersey (Exxon), and DuPont – were described and analyzed in particular detail. When these four firms changed their basic and overall strategy (i.e. corporate strategy), from focusing on a well-defined core business to expanding the business into new competitive arenas, very complicated problems of co-ordination started to emerge. Among them were difficulties in co-ordinating production and resource allocation within the corporation. A decentralized, divisionalized structure was adopted in response to these problems. Operational decisions were delegated to the divisions and their management, while corporate management and their staff were responsible for over-all planning and co-ordination. Instead of co-ordinating functions and departments, it was now necessary to persuade the divisions to collaborate and share important activities (i.e. to exploit synergies).

Chandler's conclusion that the firm's internal structures must be adapted to its strategies was one of the fundamental assumptions in Andrews' basic normative textbook on Business Policy (Learned et al., 1965). Another researcher who appears to have influenced Andrews is Selznick (1957) with his theories of "distinctive competencies" and the need to match the firm's "internal state" with its "external expectations" (Mintzberg, 1990; Mintzberg et al., 1998). Andrews argues strongly that the firm's strategy should be based on a thorough analysis of threats and opportunities in its environment. Similarly, management must conduct an internal assessment in which the strengths and weaknesses of the firm are identified. Rumelt et al. (1994, p. 17) argue that the objective of this exercise is to devise a strategy in which the competencies of the firm are adapted so as to avoid the threats and exploit the opportunities. The ultimate choice of strategy is also influenced by managerial values and social responsibility. Figure 2.1 illustrates essential elements of the process described by Andrews.

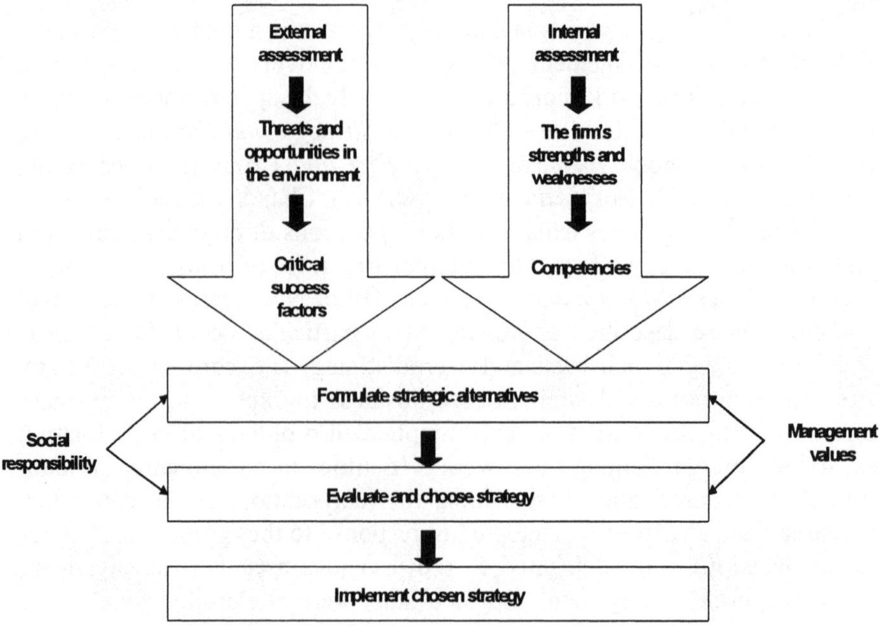

Fig. 2.1. Essential elements of strategic planning and implementation according to the design school. Source: Mintzberg H, Alhstrand B, Lampel J. 1998. Strategy Safari. p. 26 (modified)

The SWOT analysis – that is, the assessment of Strengths and Weaknesses of the company in the light of the Opportunities and Threats in its environment – was presented as a significant aid in the formulation of strategic alternatives (*cf.* Figure 2.1). Minztberg et al. (1998, p. 29 ff) maintain that the belief in strategy formulation as a "deliberate process of conscious thought," where the chief executive is viewed as the "architect of organizational purpose," was very strong. Also, the planning process was viewed as concluded when a strategy had been chosen and implementation begun. Consequently, incremental development of strategy, in which goals and business plans emerge successively, was considered inconsistent with efficient, well-structured planning (*cf.* Mintzberg and Waters, 1985). Mintzberg et al. (1998) have called this approach to strategic management the Design School. In this school of thought, according to the authors (ibid, p. 41), strategies do not change abruptly. In other words, the environment is considered to be stable, with a low degree of uncertainty. Therefore, Mintzberg (1990, p. 191) holds that the approach of the Design School is appropriate "...at the junction of major shift for an organization, coming out of a period of changing circumstances and into one of operating stability."

On the basis of personal experience as an executive, Ansoff also chose to discuss how strategic planning should be designed (Ansoff, 1965). Like Andrews, Ansoff maintained that the purpose of strategic planning is to achieve a "fit" between the firm's environment and its capabilities and competencies. Examples of other similarities are the belief in strategy formulation as a "deliberate process of conscious thought" (Mintzberg et al, 1998, p. 29), and the separation of formulation and implementation. One major difference is that Ansoff advocated a much more formalized, almost mechanical planning process in which each activity is broken down in detail (ibid, p. 57 ff). Another difference is that Ansoff preferred to focus on the firm's corporate strategy, particularly the decision to diversify (*cf.* Figure 2.2). Andrews, on the other hand, was more interested in evaluation and formulation of business strategies (Rumelt et al., 1994). Mintzberg et al. (1998) refer to the view of strategy represented by Ansoff as the Planning School. The authors criticize this school on the same grounds as the Design School, i.e., that a formalized planning process requires a stable environment.

While normative models continued to be developed after these initial efforts, many scholars devoted most of their research to careful observation of actual organizations. These studies concentrated mainly on extending

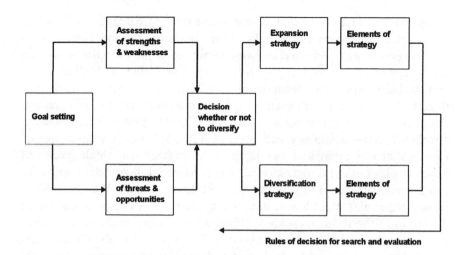

Fig. 2.2. Essential elements of strategic planning and implementation according to the planning school. Source: Bengtsson L, Skärvad PH. 1988. *Företagsstrategiska perspektiv,* in Swedish *(Business Strategy Perspectives),* p. 31

and developing the relationships identified between the business environment, strategy, and structure (Galbraith and Nathanson, 1978). One particular objective was to learn more about the ways in which the competitiveness of the firm, and ultimately its performance, are affected by matching the external environment with the internal structures.

Strategy, Structure, and Performance

In regard to developments in the area of strategy, structure, and performance, Rumelt et al. (1994, p. 21 ff) distinguish three avenues of research in their overview of the field. The first avenue, represented primarily by the so-called "brewery studies" in the early 1970s, focused on business strategies and the types of strategies with the greatest payoff in terms of competitive strength (focus on external fit). According to Rumelt et al., the findings showed that breweries with strategies better adapted to their environment than the strategies of competitors achieved better results. The studies also showed that strategy was a concept with both a theoretical and an empirical content and that it could be measured in a meaningful way.

The second avenue of research sought to find relationships between various corporate strategies, the form of organization, and the performance of the firm (focus on internal fit). In the 1970's a number of studies were conducted to test and develop the relationships between strategy and structure that Chandler had presented in 1962. Wrigley (1970) performed one of the first of these studies (Rumelt et al., 1994). As noted in Galbraith and Nathanson's (1978) review of the literature – as well as in the review by Rumelt el al. (1994),[6] Wrigley's (1970) study was replicated in Great Britain (Channon, 1973), France (Pooley-Dyas, 1972), Germany (Thanheiser, 1972) and Italy (Pavan, 1972). According to Galbraith and Nathanson (1978, p. 28) these studies showed that most companies diversified their business during the period 1950-1970. Despite this strategic shift, many firms retained the functional and holding-company structure. The tendency was especially clear in countries where competition was limited, for example by tariff barriers. After this discovery, Chandler's original theory was modified to include the proviso that a strong correlation between strategy and structure requires the presence of competition. Finally, Rumelt (1974) conducted a study of selected *Fortune 500* companies. This study confirmed previous findings but failed to show that performance is the product of a match between strategy and structure (Galbraith and Nathanson, 1978, p. 47 f).[7, 8, 9]

The last avenue of research, with Porter (1980, 1985) as one of its foremost representatives,[10] highlights the significance of external conditions for competitive strength (external fit) (Mintzberg et al., 1988, p. 99). At the same time, considerable emphasis is also placed on the structure of the firm, particularly as manifested in the so-called value chain (internal fit). Thus, this perspective illustrates the interplay between external and internal fit in creating and maintaining competitive advantage. According to Porter (1985, p 11), competitive strength is evidenced by a rate of return which consistently exceeds the industry average. He argues that even when the industry structure is unfavorable, and the average rate of return is low, it should be possible to position one's own company so that a good return will be achieved. Porter (ibid, p. 3) holds that a position of competitive strength is due to the firm's success in creating unique value for its customers.[11] Otherwise the firm may be "stuck in the middle," a position which usually means low profitability. Thus, it is very important for management to conduct a thorough analysis of the competitive arena.[12]

One problem, however, is the difficulty in translating an analysis of the environment into clear strategies. In response to this problem, and in the spirit of the Design School, with its focus on strategic analysis and intended strategies (Mintzberg, 1990), Porter (1985, p. 33) introduced the so-called value chain as a tool for analyzing how competitive advantage arises

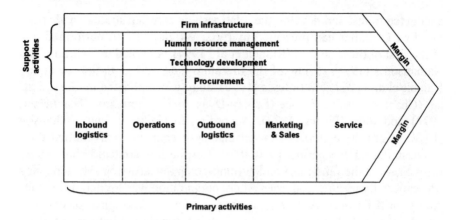

Fig. 2.3. The value chain. Source: Porter ME. 1985. Competitive Advantage. p. 37

and is maintained at the business-unit level. As shown in Figure 2.3, this model of analysis distinguishes between the businessunit's primary activities (such as operations) and its supporting activities (such as the functioning of its infrastructure). How these value-creating activities are configured and subsequently performed is critical to the creation of competitive advantage and ultimately to performance (expressed in terms of margin in Figure 2.3). For example, it is important to co-ordinate the activities of a business unit so that they are utilized efficiently, and at the same time to eliminate activities that do not create value. As mentioned previously, it may be considerably easier to configure the value chain if management has developed a clear and unique strategy. The design and use of the control systems are very important not only in the process of formulating strategies, but also in implementing them. Quite a large body of research has been devoted to the question how to adapt control systems to strategy so that the firm will be effectively managed and competitive (Langfield-Smith, 1997).

Strategy and Control

During the 1980's and 1990's, interest focused increasingly on one particular structure of the firm: the control system (i.e. management control and manufacturing control). The large-scale questionnaire studies at the time were directed at finding a relationship between strategy[13] and control at the corporate, business-unit, and functional levels. As mentioned in the introduction to this book, researchers in management control previously concentrated on studying procedures for planning and for monitoring results at the corporate and business-unit levels. Not until the end of the 1990's did control of production flows begin to attract attention. Part of the reason was the realization that decentralized decision-making requires integration of management control and operational control (*cf.* Otley, 1994). Researchers in the area of manufacturing concentrated instead on control of activities at the functional level (Vollmann et al., 1992).

The Corporate Level

Of the three organizational levels noted above, the corporate level appears to have received the least attention (*cf.* Langfield-Smith, 1997; Luft and Shields, 2003; Anthony and Govindarajan, 2004). The study by Goold and Campbell (1987a), with its case descriptions of 16 large diversified UK companies, is probably one of the most widely publicized.[14] Here the authors show that in corporate groups with low synergy potential (financial-control strategy) and a limited need for co-ordination, business units were expected to develop their own strategies and plans. The plans approved by corporate management were regarded as contracts, and monitoring of results was detailed and frequent, with little tolerance for deviations – so-called tight control. In corporate groups with high synergy potential (strategic-planning strategy), on the other hand, top management participated actively in decision-making, thus providing operational integration among different business units. As corporate management was deeply involved in the decision-making process, performance was monitored less frequently, and deviations from plan seldom carried serious consequences – so-called loose control. Finally, Goold and Campbell identified a few corporate groups with a combined strategy of financial control and strategic planning (a strategic-control strategy). These groups had certain clusters of business units where synergy potential was high and other clusters where it was low. According to the authors decision-making was decentralized, and monitoring of results was based on a mix of tight and loose control. Because of an unclear strategy and difficulties in establishing a consistent and well-functioning control-system, these corporate groups did not perform as well as the others in the study.

Goold's and Campbell's (1987a) conclusions on the relationship between corporate strategy and the design and use of control systems were one of the principal starting points for Nilsson's (2000) analysis of four Swedish corporate groups.[15] In addition to procedures for planning and re-

Table 2.1. Tendencies in the relationship between corporate strategy and control systems

Features of the Control system	Features of the corporate strategy	
	Low synergy potential	High synergy potential
Intensity of monitoring	Tight control	Loose control
Control classified by type of information used	Monetary control	Non-monetary control
Time perspective	Short-term	Long-term

porting – the focus in Goold's and Campbell's study – Nilsson included investment control, transfer prices, and key ratios in the subsystems to be studied. The findings indicate that at firms with a corporate strategy of financial control, business units were regarded as autonomous companies where profits were to be maximized. Control was rather tight, with an emphasis on short-term financial performance. At firms with a corporate strategy of strategic planning, co-ordination of business-unit operations was important in view of the substantial synergy potential. Control was loose, mostly non-monetary, and characterized by a long-term perspective. Anthony and Govindarajan (2004, p. 637 ff) noted similar tendencies in regard to the relationship between corporate strategies and the design and use of the overall control system. Their report is based on a short and high-level review of a number of empirical studies (*cf.* ibid, 1992, p. 693 ff). Although some of these were probably not directly intended to examine the relationship between strategy and control, they have indirectly provided valuable insights into this area of research. Based on our review of the literature, Table 2.1 provides a summary of certain overall tendencies in the relationship between corporate strategy and the design and use of control systems.[16]

The Business Unit Level

At the business-unit level there have been a large number of studies, based mainly on the business-strategy typologies of Miles and Snow (1978), Porter (1980), and Gupta and Govindarajan (1984). Below we discuss some of the studies.[17] Our first example is a survey conducted by Govindarajan (1988). He collected data from 75 business units of 24 firms on the Fortune 500 list. The findings showed that a de-emphasis on meeting the budget was associated with high performance in business units pursuing a strategy of differentiation. Reliance on product innovation and broad product lines was assumed to create a turbulent and uncertain environment typically associated with a differentiation strategy. In this environment, future revenues and expenses are difficult to estimate, thus limiting the importance of the budget. Similar results were obtained by Bruggeman and Van der Stede (1993) in their field research on 18 Belgian firms (32 business units). One interesting finding was that business units selling differentiated standard products were using tight control, allowing no budget revisions. Miller (1988) also reached conclusions similar to Govindarajan's (1988) in his study of 89 firms in Quebec.[18]

It has also been shown by other researchers that a control system based on loose and non-monetary control, combined with a long-term perspective, is appropriate when the chosen strategy entails uncertainty. One example is a study by Govindarajan and Gupta (1985), who examined the linkages between the strategic mission (build, hold, and harvest strategies),[19] the incentive bonus system, and effectiveness. Based on data from 58 strategic business units, they found that reliance on long-run criteria[20] and subjective approaches for determining managers' bonuses contributed to effectiveness with a build strategy but worked against it with a harvest strategy. No correlation could be found between the strategy, the use of short-term criteria, and effectiveness. Merchant (1985) found that decisions were more affected by income targets and head-count controls when a high-growth strategy was pursued than when the strategy was to maintain market share. A final example is a study by Rajagopalan (1996), who investigated how prospectors (always seeking new opportunities) and defenders (limited, low-cost product range) designed and used their incentive systems. The data showed that defenders primarily resorted to short-term, low-risk forms of incentives (that is, cash bonuses) based on quantitative criteria for evaluating performance. With prospectors, incentives were more long-term in nature and involved a higher risk.

In 1987, Simons published a study that partly contradicted several of the findings discussed above, thus attracting considerable attention. He gathered data from 76 Canadian business units in manufacturing industries; each unit could be classified as either a prospector or a defender. Simons showed that high-performing prospectors were characterized by tight control, with an emphasis on forecasts, strict budget targets, and careful monitoring of outputs. With large defenders, there was a negative correlation between performance, on the one hand, and the use of strict budget targets and close monitoring of output, on the other. Simons therefore con-

Table 2.2. Tendencies in the relationship between business strategy and control systems

Features of the control system	Features of the business strategy	
	Unique products	Standardized products
Intensity of monitoring	Loose control	Tight control
Control classified by type of information used	Non-monetary control	Monetary control
Time perspective	Long-term	Short-term

cluded that at defenders control was typically looser than at prospectors, which relied less on the formal system of management control. Similar findings were reached by Collins et al. (1997) in their study on the use of the budget by prospectors and defenders. According to Dent (1996), the explanation for the loose control at defenders was probably that control was provided by the production technology itself. The tight control at prospectors was likely due to a desire to influence the pro-innovative culture of the typical prospector with a more realistic view of the unit's opportunities for expansion. Kald et al. (2000), on the other hand, maintain that the differences in the findings more probably stem from the use of different business-strategy typologies, which makes comparison of the studies difficult. In summary, the studies at the business-unit level do not provide totally clear results. However, there appears to be relatively strong support for a relationship between a turbulent environment, a strategy with a strong focus on product uniqueness (i.e. differentiation), and a control system based on a long-term perspective and loose, non-monetary control. These general tendencies are shown in Table 2.2.

The Functional Level

The studies at the functional level are largely focused on the control of production flows. Researchers with backgrounds in management control have emphasized the relationship between manufacturing strategy and the design of performance measurement. In many of the studies, questionnaires have been used for gathering data, but unlike the studies at the business-unit level, the data collection is not based on established typologies of manufacturing strategy.[21] Instead, the researchers tend to develop unique measuring instruments adapted to the specific study, with the result that the findings are difficult to compare. One example is an explorative study by Abernethy and Lillis (1995) of 42 manufacturing firms in Australia. At companies with a manufacturing strategy based on flexibility,[22] the use of financial or other efficiency-based measures was not very extensive. On the other hand, it was important to monitor cost effectiveness at firms with a manufacturing strategy based on mass production and standard product lines. Abernethy and Lillis showed that firms with these characteristics performed better than firms with other types of relationships between manufacturing strategy and control. Perera et al. (1997) followed and extended the study by Abernethy and Lillis by examining 109 Australian manufacturing firms.[23] The study showed a significant relationship between a customer-focused strategy and the use of non-financial performance measures, but this relationship was not linked to performance.

Other researchers, like Chenhall (1997), for example, have based their work on quality-oriented manufacturing strategies. In a study of 39 manufacturing firms, Chenhall found a positive correlation between employing total quality management (TQM) and using non-financial (i.e. production-oriented) measures in evaluating managers, on the one hand, and superior performance, on the other. These results, however, are not undisputed. For example, Ittner and Larcker (1995) could not find empirical support for their proposition that the use of both TQM and "non-traditional" information and reward systems should lead to superior performance. According to the results, non-traditional information and reward systems could also be found at high-performing companies that used quality programs less extensively. The data in this study were taken from an earlier consulting-firm survey of quality-management practices, covering automobile and computer manufacturing plants in several parts of the world. The data were also used in a subsequent paper (Ittner and Larcker, 1997) discussing the extent to which firms used both monetary controls and controls focused on business development in a broader sense. Ittner and Larcker found that at American and German firms there was a relationship between quality strategies and the use of quality-related controls.[24] Japanese firms, on the other hand, combined different types of controls; therefore, the link to the manufacturing strategy was not always clear. According to Ittner and Larcher this finding was similar to the results presented in Daniel and Reitsperger's (1991) paper on the use of quality targets and feedback at Japanese manufacturers.

Compared to the studies based on theories from the area of management control, researchers in the field of manufacturing have not shown an equally strong interest in linking performance measures and strategy (cf. Voss, 1995; Dangayach and Deshmukh, 2001). Instead, there seems to have been a strong focus on studying how to design planning systems depending on the choice of manufacturing strategy, and particularly on the requirements of technical flexibility (*cf.* Kim and Lee, 1993).[25] One example is a normative study by Olhager et al. (2001) which treats the relationship between flexibility and capacity planning (planning horizon 1-5 years) and manufacturing planning (sales and operations planning). The study shows that in a turbulent environment, where there is a great need for flexibility, it is important to forecast future capacity needs (lead) and rapidly to adjust the manufacturing plan for the period to new patterns of demand (chase). In a stable environment there is less need for flexibility, and capacity is adjusted only after an increase in demand has been noted (lag). Moreover, the stable demand situation means that the manufacturing plan for the period seldom has to be changed and can focus on maintaining a pre-set volume (level).

Two other important concepts used in studies of the relationship between manufacturing strategy (i.e. need for technical flexibility) and control should be mentioned: the customer-order decoupling point and the control concept (Vollmann et al., 1992). Olhager and Rapp (1985, 1996) discuss the first concept, which refers to the point in time when the product is designated for a specific customer. The authors show that when the products are standardized and the demand for them is stable, manufactur-

Table 2.3. Tendencies in the relationship between manufacturing strategy and control systems

Features of the control system	Features of the manufacturing strategy	
	High technical flexibility	Low technical flexibility
Control classified by type of information used[26]	Non-monetary control	Monetary control
Capacity / S&O planning	Lead / Chase	Lag / Level
Customer-order decoupling point	Make to order	Make to stock
Control concept	Materials-requirement planning	Just-in-time

ing to a stock of finished goods is most appropriate (MTS). Unique products, for which the demand is very difficult to forecast, require manufacturing entirely to customer order (MTO). The authors found that with MTO planning is characterized by higher uncertainty, and a greater need for technical flexibility, than with MTS.

As for the control concept, most studies focus on the ways in which the need for technical flexibility affects the planning of materials flow. Vollmann et al. (1992, p. 361 ff), in their normative textbook, maintain that JIT (just-in-time) is a suitable control concept when there is little need for flexibility. According to the authors (ibid), the focus of JIT is on continuous flow with short lead-times and products that pass sequentially through the manufacturing process. In cases where the volume of production and the product mix vary considerably, it is better to use MRP (materials-requirement planning). This concept of control is characterized by planning based on batches, in which articles are processed in parallel (ibid). Based on our review of the literature, Table 2.3 summarizes a number of general tendencies in the relationship between manufacturing strategy and the design and use of control systems.

Toward a more Complex Theory

As already pointed out, our review of the literature is not complete. However, it includes many important and well-known studies in the field. It shows that most of the studies treating the relationship between strategy and control focus only on the ways in which this matching affects competitive advantage (i.e. performance) in a selected part of the company. As is apparent from the introductory discussion in Chapter 1, this conclusion is consistent with other reviews of the literature on management control (cf. Langfield-Smith, 1997; Ittner and Larcker, 2001; Luft and Shields, 2003). To study in isolation how a certain manufacturing strategy, for example, affects the control systems at the operational level is to ignore the larger context in which this critical function is performed. Particularly in complex organizations, with multiple production units and multiple products, there is need for co-ordination – both in the choice of overall strategy and in the implementation of strategies (Goold and Campbell, 2002b). As previously noted, however, few empirical studies consider that there are strategies at several organizational levels and that integrated control systems can facilitate the implementation of these strategies. Nevertheless there are some interesting case studies with results that contribute to the development of our knowledge in this area.

The case studies by Goold et al. (1994) are one illustration that strategic congruence can be advantagous.[27] A well-considered overall strategy means that there is a common business logic, for example in the form of a limited number of critical success factors. Such a situation is favorable to the creation of a uniform management style. However, there are difficulties in establishing such a management style without a high degree of strategic congruence. The reasons for such problems at GEC and Ferranti, two British companies, are analyzed in the following excerpt:

GEC and Ferranti faced problems in adding value to the business in their portfolios. Their electronics, defense, and telecommunications businesses were confronting stiff competition from global-scale competitors. This type of competitive battle is not well suited to a style of management focused largely on shorter-term financial results and committed to an organization structure based on separate, stand-alone business units (Goold et al., 1993a, p. 50).

The passage cited suggests that overly large differences in business-unit strategies make it difficult to establish an appropriate organization structure with corporate-wide procedures for monitoring results. In the case above, there seems to be a misfit between the control systems of certain business units, which because of the turbulent environments in which they operate must review performance on a long-term basis, and the corporate monitoring of short-term financial results. Thus, integrated control – that is, coherent strategic planning and monitoring of results throughout the firm – can be assumed to be an important feature of competitive firms. In the excerpt below, Goold et al. (1993a, p. 58) analyze how the planning process at BP helped to create value in the business units belonging to the core business. It is also apparent from the excerpt that this corporate-wide planning process is not equally appropriate for all units of the firm.

Its thorough planning process and its experienced and knowledgeable corporate managers contributed to the company's ability to make sound decisions about the large, risky and long-term investments required in the oil industry. At the same time, however, BP suffered from some of the disadvantages of the Strategic Planning style:[28] non-oil businesses benefited less from the time-consuming planning process; there were signs that BP's success in its core business led it to tolerate poor performance in some businesses for too long; and many managers were impatient with the company's bureaucracy and hierarchy (ibid).

The examples from GEC, Ferranti, and BP indicate that without congruity between strategies and control systems it can be difficult to add value to all businesses in the corporation. Thus, it is not sufficient to establish strategic planning and monitoring systems that are consistent throughout the firm, as BP succeeded in doing. In addition, the design and use of the processes and structures of the control system must be appropriate for most of the business units in the firm. As shown in the examples above, however, this requirement is very difficult to meet at large firms where there are often operations outside the core business. Consequently, a high degree of strategic congruence will make it much easier to establish a system of integrated control. For example, in similar environments, there will be convergence in the degree of uncertainty for the business units and their functions, although it is probably impossible to reach a situation in which all business units and functions operate under the same degree of uncertainty. Lawrence and Lorsch (1967) have shown that differences in the subenvironments of departments can lead to somewhat differing styles of organization at the functional level. On the other hand, it is both possible and desirable that critical functions, such as business-unit manufacturing, be adapted to the need for flexibility in the chosen competitive arena (*cf.* Thompson, 1967).[29] In previous sections we have shown how environmental turbulence, and the accompanying need for technical flexibility, affect the characteristics of the control systems at both the business-unit and functional levels.

In light of the above, there are compelling reasons to devote special study to the importance of strategic congruence and the degree of integrated control for the creation of competitive advantage. To provide a clear theoretical starting point and structure for this discussion – and the remainder of the book – a model has been developed (Figure 2.4) The model is influenced by contingency theory and summarizes important variables and relationships in the discussion thus far. Similar models have been presented earlier, by for example, Hrebiniak et al. (1989, p. 5) and Galbraith and Nathanson (1978, p. 2). However, to the best of our knowledge, few scholars have treated the question how strategic congruence and integrated control together affect the creation of a strong competitive position. An explanation for this situation can probably be found in our review of the literature and in such reviews by others (Langfield-Smith, 1997; Ittner and Larcker, 2001; Luft and Shields, 2003). These reviews show that in the area of management control it is rarely considered how control at a higher organizational level affects control at a lower level. Consequently, it is also difficult to conduct a more detailed discussion on integrated control and its relationship to the existence of strategic congruence.

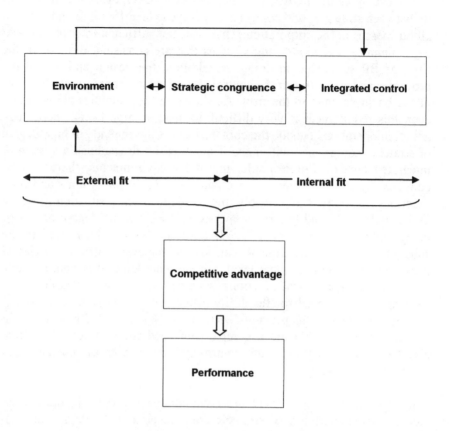

Fig. 2.4. Variables and relationships of interest in the subsequent discussion

As indicated in Figure 2.4, and in consistency with previous research and models used in this area, the relationships between the different variables are assumed to affect and shape each other (see, for example, Peters and Waterman, 1982; Pettigrew and Whipp, 1991). With this mutual dependence, strategy both influences and is influenced by the business environment. Nor is the management-control system solely a reflection of the chosen strategy; the control system also limits and affects the range of strategies that are considered (Hall and Saias, 1980; Simons, 1990). The sections to follow will develop this discussion further by describing the different variables of the model and their relationship to each other.

Environment

From the introduction and the review of the literature, it is apparent that we view the firm as an open system. We thus assume that the environment influences the firm, but also that the firm to some extent can affect its environment. An example of the former is new legislation that limits what the firm and its management actually can accomplish (consider the enactment of a tax on new construction). An example of the latter type of influence is found when the firm introduces a new model of business, leading to a change in the competitive situation (consider the effect of budget air travel on European air fares). Thus, it is reasonable to assume that management cannot fully control all factors having an impact on, or relevance to, the company. We shall refer to those elements of the environment with which the firm chooses to interact, such as customers and suppliers,[30] as the domain (cf. Ford et al., 1988). It may be noted that in certain cases the interaction between domain and firm may be far-reaching, though falling short of the firm's absorbing either its customers or its suppliers. In a tightly woven network of this type, the boundaries between environment, domain, and firm may become indistinct.[31]

Customers, suppliers, and other significant factors also affect the basic features of the environment. As previously mentioned, both contingency theoreticians and researchers in strategic management have devoted considerable attention to one feature in particular: the degree of uncertainty. By uncertainty is meant the extent to which it is possible to foresee both major and minor changes in the firm's environment. At a firm with considerable R&D, for example, changes in customer preferences create uncertainty since the firm must spend money on developing projects without knowing future demand patterns (Shank and Govindarajan, 1993). Supplier relationships characterized by imprecision in deliveries lead to an uneven flow of materials and are thus another source of uncertainty (Thompson, 1967). We consider this type of high uncertainty, with its attendant limitations on detailed planning of operations, to be typical of a turbulent environment. A low degree of uncertainty and ample time to take appropriate action are distinguishing features of a stable environment (cf. Burns and Stalker, 1961). In our model, the degree of uncertainty is taken as a central property of the environment and is thus a factor of considerable importance in matching external demands with internal resources.

Strategic Congruence

From Figure 2.4 it can be seen that the environment is considered to impact internal resources, such as the control systems, primarily via the mediation of strategy as formulated by management (*cf.* Archer and Otley, 1991). It is thus assumed that management is in a position to choose a strategy well adapted to the environment in which the firm operates (external fit). It is also assumed that in a longer-term perspective management can affect, at least to some extent, the degree to which the firm will operate in a turbulent or a stable environment. We thus regard strategy formulation as a "deliberate process of conscious thought" (*cf.* Mintzberg et al., 1998, p. 29 ff), although we do not thereby mean that all strategies are the product of management intentions. In this book, the focus is primarily on ways for management to achieve a fit between the firm's environment and its strategy, rather than the planning process itself.[32] As is evident from previous sections, it is often not enough that such congruence exist in a small portion of the company. To co-ordinate the firm's business units effectively, and to focus on activities that build competitive strength, it is advantageous if strategies at all organizational levels are based on a common business logic. The requirements for establishing a common business logic, and thus a high degree of strategic congruence, are developed in detail in the next chapter (Chapter 3).

Integrated Control

One central assumption in this book is that the firm's control systems are management's primary instrument for implementing chosen strategies. As shown in Figure 2.4 and in discussions in preceding sections, the control systems also fulfill an important function in the development of new strategies – for example, by identifying activities that do not create value (Porter, 1980, 1985).[33] Today, few believe in the sharp boundary between formulation and implementation of strategy, which was drawn by scholars like Anthony (1965) and Andrews (Learned et al., 1965) and which in practice limits control systems to being a tool for implementation. Instead, the focus is on the use of control systems to help establish an internal fit – that is, an appropriate matching of the firm's overall strategy, internal capabilities, and expected performance. Achieving such congruence can be facilitated by the introduction of uniform concepts and similar principles of control. Integrating the principal control systems – such as management control and manufacturing control – can also help to enhance transparency in the process of planning and monitoring results, thereby interlinking strategies at different organizational levels. The systems of control are thus important both when strategies are developed and when they are implemented. How to achieve this type of integrated control is further developed in Chapter 4.

Competitive Advantage

In previous sections we have discussed competitive advantage on the basis of Porter's (1985, p. 3) definition, according to which the distinguishing feature of a firm with a strong market position is that its products create unique value for purchasers. Porter argues that in order to be able to create competitive advantage, a thorough knowledge of the current competitive arena is required (external fit); it is also necessary to understand in detail how the firm best can utilize its internal structures in positioning the product offering (internal fit). In this book, the emphasis is on this interplay between external fit (a fit between environment and strategy) and internal fit (a fit between strategy and control systems). As noted in the discussion so far, a strong competitive position can arise only if there is a high degree of congruence between environment, strategy, and control systems. Consequently, a strategy well adapted to the firm's environment, but without control systems that provide support for its business approach, will not create value, nor vice versa.

Performance

By performance is meant the value that is created for the firm's most important stakeholders. Both practitioners and scholars commonly define performance in terms of total shareholder return (dividends plus share-price appreciation). Donovan et al. (1998, p. 18 ff) argue, however, that it is not sufficient to focus solely on shareholders; due consideration must also be given to other major stakeholders, most notably customers and employees. In the view of these authors, there is competition for all three categories of stakeholders, and every firm must create value for each in order to prosper. Finding this view persuasive, we have chosen to define performance according to the degree to which value is created for employees, customers, and shareholders. In our opinion, lasting high performance is the result of a strong competitive position in respect to all three groups.

Summary

In this chapter we have reviewed empirical research on strategic management from a contingency-theory standpoint. This research focuses on the question how a good fit between the environment, strategy, and structure affects the creation of competitive advantage, and ultimately performance. In the second half of the chapter, the studies in the areas of strategy, management control, and manufacturing are integrated into a model. One objective of this model is to highlight central concepts in the review of the literature and to relate them to each other. A second objective is to establish a clear theoretical foundation and a structure for the remainder of the book.

The model is based on the assumption that the firm is an open system which both affects its environment and is affected by it. Thus, the firm is influenced by events outside its control; at the same time, it is in a good position to exercise control over its own development. The long-term objectives of the firm should therefore be the basis for designing suitable strategies, even though the environment can impose certain limitations in the short run. Consequently, it is assumed that management can choose a strategy well adapted to the environment in which the firm operates. It is also assumed that in the longer run management can affect whether the firm will operate in a turbulent environment or a stable one.

In the model, the matching of environment and strategy is referred to as external fit. There are reasons to believe that such a fit – established throughout the firm – contributes to the creation of a strong competitive position. Management should therefore seek strategic congruence – that is, mutually consistent corporate, business, and functional strategies. In this effort, the systems of control have an important function in regard to both the formulation and the implementation of strategies. So-called integrated control systems are particularly appropriate for establishing an internal fit – in other words, a high degree of consistency between strategies, internal capabilities, and performance. A typical feature of such control systems is that strategic planning and monitoring of results are coherent throughout the firm. In the model, it is emphasized that neither a good external fit nor a good internal fit is sufficient to establish a strong competitive position. Required are both a thorough knowledge of the chosen competitive arena and a detailed understanding of the ways in which the firm best can utilize its internal structures to position the product offering successfully.

Notes

1. The mechanistic form has its origin in the so-called machine theory. For a detailed discussion of the machine theory, especially its strengths and weaknesses, we refer the reader to Morgan (1986).

2. According to Morgan (1986, p. 56 f) the organic form bears a certain resemblance to an "adhocracy" (i.e. an adaptive and temporary system). A typical adhocracy is the project organization.

3. The environment is customarily regarded as one of the principal contingency factors. Examples of other contingency factors are technology, industry, and size (see also Chapter 1, Footnote 8).

4. For a review of some early studies in the field of contingency theory, see Galbraith and Nathanson (1978, chapter four).

5. Chandler (1962, pp.13 ff.) defines strategy as "the determination of the basic long-term goals and objectives of an enterprise, and the adoption of courses of action and the allocation of resources necessary for carrying out these goals. Decisions to expand the volume of activities, to set up distant plants and offices, to move into new economic functions, or become diversified along many lines of business involve the defining of new basic goals...Structure can be defined as the design of organization through which the enterprise is administered. This design, whether formally or informally defined, has two aspects. It includes, first, the lines of authority and communication between the different administrative offices and officers, and, second, the information and data that flow through these lines of communication and authority."

6. Hrebiniak et al. (1989) have also compiled empirical research on the relationship between strategy, structure, and performance in the 1980's.

7. According to Galbraith and Nathanson (1978, p. 31) the study by Rumelt (1974) shows that a strategy of controlled diversity is associated with high performance.

8. See Galbraith and Nathanson (1978, pp. 35 ff.) for a review of other studies from the 1970's that examine how a fit between strategy and structure affects performance.

9. See Chapter 1, Footnote 4, for a discussion of the concept of structure.

10. According to Mintzberg et al. (1998), Michel Porter is a leading representative of the so-called Positioning School. This school has origins in both the Planning and Design Schools.

11. Porter (1980, 1985) maintains that only three strategies are possible at the business-unit level: differentiation, cost leadership, and focusing (these strategies are described in detail in Chapter 3). Other schools of thought in strategic management – such as the Design and Planning Schools – put no limits on the number of possible strategies (Mintzberg et al., 1998).

12. See Chapter 1, which describes how this analysis can be conducted with the aid of Porter's (1980) five-force framework.

13. The following section contains an overall discussion of different corporate, business, and functional strategies. The reasoning is developed further in Chapter 3, particularly in regard to the distinguishing features of each strategy.

14. The results from the study by Goold and Campbell (1987a) were further analyzed and refined in Goold et al. (1994).

15. Nilsson (2000) studied only corporate groups with a strategy of either financial control or strategic planning. He also discussed the design and use of the management control systems at the business unit level. In Nilsson (2002) the analysis is further refined with a focus on how – and to what extent – management control changed following take-over.

16. The studies by Goold and Campbell (1987a) and Nilsson (2000) are case studies. As with all types of case studies, it is not possible to generalize the results to a larger population. In addition, the results are often open to somewhat varying interpretations. Nevertheless the studies can give some indication of tendencies regarding the relationships between corporate strategy and control systems, especially when they are compared to the results of other studies (cf. Yin, 1989).

17. For an excellent overview of the field, we recommend the article by Langfield-Smith (1997). Other researchers providing overviews in this area include Kald et al. (2000) and Anthony and Govindarajan (2004, p. 698 ff).

18. The study by Miller (1988) investigates the relationship between Porter's business strategy and a broad set of structural variables. In other words, this is not a study focused primarily on the link between strategy and control systems. Nevertheless, it has produced some interesting findings. For example, Miller (1988) demonstrates that there is a positive correlation between a cost-leadership strategy and the use of formal control. This correlation was significant at the companies that were successful.

19. The business-strategy typology of build, hold, and harvest was developed by Gupta and Govindarajan in 1984. Basically it relates business strategy to the so-called product life cycle. See Chapter 3 for a more detailed description.

20. Examples of long-run criteria used by Govindarajan and Gupta (1985) are sales-growth rate, market share, new-product development, market development, and personnel development. Examples of short-run criteria are operating profits, profit-to-sales ratio, cash flow from operations, and return on investment.

21. Examples of frequently encountered typologies of manufacturing strategy are discussed in Chapter 3. These typologies have been developed by researchers in the area of manufacturing control.

22. According to Abernethy and Lillis (1995), manufacturing flexibility is reflected in a firm's ability to respond to market demands by switching from one product to another and its willingness or capacity to offer product variations.

23. The authors maintain that this study is more generalizable than Abernethy and Lillis (1995). In finding the association between manufacturing strategy and non-financial performance measures, the authors used four components of a customer-focused strategy rather than one, a different survey methodology, and a broader-based random sample of manufacturing firms.

24. Strategic control includes strategy-implementation practices (for example, the importance of plans and targets), internal-monitoring practices (for example, the type of feedback given) and external-monitoring practices (for example, the use of external benchmarks).

25. According to Kim and Lee (1993), technical flexibility refers to flexibility in the use of machinery, flexibility in processes, product flexibility, routing flexibility, flexibility of volume, flexibility of expansion, and process sequence flexibility. In the subsequent discussion of studies on manufacturing control, and of articles where typologies of manufacturing strategy are presented, we have chosen to highlight how the authors – directly or indirectly – have related control models and strategies to changes in volume and to the introduction of new products and variants of existing products. A narrow range of products with stable product designs and manufactured in high volumes requires a different degree of technical flexibility than custom-made products made in a wide variety and in low volumes.

26. The tendencies in regard to the type of information used in the control system are linked to the studies that explicitly discuss this dimension in relation to a manufacturing strategy based on flexibility (i.e. Abernethy and Lillis, 1995; Perera et al., 1997).

27. Goold et al. (1994) do not discuss in much detail how management needs in regard to the systems of control may differ between the business-unit level and the corporate level. To judge from the authors' general reasoning, they appear to recommend limiting the freedom of the business unit to adapt its system of control to its own situation (Goold et al., 1994, p. 418). See also Footnote 13 and 14 in Chapter 1.

28. Strategic Planning is one of the three successful corporate strategies discussed by Goold et al. (1994). These corporate strategies are described in detail in Chapter 3.

29. The so-called protective buffers discussed by Thompson (1967) can probably not totally insulate manufacturing from environmental influences; some adaptation of organization and control is probably always required.

30. Ford et al. (1988, p. 397 ff) identify the following environmental elements at the highest level: (1) sociocultural elements such as the government and the general public; (2) economic elements such as

capital markets, customers, and competitors; (3) physical elements such as minerals, metals and water; and (4) technological elements such as improved processes, machinery, and equipment.

31. Thompson (1967, p. 34 ff) discusses three different strategies which a firm may follow in managing cooperation with important elements in its environment. According to Thompson, it is characteristic of the first strategy, which is termed Contracting, that the firm tries to formalize its relationship with the elements selected. With the second strategy, Co-opting, the firm absorbs the element in question. The third strategy is called Coalescing by the author; it means that the original firm and the element together create a new organization.

32. For a thorough and detailed description of the planning process itself, we recommend *Corporate Strategy*, by H. Igor Ansoff (1965). The Planning School is described in the section entitled "Strategic Management" in Chapter 2.

33. One reason why Porter (1985) introduced the concept of the value chain was to facilitate analysis of the firm's primary and secondary activities. In the field of management control, the concept of activity-based costing (ABC) was subsequently launched (Bromwich and Bhimani, 1994).

3 Strategic Congruence

One central point of departure for this book is that strategic congruence is a necessary precondition for being competitive. In this chapter the concept of strategic congruence is defined and related to other important concepts in the research area of strategy. The chapter also contains a description and discussion of the three principal levels of strategy: corporate strategy, business strategy, and functional strategy. Since both researchers and practitioners have adopted their own individual interpretations of each of these levels, a large number of strategic typologies have been developed. We have therefore chosen to limit our discussion to a selection of well-recognized, established typologies and to comment upon them thoroughly with regard to archetypes, features, and contributions within and outside the scholarly field directly concerned. The purpose of the chapter is to discuss more extensively the concept of strategic congruence and from this discussion to select the typologies – one for each strategic level – that are particularly appropriate for use in the tentative model.

Strategic Congruence Defined

By strategic congruence we mean that the corporate, business, and functional strategies of the firm are mutually consistent, with strategy at each organizational level appropriate to the firm's competitive arena and overall strategic aims (*cf.* Hofer and Schendel, 1978; Fry and Smith, 1987; Nath and Sudharshan, 1994). The need to co-ordinate strategies at different organizational levels emerged as major companies began to diversify their businesses during the 20th century. As firms enlarged their sphere of operations from a single, often very clearly defined core business to include a variety of different businesses and products, the problems of co-ordination became more complex (Chandler, 1962). One of those who illustrated these problems was Skinner in his article on the necessity of linking manufacturing strategies to business and corporate strategies (Skinner, 1969). At the end of the 1960's, there were few US firms where the manufacturing function was governed by the priorities of corporate and business strategy. Instead, operating decisions were guided by concepts like "total productivity" and "efficiency."[1] The absence of strategic congruence often resulted in suboptimization and difficulties in meeting customer needs. Skinner's solution to these problems was centralized planning, in which corporate and business strategy would be used to formulate the firm's manufacturing strategy.

Skinner is not alone in recommending that strategic congruence be achieved by breaking down corporate goals and strategies to the business-unit level, and then to the level of each function. Many leading scholars and practitioners hold that decomposing strategy is a central activity in the co-ordination of corporate operations. For example, representatives of the so-called Planning School, with Ansoff in the forefront, have developed guidelines for designing this process (Mintzberg et al., 1998). According to these normatively focused researchers, overall corporate goals and strategies are the starting point for all co-ordination. As shown in Figure 3.1, co-ordination of corporate and business-unit strategies is the first step in the process of breaking down goals and strategies. Goals for return on capital and the positioning of the business unit in the chosen arena are examples of areas that corporate management must discuss with business-unit management. The value chain (Porter, 1985) and SWOT analysis (Learned et al., 1965) are two tools that have been developed for the purpose of facilitating this discussion.[2]

However, creating strategic congruence by breaking down goals and strategies has proven difficult (cf. Pettigrew and Whipp, 1991, p. 175 ff).

Fig. 3.1. Levels of strategy and their co-ordination

In many cases it has only been possible to achieve consistent strategies at different levels in certain parts of the firm. For example, many acquisitions are justified on the ground that there are synergies with one single business unit of the corporation.[3] The problem is that often these synergies are in fact limited to that particular business unit and that the newly acquired company operates in a substantially different competitive arena than most other corporate business units (*cf.* Nilsson, 2002). Thus, the acquired company may have a strategy that is quite well adapted to the environment in which it operates (external fit) but that is only appropriate for some of the other corporate business units (*cf.* Wheelwright, 1984). The possibility that relationships identified at a lower level (the business unit) may not be valid at a higher level (the corporation) – and vice versa – was explained back in 1967 by Lawrence and Lorsch, who referred to differences in the environment, particularly regarding the degree of uncertainty. Subsequently, the effect of the environment on the potential for creating strategic congruence has interested many scholars – two examples are the studies by Stobaugh and Telesio (1983) and by Kotha and Orne (1989). In both studies, the authors analyzed in detail the connection between business and manufacturing strategies, while only referring indirectly to the corporate-strategy level. They discussed the external environment extensively, but did not devote the same attention to the appropriate design and use of control systems (internal fit).[4] It may be noted that many empirical contributions in the field have a similar focus.

However, numerous authors maintain that to be highly competitive, management needs a thorough understanding both of the environment in which the business units operate, and of the ways in which the corporation should use its internal structures to position the product offering (see, for example, Porter, 1987). As discussed in previous sections, it can be difficult to acquire this understanding in either respect at firms where corporate, business, and functional strategies are not congruent. Case studies by Goold et al. (1994) indicate that at corporations focused on businesses in certain well-chosen markets and industries (so-called "heartlands"), such concentration contributes to good financial performance. In addition, these corporate groups seem to have limited their holdings to business units with similar competitive arenas, units that would be quite closely related in regard to the nature of synergies and typical decision-making situations. With the corporation's businesses based on a common logic, the mechanisms that create value are clearly discernible. One advantage of such focusing is that it permits integrated planning and follow-up, thus making it easier to co-ordinate the goals and strategies of the different organizational levels. Among other benefits, corporate management can ensure that synergies are exploited and can participate more effectively in the development of individual business units. Thus, strategic congruence can be assumed to improve the possibilities of matching strategies with the environment and of establishing a system of control that supports implementation of these strategies.

One problem, however, is that in many instances corporate management seems to have abdicated its role of leading and developing the enterprise. An illustration is the trend toward partly abandoning co-ordinated strategic planning in favor of decentralizing many decisions to the tactical and operating levels. Poor co-ordination of corporate activities has been a frequent side-effect of such attempts by corporate management to make business units more flexible and adaptable. Business units have been left to their own devices in regard to their development, with consequent erosion of the gains justifying the existence of the corporate whole. For the individual firm, the result is a low return on capital for shareholders – not infrequently leading to a takeover by so-called corporate raiders and to subsequent dismemberment of the company. A challenge to corporations is thus to grant business units sufficient freedom in tactical and operational decision-making while maintaining well-functioning overall co-ordination of business unit strategies (*cf.* Goold and Campbell, 2002b).

We argue that corporate management must be active in the process of establishing a clear heartland and thereby achieving a high degree of strategic congruence. Perhaps the most important task in this endeavor is to choose which business units should belong in the corporation; it is these units and their strategies that compete on the market, not the corporation as a whole.[5] Special attention should be paid to the environment, which can limit the range of feasible strategic alternatives in the short run. As is apparent from our theoretical premises, the basic properties of the environment are affected by such important factors as customers, suppliers, and in particular the degree of uncertainty. The chosen business strategy specifies those elements of the environment with which the unit chooses to interact, the so-called domain. Thus, management is in a position to influence whether the business unit will operate in a turbulent or more stable environment, at least in the longer term. This choice will determine, for example, how production should be organized, how control systems should be designed and used, and to what degree decisions can be decentralized (Galbraith and Nathanson, 1978). In a firm where business units are exposed to differing degrees of uncertainty, it will probably be difficult to co-ordinate strategies and to create a uniform corporate-wide organization and control system (*cf.* Lawrence and Lorsch, 1967). For example, a business unit in a turbulent environment, with many newly launched products and demand that is difficult to forecast, will require quite a different kind of control than a unit in a stable, mature industry. Therefore, it is reasonable to assume that strategic congruence requires that the business units operate in environments where approximately the same degree of uncertainty prevails.

In summary, this review shows what a high degree of strategic congruence can mean for the creation of competitive advantage. Many studies discuss the value of a fit between strategies at different organizational levels. However, we think it is possible to provide even better guidance as to what actually creates "fits" and "misfits." Consequently, there is a need to explore the concept of strategic congruence in greater depth. To facilitate our discussion, we will need a common frame of reference for the concepts of corporate, business, and functional strategy. In the following three sections, we shall review these concepts on the basis of generally accepted strategic typologies. The focus in these sections will thus be on pure forms of different corporate, business, and functional strategies. The detailed description of the characteristics of each strategy will serve as the starting point for the elaboration of the tentative model in Chapter 5.

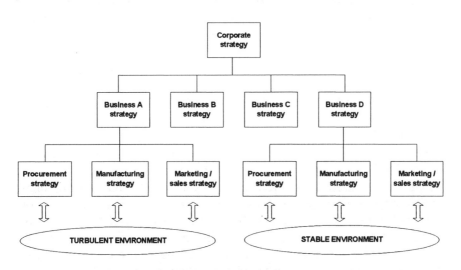

The matching of strategies and the environment
affects control systems and the organization at the
corporate, business-unit and functional levels

Fig. 3.2. The environment and strategic congruence

Corporate Strategy

The goals of a corporation are often financially oriented and closely linked to the manner in which value is to be created for owners, customers, and employees.[6] Corporate strategy indicates how the goals are to be achieved, and in particular why a solution with several business units is preferable (Hofer and Schendel, 1978).[7] According to Porter (1987) the costs of various co-ordinating activities to a corporate organization must be offset by the benefits of co-ordination. Examples of such benefits cited by the author are corporate contribution of professional management resources and technology, lower costs of capital for business units, and the opportunity to reduce costs through operating co-ordination of business-unit value chains. These benefits of co-ordination, which result from sharing the firm's resources among several business units, are called synergies. The value of synergies can be expressed as the increase in performance of the combined firms in the form of reduced costs and / or increased revenues.

In a traditional classification of corporate strategies, synergy potential – and particularly the degree of diversification – is treated as a reflection of general corporate strategy (cf. Rumelt, 1974). In these schemes of classification, the opportunities for synergies are greatest in corporations where the business units have similar operations – in other words, where the degree of diversification is low. In corporations with a high degree of diversification, and thus a wide range of focus for the various business units, there is less synergy potential. As for costs of co-ordination, these are lower in corporations with a substantial degree of diversification. Synergy potential and degree of diversification are also important dimensions, directly or indirectly, in the corporate-strategy typologies developed in the latter half of the 1980's. Examples of well-known typologies are those of Porter (1987), Goold et al. (1994), and Prahalad and Hamel (1996). Like the typologies developed in the 1970's, they address the fundamental question of corporate strategy: what businesses should be included in the corporation? Table 3.1 summarizes the principal features of these three typologies of corporate strategy. In the following sections, we provide relatively detailed descriptions and summaries of those portions of the corporate-strategy typologies that we find the authors of each study to consider important. Our reason for being so thorough at this stage in the presentation is partly to lay a solid foundation for our comparative analysis of typologies, and partly to facilitate deeper analysis of the question which cor-

Table 3.1. Schemes of classifying corporate strategy. Source: Based on Porter (1987), Goold et al. (1994) and Prahalad and Hamel (1996)

Study by	Arche-types	Features
Porter	Portfolio manage-ment	Acquires undervalued companies. Highly autonomous business units. Corporation supplies capital and sophisticated management techniques.
	Restructur-ing	Acquires undeveloped companies. Corporation transforms companies by changing management, strategy etc. Transformed companies are sold to finance acquisitions.
	Transfer-ring skills	Acquires companies with the potential to transfer skills or expertise. Corporation creates appropriate organizational mechanisms to facilitate cross-unit interchange.
	Sharing activities	Acquires companies with the potential to share activities between value chains. Corporation creates a context in which collaboration is encouraged and reinforced.
Goold et al.	Financial control	A corporate strategy based on stand-alone influence, i.e. low synergy potential. Value is created by developing the operations of individual business units.
	Strategic planning	A corporate strategy based on linkage influence, i.e. high synergy potential. Emphasis is placed on exploiting synergies through various forms of operational integration among business units.
	Strategic control	A corporate strategy that combines linkage influence and stand-alone influence. The company will have clusters of units with high synergy potential and clusters with low synergy potential.
Prahalad and Hamel	Portfolio of businesses	Management focuses on organizational units, which means that capital is allocated business by business. The product-market is important in defining the organizational boundaries of business units.
	Portfolio of competen-cies	Management focuses on competencies; this focus is also the basis for the allocation of capital and talent. Competencies and core products are important in defining organizational units.

porate, business, and functional strategies are congruent. It is also worth noting that the "Business Strategy" and "Functional Strategy" sections are organized in the same manner.

The Porter (1987) Typology of Corporate Strategy

This typology is based on an empirical study of the ways in which 33 large US corporations diversified their operations.[8] Porter selected the firms at random from many sectors of the economy, and he studied their diversification history for the period 1950-1986.[9] The study covered all acquisitions, joint ventures, and start-ups undertaken during the period covered. On average, each company in the study entered 80 new industries and 27 new fields.[10] Of the acquisitions in new industries, more than 50% were divested – a full 60% when entirely new fields had been entered.[11] According to Porter, these data show that successful diversification calls for a clear strategy and also the capacity to implement it. On the basis of this study, Porter identified four corporate strategies which had proven successful under the right circumstances: portfolio management, restructuring, transferring skills, and activity sharing. He stresses that although these strategies are overlapping, they create value in different ways.

According to Porter, a corporation with a strategy of portfolio management buys undervalued but well-managed companies where management agrees to continue working for the firm after the acquisition. The degree of diversification is high; in other words, the firms operate in a large number of unrelated industries (see Figure 3.3). Thus, synergy potential is limited, and the units continue to be managed as basically stand-alone firms. With a strategy of portfolio management, value is created in a number of different ways. In the article by Porter, four examples are given. First, corporate management uses its knowledge and its arsenal of methods to identify attractive firms to acquire. Second, the corporation can supply the units with capital on better terms than they could have obtained had they been independent companies. Third, the units gain access to more sophisticated management skills and techniques through the corporation. Finally, corporate management can help to improve the strategies of the units by thorough and unemotional reviews.

A restructuring strategy is similar to one of portfolio management, except that the policy is to divest companies after radical restructuring. For this reason it is important that the companies have a large potential for improved performance. The basic procedure with this strategy is that once the

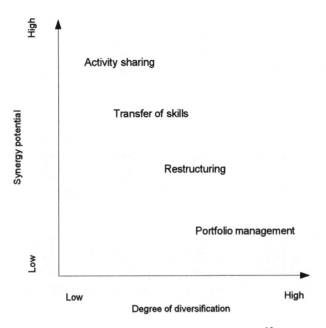

Fig. 3.3. The Porter (1987) typology of corporate strategy.[12] Source: Nilsson F. 1997. Strategi och ekonomisk styrning (in Swedish, "Strategy and Management Control: a Study of the Design and Use of Management Control Systems Following Takeover," p. 27)

acquisition is completed, corporate management takes a number of steps to turn the company around financially. Porter gives examples of some typical steps such as a change of management, a change of strategy, or the introduction of new technology. Restructuring can then be continued by acquisition of more companies to enlarge the business and make it stronger through economies of scale. According to Porter, restructuring is most successful when the company takes the lead in transforming an entire industry. Often the result of the transformation process is that the strategic position of the acquired companies is radically changed. Porter maintains that at this point the restructuring firm normally chooses to sell the acquired company because corporate management can add no further value. Since competence in successfully restructuring a business is limited to certain categories of industries, the degree of diversification is lower with this type of strategy than with one of portfolio management (see Figure 3.3).

With a strategy of transferring skills, the degree of diversification is low, and synergies arise primarily from the potential for transferring skills between similar activities (see Figure 3.3). Although each unit has its own unique value chain, it is important to establish procedures and incentive systems for effective inter-unit transfer of skills in conducting essential activities. Through these types of internal structures, the skills possessed by one cluster of business units can be shared by other units in the company. However, for competitiveness to be created through the transfer of skills, the activities involved in the businesses must be similar enough. According to Porter, general similarities, which will not help the corporation in building a strong and unique market position, are not an adequate basis for expanding operations. In addition, Porter stresses that the skills transferred must relate to the most critical areas, that is, activities of importance to the corporate, business and functional strategies. Moreover, these skills must be of a kind that will make the firm more competitive and thus not easily imitated by competing firms. Finally, Porter emphasizes, many companies fail with a transfer-of-skills strategy because they were not capable of establishing the culture, organization, and control systems required for spreading and sharing critical skills.

A strategy of activity sharing implies that the differences among the various activities of the firm are small enough to permit the sharing of certain activities, as in a joint R&D function, for example. Compared with other corporate strategies, the strategy of activity sharing features the lowest degree of diversification and offers the greatest opportunities for synergies (see Figure 3.3). Porter stresses that the principal reason is the relationship between this corporate strategy and the business strategies of cost leadership and differentiation.[13] Through co-ordinated and shared technological development, resource procurement, marketing functions, etc., economies of scale are achieved. Units can thereby lower their costs of production – an achievement of paramount importance with a cost-leadership strategy. Sharing activities can also help in differentiating the product offering; for example, shared service centers can often provide a very high service level. These examples of activity sharing, by Porter, create added value, but also add to the cost of co-ordinating business-unit operations. Whether the value added exceeds the costs of co-ordination depends on the possibilities of charging a premium price or of lowering the costs of production.

The Goold et al. (1994) Typology of Corporate Strategy

This strategic typology is based on 16 in-depth case studies of major British corporate groups. At the time of the study, they were all publicly quoted and covered a range of manufacturing and service sectors. Goold et al. (1994, p. 5) found that financially successful firms attached considerable importance to the following questions: "In what businesses should the company invest its resources, through ownership, minority holdings, joint ventures, or alliances? And how should the parent company influence and relate to the businesses under its control?" The purpose of these questions was to further the creation of a corporate strategy based on a common business logic – referred to by Goold et al. (1994) as Parenting Advantage. In this connection, one fundamental consideration is the manner in which the corporation creates value. On the basis of their case studies, the authors distinguish four different, though partly overlapping, types of value creation, cited below (ibid, p. 78):

1. Stand-alone influence, through which the parent enhances the standalone performance of the business units.

2. Linkage influence, through which the parent enhances the value of linkages between the business units.

3. Functional and service influence, through which the parent provides functional leadership and cost-effective services for the business units.

4. Corporate development activities, which create value by altering the composition of the portfolio of business units.

A corporate strategy can be based on a single type of value creation or on a combination of several different types. The authors emphasize that while not all of these types offer the same synergy potential, other circumstances determine whether the corporate strategy will be successful. Goold and Campbell (1987c) have shown that corporate strategies based on stand-alone influence, that is, a conglomerate-like strategy with limited synergies, are associated with a higher return on capital than strategies based on linkage influence.[14] Other studies of British companies have also shown that corporate groups with extensive diversification and limited synergies achieve high profits (Johnson and Thomas, 1987).

On the basis of these findings, Goold and Campbell (1987c) contend that the concept of synergy is too narrow to serve as the sole explanation for success. They argue that it is important for the business units to have largely similar critical success factors if corporate management is to participate effectively in the development of the business (Campbell et al., 1995). According to Goold et al. (1994, p. 278 ff), a common business logic is easier to establish if the corporation focuses on certain markets and industries – so-called heartlands. One advantage of such concentration is that it permits the corporation to establish a clear management style, manifested in a unified system of strategic planning and follow-up. This system must be adapted to the manner in which corporate management wishes to influence the design of business-unit strategies (planning influence) and to follow up business-unit performance in relation to strategy (control influence) (ibid, p. 411). The authors maintain that these two dimensions are important for describing the work of corporate management in developing the business units and creating value. Although these dimensions represent central features of the corporate control system, they are used here as the basis for the corporate-strategy typology of Goold et al. (1994). Figure 3.4 shows the three types of successful corporate strategies, referred to as Parenting Styles.[15]

Financial control is the strategy of corporations in which the business units operate independently of each other and the synergy potential is low (value creation through stand-alone influence).[16] According to the reasoning of Goold et al., business units are encouraged to act as independent firms which co-operate only if there are very clear benefits in so doing. As shown in Figure 3.4, most strategic decision-making is left to the business units (low planning influence). Goold et al. stress that considerable importance is attached to the budget, which corporate management carefully evaluates before approving it – often only after the financial goals have been raised to a higher level. Therefore, following up the annual budget is very important, and deviations are tolerated only in exceptional circumstances. Thus, the control process focuses primarily on the responsibility of the business-unit manager to achieve the financial results agreed on in the budget process (influence through tight financial control). According to the authors, this corporate strategy is based on the assumption that the business units of the corporation are best managed by using short-term, monetary controls. The cases show that it is appropriate in stable, mature industries where the need for massive, long-term investment is limited.

Strategic planning is characterized by the considerable potential for synergy gains from co-ordinating business-unit operations (value creation through linkage influence). The business units described in the case studies

Fig. 3.4. The Goold et al. (1994) typology of corporate strategy. Source: Goold M, Campbell A, Alexander, M. 1994. *Corporate Level Strategy.* p. 412

are therefore strongly encouraged to co-operate. As an aid, corporate management has implemented different kinds of co-ordinating mechanisms, such as overlapping and matrix responsibilities. Figure 3.4 shows that corporate management is highly involved in preparing the strategic plans of the business units. The authors maintain that typically corporate management is thoroughly familiar with the different businesses in the firm and actively tries to influence their long-run development (high planning influence). As corporate management has been involved in the decision-making process, follow-up will be based largely on non-monetary information. Given the importance attached to the long-term development of the firm's businesses, short-term monetary controls are only one aspect of the overall evaluation of business performance (influence through flexible control). According to Goold et al, this type of corporate strategy is often based on the possibilities of co-ordinating operations and exploiting synergies. The cases show that it is appropriate in high-risk industries where a long-term approach is prerequisite to success.

With strategic control, corporate management seeks to combine the advantages of the two other corporate strategies (value creation through both stand-alone and linkage influence). Since the degree of diversification is high, management usually seeks to create clusters of homogeneous business units. The cases indicate that the purpose is to adapt corporate-wide planning and follow-up to each cluster. In practice, such attempts have proven difficult, and the result has often been unclear control (see Figure 3.4). Goold et al. characterize the planning process as a relatively decentralized one where business units are expected to propose appropriate strategies accompanied by a budget. Thus, the role of corporate management is to examine these plans critically to make sure that they are of acceptable quality (moderate planning influence). In follow-up, both short-term monetary controls and longer-term strategic milestones are used (influence through tight strategic control). According to the authors, this style of management is intended to permit managing extremely diverse businesses. It has been shown, however, that the business units should have certain features in common for strategic control to be effective (Goold et al., 1993b). In addition, corporate management must be capable of adapting its management style to the needs of each cluster. The following passage describes the approach taken by one of Goold's and Campbell's (1987b) case companies:

We adapt our style to the different companies in our portfolio. We use Strategic Planning where we are building businesses with a 5-10 year payback. Strategic Control is our normal style and an active strategic dialogue takes place between the Group and the operating companies. And we use Financial Control for our "dog" companies, when we are sorting out and preparing for disposal operations which do not fit our long-term requirement (Goold and Campbell, 1987b, p. 47).

The Prahalad and Hamel (1996) Typology of Corporate Strategy

Prahalad and Hamel (1996) criticize the corporate-strategy typologies based solely on degree of diversification and synergy potential. In their view, competitiveness is dependent on access to competence and on the ability to utilize it in a manner that creates value. Using case studies primarily involving US businesses, Prahalad and Hamel focus instead on what they term "core competencies." A core competence consists of "the collective learning in the organization, especially how to co-ordinate diverse production skills and integrate multiple streams of technologies (ibid, p. 222)." Other important characteristics of a core competence mentioned by the authors are the following: it gives access to many different competitive arenas, it enhances the value customers attach to the product, it cannot be easily imitated.[17] The ability to create and develop new and revolutionary products in a cost-effective manner are another attribute of core competence that Prahalad and Hamel stress in their article.

As an example, the authors cite Honda's core competence in engines that has given that company a clear competitive advantage in a number of rather disparate businesses. According to the authors, companies should seek a strong and global competitive position in a well-specified class of product functionality – such as Honda's light-weight engines. Prahalad and Hamel are very skeptical about the possibility of "renting in" this competence through various forms of out-sourcing agreements.[18] Companies that enter into such agreements risk severe problems in the event of a shift in technology. Another example mentioned by the authors is the situation where a supplier chooses to become a competitor.

With this point of departure, a corporate strategy can be based either on a portfolio of businesses or on a portfolio of competencies. Prahalad and Hamel maintain that there are a number of drawbacks to the former approach. First, there is the likelihood that the investments required to build and develop core competencies will not be made, the reason being that no single business unit will consider itself responsible for investments of

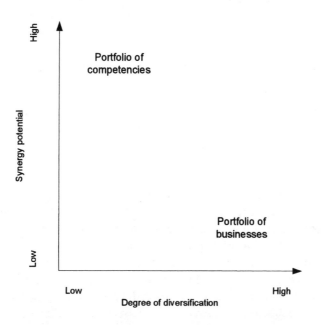

Fig. 3.5. The Prahalad and Hamel (1996) typology of corporate strategy. Source: Based on Prahalad CK, Hamel, G. 1996. *The Core Competence of the Corporation*

this kind. Second, there is a substantial risk that competencies will be locked into individual business units. Third, there is the possibility that the degree of innovation will be lower because SBU:s will pursue only opportunities in areas familiar to management. The authors conclude that a corporate strategy based on a portfolio of businesses may be appropriate for a conglomerate where the degree of diversification is high and synergies among business units are exclusively financial (see Figure 3.5). In corporations where the opportunities and ambitions to exploit synergies are greater, corporate management must develop what Prahalad and Hamel, have chosen to call a "corporate-wide strategic architecture." According to the authors, one of the purposes of such a structure is to help management in identifying the type of linkages between business units that can contribute to the development of a strong competitive position in the market. With this type of competence-based strategy, in contrast to a corporate strategy based on a portfolio of businesses, critical skills are a strategically very important, corporate resource. Core competencies should therefore, in the opinion of Prahalad and Hamel, be allocated among the divisions in the same manner as capital. Consequently, top management must be well acquainted with the operations of the business units; such familiarity is easier to achieve if the degree of corporate diversification is low (see Figure 3.5).[19]

Comparative Analysis of the Typologies of Corporate Strategy

From this review it is apparent that Porter (1987), Goold et al., (1994), and Prahalad and Hamel (1996) disagree on the importance of synergy potential in creating added value. At the same time, however, careful examination of these three schemes of classification shows that there are also considerable similarities. While Porter focuses on synergy potential, Goold et al. concentrate on analyzing which management style is appropriate for different kinds of relationships between businesses. Thus, Porter answers the question which corporate strategy can be expected to yield the highest return. Goold et al., on the other hand, seek to explain how corporate management, with the help of appropriate control systems, can realize synergies and thus successfully implement the chosen strategy. Prahalad and Hamel, in turn, try to show which synergies may be present in a business and how they can be exploited. Instead of treating synergies from the standpoint of activities, the authors emphasize that the firm's core competencies should permeate the entire organization and not be concentrated in individual business units. Figure 3.6 shows how the three typologies of corporate strategy can be related to each other on the basis of synergy potential and diversification degree.

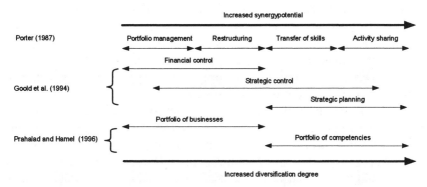

Fig. 3.6. The relationship among three typologies of corporate strategy[20]

As the previous description shows, financial control emphasizes decentralized decision-making and tight financial control. According to Goold et al. (1994), this corporate strategy is suitable when the business units are independent of each other and the need for co-ordination is limited, in other words, the type of corporate strategy that Porter (1987) would term portfolio management. With strategic planning, decision-making is centralized, and control is loose and flexible. In order to benefit from the considerable synergy potential, co-ordination of business-unit operations is heavily emphasized. Transfer of skills and activity sharing are the terms used by Porter (1987) to designate corporate strategies where there is a high synergy potential and a substantial need for co-ordination of business-unit operations. Prahalad and Hamel (1996) prefer the term Portfolio of Competencies to designate a strategy based on the sharing of essential skills by several business units. For such sharing to take place, there is a need for comprehensive co-ordination and a structure that can identify and allocate core competencies in the same manner as capital. A corporate strategy where there are no real synergies and where the units are managed like independent companies is termed a Portfolio of Businesses by Prahalad and Hamel. As with financial control and portfolio management, the need for co-ordination is limited with this type of corporate strategy.

In the presentation to follow, Porter's (1987) scheme of classification will be used. The principal reason is that Porter, unlike Goold et al. (1994) and Prahalad and Hamel (1996), has also developed a typology of business strategy. The strong link between his corporate- and business-strategy typologies, and particularly the similarity of their theoretical foundations, is a pedagogical advantage in the discussion of strategic congruence in Chapter 5. A second reason is that Porter's typology is based on well-established dimensions of corporate strategy such as degree of diversification and synergy potential. Goold et al. (1994) have chosen to include control systems, organization, and management style as bases for their classification. These structural variables are normally considered important in creating internal fit and thus in facilitating the implementation of strategy. Although this mixture of strategic and structural variables is innovative, there is a risk that the discussion of the concepts of strategic congruence and integrated control will be less clear than when these variables are considered separately.[21, 22] As for Prahalad's and Hamel's (1996) typology, it is innovative in many respects, but also relatively one-sided in its focus on core competence as virtually the sole basis for value creation. For the sake of clarity in the subsequent presentation, we have decided to focus on two strategies in Porter's typology: portfolio management and activity sharing. The reason for this choice is that these corporate strategies represent two opposite extremes in regard to degree of diversification and synergy potential.

Business Strategy

According to Hansson and Skärvad (1992, p. 513), the distinguishing features of a business unit can be summarized as follows: it has a competitive arena with well-defined competitors, it has a strategy of its own, and the products are sold directly to an external market. These criteria mean that the business unit includes the same primary activities of the value chain[23] as those required of an independent company. However, if a large proportion of activities are shared, the question of merging the business units involved should be considered (Goold and Campbell. 2000). Thus, within the unit there must be an identifiable process of adding value if a business unit is to qualify as such. This requirement means that production and other related activities are to be performed within the business unit.[24]

Since it is the business units that compete directly on the market, they are the most important elements of a corporation (*cf.* Goold et al., 1994). This fact also explains why the goals of the business units must be closely linked to the goals and strategies of the corporation, and especially to the manner in which value is to be created for owners, customers, and employees. The business strategy indicates what the individual business unit

Table 3.2. Schemes of classifying business strategy. Source: Simons (1990, p. 130), modified

Study by	Arche-types	Features
Porter	Differentia-tion	Product uniqueness permits higher prices. Emphasis on marketing and research.
	Cost lead-ership	Low price with focus on high market share, standard-ized products, and economies of scale.
	Focus	Focus on defined buyer group, product line, or geo-graphic market.
Gupta and Govinda-rajan	Build	Mission is to increase market share through invest-ment in higher capacity. Low relative market share in a high-growth industry.
	Hold	Mission is to keep existing market share. High rela-tive market share in a mature industry.
	Harvest	Mission is to maximize short-term earnings; invest-ments will therefore decrease rapidly. High relative market share in a declining industry.
Miles and Snow	Defender	Stable domain with limited product range. Competes through low cost or high quality. Efficiency para-mount. Company uses a centralized structure.
	Prospector	Turbulent domain where the company always seeks new product and market opportunities. The environ-ment is uncertain. The company uses a flexible struc-ture.
	Analyzer	Hybrid with a core of traditional products. Enters new markets after viability established. The company uses a matrix structure.
	Reactor	Lacks coherent strategy, and structure is inappropri-ate to purpose. Therefore, the company misses op-portunities. The company is viewed as unsuccessful.

should do to achieve its overall objectives and particularly the way in which it is to gain competitive advantage on its own market. Most typologies of business strategy, therefore, are based on the product offering of the business unit (Hofer and Schendel, 1978). One widely recognized typology of this kind was developed by Porter (1980). Another well-known example can be found in the discussion by Gupta and Govindarajan (1984) on strategic objectives in terms of the product life cycle. A more inwardly focused typology is presented by Miles and Snow (1978) in their discussion of interrelationships between domain, technology, and organization. Through explicit discussion of the interplay between external and internal fit, this typology will show with particular clarity the importance of the uncertainty created by the competitive arena of the business unit. Table 3.2 summarizes the features of the three typologies.

The Porter (1980) Typology of Business Strategy

This typology is derived from a factual base of hundreds of case studies.[25]

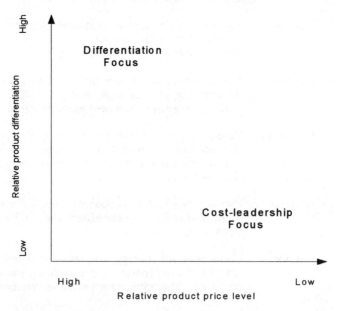

Fig. 3.7. The Porter (1980) typology of business strategy. Source: Nilsson F. 1997. Strategi och ekonomisk styrning (in Swedish, "Strategy and Management Control: a Study of the Design and Use of Management Control Systems Following Takeover," p. 27)

With this data as the point of departure, Porter (1980, p. 35) contended that a return on capital in excess of the industry average is possible only when one of the following strategies is pursued: differentiation, cost leadership, or focusing. One of the two criteria used by Porter in classifying these strategies is whether the customer considers the product to be differentiated; the other is whether the customer considers it to have a low price. The relationships involved are shown in Figure 3.7.

According to Porter (1980, p. 37; 1985, p. 14), the distinguishing feature of a differentiation strategy is that the business unit differentiates its product offering in respect to product attributes which it finds that purchasers strongly appreciate. By meeting purchaser needs in a unique way, the firm can often charge a price above the established level. The environment is turbulent (Miller 1986, 1987, 1988), and uncertainty is created by a comprehensive product assortment, difficulties in predicting demand, and dependence on successful R&D (Shank and Govindarajan, 1993, p. 105). Porter (1980, p. 35; 1985, p. 12) characterizes a cost-leadership strategy as one where the business unit seeks to achieve the lowest manufacturing cost in its industry through standardized products that are manufactured in long production runs. If the products can be sold at a price close to the established level, the firm will earn a return above the industry average. The environment is stable (Miller, 1986, 1987, 1988), and the uncertainty faced by the business unit is relatively limited, for reasons that include a narrow product range and stable demand (Shank and Govindarajan, 1993, p. 105). A focusing strategy is followed by business units with a strategy of differentiation or cost leadership that choose to concentrate on one segment of their industry (Porter, 1980, p. 38).

Porter (1985, p. 18 ff) holds that a differentiation strategy and a cost-leadership strategy are mutually exclusive. This should not be interpreted to mean that a business unit with a differentiation strategy can disregard costs of production; cost-effectiveness is merely not the primary success factor. However, there are some special situations where it might be possible to combine the two different types of business strategy (ibid,):

1. Competitors have chosen not to adopt either a differentiation or a cost-leadership profile, thus leaving the way open for skillful management to position its own unit by following both types of business strategy.

2. Cost leadership is achieved through holding a very high market share. In such a case, economies of scale can offset the cost of differentiation.

3. The business units introduce revolutionary new technology, in logistics, for example. However, it will no longer be possible to pursue two business strategies at the same time once the same technology becomes available to competitors.

Porter (1985, p. 20) holds that the circumstances described above are in most cases transitory. Thus, it is very difficult to maintain both differentiation and cost leadership over an extended period of time. Johnson (1992) is one researcher who disagrees:

From now on, the strategic choice is not beating competitors on cost or differentiating from competitors to offset higher costs with additional revenue. Competitive excellence in the global economy means companies must differentiate and beat competitors on cost, no trade-off (Johnson, 1992, p. 101).

Miller and Friesen (1986), Miller (1992) and Cooper (1996) are examples of researchers who have drawn conclusions similar to Johnson's. Cooper conducted a study on 19 major Japanese companies.[26] In the following quote the results and conclusions of the study are evident:

... especially in markets faced by the Japanese companies described in this study, competition is simply not like that. Customers have become more informed, rivals more aggressive and survival zones have been squeezed. In such a situation, the traditional approach of selecting whether to use a cost-leadership or differentiated product strategy is no longer available. If a firm wants to survive, there is no alternative but to compete head on in terms of cost, quality and functionality[27] (Cooper, 1996, p. 220).

Hall (1980) reached the opposite conclusion. In a study of 64 large US companies, he showed that very few of the most successful firms in the sample were capable of combining differentiation and cost leadership. Gilbert and Strebel reached a conclusion similar to Hall's in their study of the global automobile industry during 1980-1983.[28]

Nayyar (1993) presented an interesting approach to the problem of conflicting results concerning the possibilities of combining differentiation and cost leadership. In his view, it should be possible to explain the ambiguous results by analyzing the measuring instruments used. The conventional instruments are often based on the total product offering of the business unit (see, for example, Govindarajan, 1988). As a consequence, business units with both differentiated products and low-price products may be considered to follow a combined strategy. According to the author, this classification is perhaps correct at the business-unit level, but not appropriate at the product level. Porter (1996) maintains that it is difficult to combine these strategies even at the business-unit level, warning that the absence of trade-offs is a half-truth that managers must unlearn.

In general, false trade-offs between cost and quality occur primarily when there is redundant or wasted effort, poor control or accuracy, or weak coordination. Simultaneous improvement of cost and differentiation is possible only when a company begins far behind the productivity frontier[29] or when the frontier shifts outward. At the frontier, where companies have achieved current best practice, the trade-off between cost and differentiation is very real indeed (Porter 1996, p. 59).

The Gupta and Govindarajan (1984) Typology of Business Strategy

Closely related to Porter's (1980) discussion on the strategic position of

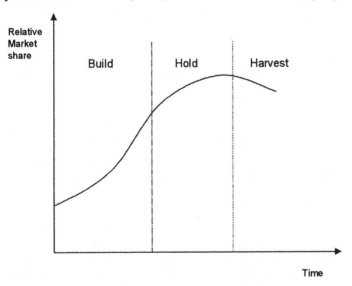

Fig. 3.8. The Gupta and Govindarajan (1984) typology of business strategy. Source: Based on Gupta AK, Govindarajan, V. 1984. Business Unit Strategy, Managerial Characteristics, and Business Unit Effectiveness at Strategy Implementation. Similar figures have been presented by for example, Porter (1980, p. 158)

the firm is the so-called product life cycle, in which the development of an industry is reflected in four phases: introduction, growth, maturity, and decline (ibid, p. 158). On the basis of the conflict between market-share growth and short-run profit maximization, Gupta and Govindarajan (1984) identified three business strategies: build, hold, and harvest. This classification is intended to apply at the business-unit level and thus to the development of the market and the life-cycle phase of the products of a specific unit. Since the product life cycle is based on the assumption that products go through different phases, in which demand and market share vary, a company's strategic mission[30] will also change over time. According to Gupta and Govindarajan (1984), this means that at one end of the spectrum one will find business units with a mission of increasing their market share, even if so doing will entail negative economic consequences in the short run. The authors characterize these units as holding a weak competitive position on a market with high relative growth (i.e. Build strategies). At the other end of the spectrum, one will find business units with a mission of maximizing cash flow even if the consequences will be negative in the long run. The authors classify these units as having a strong position on a market with declining demand and severe price competition (i.e. Harvest strategies). These conditions are shown in Figure 3.8.[31]

As for the relationship between business strategy and degree of uncertainty, Gupta and Govindarajan (1984) maintain that a build strategy leads to a more turbulent environment than a harvest strategy. According to the authors, a build strategy, is based on an effort to increase the market share of the business unit, while a unit with a harvest strategy can at best maintain its share of the market. Gupta and Govindarajan argue that since the pursuit of market share is a zero-sum game, a build strategy will expose the unit to considerably stiffer competition than a harvest strategy. In addition, Gupta and Govindarajan hold, that a decision to increase market share (build strategy), rather than gradually to reduce it (harvest strategy), will make the unit more affected by outside parties and their decisions. The authors add that an effort to increase demand will also require a higher input of resources and volume of production, which in turn results in strong dependence on external relations.

Finally, it is important to note that typologies like the one developed by Gupta and Govindarajan (1984) have also been discussed by the Boston Consulting Group (Henderson, 1972), among other sources. As previously mentioned, these authors, unlike Gupta and Govindarajan, focus on the entire portfolio of business units. For example, the Boston Consulting Group classifies business units according to the following categories: cash cows (low market growth, high relative market share), dogs (low market growth, low relative market share), question marks (high market growth, low relative market share), and stars (high market growth, high relative market share). This classification is intended to serve as the basis for creating a balanced portfolio of business units – in effect, the type of corporate strategy that Porter (1987) terms portfolio management. Anthony et al. (1992, p. 335 ff) argue that in a diversified firm, liquid assets are transferred from cash cows to question marks to enable the latter to increase their market share. Question marks that cannot be developed in this manner should be terminated or sold.

The Miles and Snow (1978) Typology of Business Strategy

In the introduction to *Organizational Strategy, Structure and Process*, published in 1978, Miles and Snow describes the two principal parts of their framework: "(1) a general model of the process of adaptation that describes the decisions needed by the organization to maintain an effective alignment with its environment; and (2) an organizational typology[32] that portrays the different patterns of adaptive behavior used by organizations within a given industry or other grouping" (ibid, p. 5). This framework is the result of three empirical studies, of which the first was conducted on 16 firms in the college-textbook-publishing industry. The publishing industry

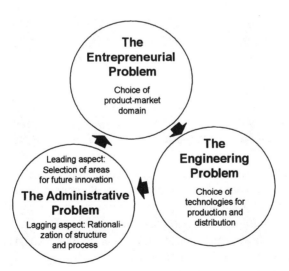

Fig. 3.9. The adaptive cycle. Source: Miles RE, Snow CC. 1978. *Organizational Strategy, Structure and Process.* p. 24

was chosen because it was undergoing major changes which the authors believed would lead to many organizational adjustments. The second study involved 49 organizations in the electronics and food-processing industries. These two industries were selected for the substantial differences between them in regard to technological change and environmental uncertainty. According to Miles and Snow, the cases were intended to provide a comprehensive exploration of the link between domain, structure and processes. Finally, a study of 19 voluntary hospitals was conducted to test the complete theoretical framework (ibid, p. 9 ff).

From their empirical research, Miles and Snow identified a number of issues confronting management. As shown in Figure 3.9, these issues can be summarized as three fundamental problems: the entrepreneurial problem, the engineering problem, and the administrative problem. According to Miles and Snow (1978, p. 21 f), the entrepreneurial problem concerns which products and markets should be developed, whereas the engineering problem is about the selection of a suitable technology. The administrative problem is one of reducing the amount of uncertainty affecting the organization. The authors stress (ibid, p. 23) that the task of management is in part to stabilize the activities that have contributed to the successful solution of problems in the entrepreneurial and engineering phases (lagging aspect), and in part to create structures and processes which will enable the organization to continue evolving (leading aspect). As the company encounters uncertainty and a need for change, solutions to the entrepreneurial, engineering, and administrative problems must be adapted to each other. If these problems are resolved in a consistent manner, a strategic pattern that is stable over time will emerge.[33]

The typology of Miles and Snow (1978, p. 29) is based upon groups of companies that have chosen to deal with the three problems in a similar fashion. The respective categories may be classified according to the following strategic typologies: defenders, prospectors, analyzers, and reactors. Miles and Snow showed that a defender has a narrow product range and operates in a stable domain. Management focuses primarily on reducing costs of manufacturing while maintaining or improving the standard of quality – for example by a high level of service. The cases indicate that growth results from further penetration of existing markets. They also show that defenders are characterized by a high degree of stability in regard to technology, structure, and processes.

According to Miles and Snow (ibid), prospectors are active in domains characterized by continual development and large changes. The authors stress that management is looking for new business and is not afraid of experimenting with different responses to threats and opportunities. In addition, the cases show that a continually changing domain means that the prospector is not able to build up the stable structures of a defender.

An analyzer operates in both stable and turbulent competitive arenas. These organizations are thus a combination of defender and prospector and show features consistent with each. Miles and Snow (ibid) found that analyzers on their stable markets typically show highly formalized and efficient structures and processes. On their turbulent markets, the cases showed that management responds only to moves by competitors after a thorough analysis. Finally, Miles and Snow identified a group of companies that they termed reactors; these are firms with no business strategy.

Comparative Analysis of the Typologies of Business Strategy

The classification schemes of Porter (1980), Gupta and Govindarajan (1984) and Miles and Snow (1978) proceed from a similar point of departure: the opportunity for management to choose a suitable strategy. As mentioned in earlier chapters of the book, the strategies and structures of the unit are not predetermined by the environment; in the long run, management often has the opportunity to affect the competitive arena of the business unit *(cf.* Child, 1972*)*. Thus, to some extent at least, management can influence whether a business unit will operate in a turbulent or a stable environment. As noted in the preceding discussion, the competitive arena of the unit, and the degree of uncertainty created by this environment, are an important dimension in the business-strategy typologies of Porter (1980), Gupta and Govindarajan (1984), and Miles and Snow (1978).

Another central dimension of the three typologies is the product offering of the business unit. Although the strategic typologies are based on many of the same assumptions regarding the product offering, they focus on different characteristics of business strategy: namely, strategic position, strategic mission, and strategic pattern. In a strategic pattern it is vital to choose whether the management of the company should try to find a completely new market or concentrate on developing the present one. If the focus is on strategic position, management has to decide whether to emphasize cost-effective production and be able to offer a low price or instead try to compete with the features of the product. Figure 3.10 shows how the three typologies of business strategy can be related to each other on the basis of the concepts of uncertainty and product offering.

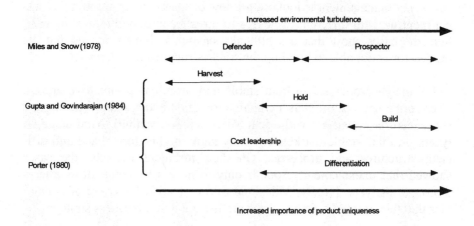

Fig. 3.10. The relationship among three typologies of business strategy

Figure 3.10 shows that the business-strategy typologies developed by Miles and Snow (1978), Gupta and Govindarajan (1984), and Porter (1980) are not mutually exclusive. In fact, there are many similarities among the typologies – particularly when the dimensions of uncertainty and product offering are considered. As noted in the preceding discussion, and in the analysis by Kald et al. (2000), a defender, in its purest form, is characterized by a stable domain and a limited product range. Since most of the products are mature, and price competition is keen, the strategic mission is often harvest. Efficiency is extremely important, and the degree of centralization is high – typical features of a cost-leadership strategy. At the other end of the spectrum, there is the pure prospector, operating in a turbulent domain where it constantly seeks to introduce interesting new products. A high proportion of newly launched products is a typical feature of units with a build strategy. A strong market focus, and innovative products that play an important part in creating competitive advantage, are distinguishing properties of differentiators.

In between the two pure forms of defender and prospector, one finds business units with other combinations of strategic patterns, strategic missions, and strategic positions. In their theoretical analysis, Kald et al. (2000) argue, for example, that a defender which strongly emphasizes product quality and customer service may be expected to seek differentiation as its strategic position. In this case, the unit will focus its product development on refining its existing product assortment (Porter, 1980).

Growth is assumed to occur through development of existing markets, with a special focus on certain products. According to Kald et al., this situation is similar to product differentiation, since the competitive advantage of the business unit is dependent on "...its ability to maintain aggressively its prominence within the chosen market segment" (Miles and Snow, 1978, p. 37). Since few completely new products are launched, the business unit seeks to prolong the life of its products; it thus follows a hold strategy. In their analyses of different combinations of business strategy, Kald et al. show that there are many similarities among the three typologies, but also important differences. Thus, one cannot equate the strategies of a defender and a cost leader.[34]

In the subsequent discussion, Porter's (1980) business-strategy typology will be used since it is clearly linked to his typology of corporate strategy (Porter, 1987).[35] As noted in the preceding section, it is advantageous to do so when discussing strategic congruence and integrated control in Chapter 5. Moreover, Porter's (1980) frame of reference is widely accepted among scholars and is considered to be internally consistent (Govindarajan, 1988). In addition, this typology has received empirical support in a number of studies (see for example, Gilbert and Strebel, 1988; Campbell-Hunt, 2000). Finally, the theoretical analysis by Kald et al. (2000) shows that Porter's (1980) typology, compared to those of Miles and Snow (1978) and Gupta and Govindarajan (1984), probably furnishes a better explanation of the design and use of management-control systems. Their hypothesis is that regardless which combination of strategic pattern, strategic mission, and strategic position is chosen, the latter variable determines whether control will be tight or loose.[36]

Functional Strategy

A functional strategy indicates how a specific function is to achieve its objectives. Common examples of functional strategies are purchasing strategy, manufacturing strategy, sales strategy, and R&D strategy. Within each business unit, business and functional strategies can be co-ordinated so that the latter are linked to the goals of the unit. These goals are often based on a particular product offering and on management's choice between a differentiation strategy and a cost-leadership strategy in positioning the unit (cf. Hofer and Schendel, 1978; Miller and Roth, 1994). In the effort to become highly competitive, the manufacturing function and its activities are considered especially important (Voss, 1995). Concepts like "world-class manufacturers" and "lean and mean enterprises" have been coined to designate firms where a well-developed manufacturing function is one of the principal reasons for their financial success (Cooper, 1996). In our subsequent presentation, we have therefore chosen to focus on manufacturing strategies and on typologies developed to describe them. According to Bozarth and McDermott (1998, p. 429), referring to Hill (1994), manufacturing strategy should be based on the assumption that performance is optimized when "(1) the manufacturing process is aligned with market requirements (environmental fit), and (2) the elements which define the manufacturing organization are mutually supportive (internal

Table 3.3. Schemes of classifying manufacturing strategy. Source: Based on Hayes and Wheelwright (1979a) and Ward et al. (1996)

Study by	Archetypes	Features
Hayes and Wheel-wright	Job shop	Low volume and low standardization of products. The high degree of product uniqueness is handled by relatively general-purpose equipment.
	Batch	Multiple products produced in low volumes. Batches of a given product proceed through a series of work stations.
	Assembly line	A few major products produced in higher volumes. Production process relatively mechanized and inte-grated.
	Continuous flow	High volume and high standardization of products. Continuous process in a very inflexible and capital-intensive plant.
Ward et al.	Niche dif-ferentiator	Offers a unique product. Customization is one way in which differentiation is achieved. Flexible produc-tion by using general-purpose equipment.
	Broad dif-ferentiator	Broad product offering, competes on the basis of quality and service. Manufacturing in batches to maintain flexibility.
	Cost Leaders	Large-scale production at low cost and with high quality. Highly mechanized flow process in which work-in-process inventory is minimized.
	Lean Competitor	Combines differentiation and cost effectiveness. Fo-cus on developing capabilities within such areas as quality, cost and flexibility.

fit)" (*cf.* Voss, 1995, p. 5 ff). External fit is often discussed in terms of central strategic dimensions such as cost, quality etc. Internal fit can be divided into structure (process, capacity etc.) and infrastructure (control systems, organizational design etc.) (Dangayach and Deshmukh, 2001; Rudberg, 2002). A well-known typology of manufacturing strategy with this focus is the one developed by Hayes and Wheelwright (1979a). Also included is the typology of Ward et al. (1996) since it provides an interesting discussion of production strategies aimed at combining the competitive priorities of differentiation and cost leadership (*cf.* Bozarth and McDermott, 1998). Table 3.3 summarizes the features of these two typologies.

The Hayes and Wheelwright (1979a) Typology of Manufacturing Strategy [37]

Hayes and Wheelwright have based their typology on the combination of two familiar concepts: the product life cycle and the process life cycle. In their view, just as a product and a competitive arena pass through

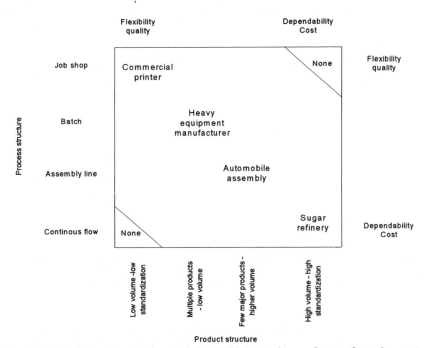

Fig. 3.11. The Hayes and Wheelwright (1979a) typology of manufacturing strategy. Source: Hayes RH, Wheelwright SG. 1979a. *Link Manufacturing Process and Product Life Cycles*, p. 135 (modified)

different phases of development, so a manufacturing process also undergoes changes. According to the authors, the course of these two types of changes typically begins with a manufacturing function where the process is flexible, small-scale, and with relatively high production costs. Thereafter, manufacturing becomes increasingly standardized and mechanized, ending with a process that is extremely cost-effective but almost totally inflexible. From this foundation, Hayes and Wheelwright (1979a) developed the so-called Product-Process Matrix (*cf.* Figure 3.11) in which the interaction of both product- and process-life-cycle stages can be represented. The vertical dimension of the matrix represents the steps through which Hayes and Wheelwright (1979a) assume that a typical manufacturing process may pass – from flexibility to mechanization. The horizontal dimension represents the different stages of the product life cycle, where unique products in low volumes are gradually replaced by, or developed into, standardized high-volume products. On the basis of this matrix,[38] Hayes and Wheelwright (1979a) identified four manufacturing strategies: job shop (jumbled flow), batch (disconnected line flow), assembly line (connected line flow), and continuous flow. As these terms suggest, they are taken from the vertical dimension of the matrix and thus reflect the nature of the internal manufacturing structure.

In Figure 3.11, each strategic position is represented by an example of different types of manufacturing units (commercial printer, heavy-equipment manufacturer, automobile assembly, and sugar refinery). According to Hayes and Wheelwright (1979a), with a job-shop strategy each product is unique, the volume of production is low, and quality is important. The uniqueness of the product rules out manufacturing to stock, since demand is virtually impossible to forecast. At the same time, the lead-time in manufacturing must not exceed what is reasonable and desirable (Olhager and Rapp, 1985, 1996). Since production must therefore be flexible, the machinery and labor force are not very specialized. When the volume of production has increased and products have become more standardized, Hayes and Wheelwright (1979a) consider a batch strategy to be more appropriate. Greater standardization means that the products can be processed in batches at different work stations. Further standardization of the product offering permits substantial economies of scale that require a highly mechanized and integrated manufacturing process; these are essential features of a what the authors have chosen to call an assembly-line strategy. Such a strategy is particularly appropriate when the product has reached a phase of maturity, and a strong competitive position is dependent on cost-effective manufacturing. Finally, Hayes and Wheelwright (1979a) discuss continuous flow. This strategy is suitable in a situation with very large volumes of highly standardized products. The authors argue that in this case a highly specialized and capital-intensive manufacturing plant will ensure dependable production with extremely low unit costs. As for production lead-time in continuous flow, it is often longer than the desired delivery time – a feature also associated with an assembly-line strategy. With stable demand, and at least partially standardized products, however, reliable sales forecasts and thus manufacturing to stock are facilitated (Olhager and Rapp, 1985, 1996).[39] The requirement of flexible production, therefore, is less stringent than with a job-shop or batch strategy.

The Ward et al. (1996) Typology of Manufacturing Strategy

According to Ward et al. (1996), the link to the business-strategy level is weak and unclear in almost all typologies of manufacturing strategy. The reason is that manufacturing strategy and business strategy are viewed as two completely different areas of research. To the authors, this situation is surprising in view of the considerable significance of manufacturing for

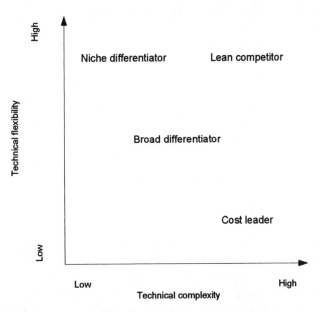

Fig. 3.12. The Ward et al. (1996) typology of manufacturing strategy. Source: Based on Ward PT, Bickford DJ, Leong KG. 1996. *Configurations of Manufacturing Strategy, Business Strategy, Environment and Structure*

the competitiveness of a business unit. From this starting point, Ward et al. (1996) have developed a manufacturing strategy typology with a clear link to the level of business strategy. In addition, the authors suggest links between manufacturing strategy and the dimensions of environment and organizational structure.[40] In the subsequent presentation of Ward et al's (1996) work, we have chosen to focus on the dimension of manufacturing strategy.

As shown in Figure 3.12, Ward et al. (1996) have identified the following manufacturing strategies: niche differentiator, broad differentiator, cost leader, and lean competitor. The authors characterize a niche differentiator as offering specialized and high-quality products to a market segment not adequately served by other firms. Low manufacturing costs are sought but are not strategically significant. Ward et al. stress that a high degree of flexibility in manufacturing is important if the business unit is to cope with rapid change in demand and offer customized products. In such a case, the unit should adopt a strategy of job-shop manufacturing, which is characterized by low technical complexity (*cf.* Figure 3.12).

The second strategy discussed by Ward et al. (1996) is that of broad differentiators. The authors characterize it as one in which business units offer an extensive, high-quality assortment of products to several different markets. By using batch production, a unit with this strategy combines relatively high technical flexibility with economies of scale. According to the authors, the difficulty with this manufacturing strategy lies in finding the right balance between the advantages of customized products through a manufacturing apparatus with high technical flexibility and the advantages of cost reduction through large-scale and technically complex manufacturing (*cf.* Figure 3.12).

The third manufacturing strategy identified by Ward et al. (1996) is that of the so-called cost leader. According to the authors, management seeks to achieve the lowest manufacturing cost in its competitive arena and therefore focuses its business on high-volume and mature products. This means that the emphasis shifts from flexibility in manufacturing to low unit costs. The authors stress that high quality in terms of conformity to standards is important since rejects and reworking entail substantial additional costs. Manufacturing can be characterized as extensively mechanized, and the integrated flow process is one of high technical complexity (*cf.* Figure 3.12).

Finally Ward et al. (1996) discuss the strategy of the so-called lean competitor. This type of strategy aims for both product differentiation and cost leadership. Economies of scale and flexibility in manufacturing are combined in a production process of rather high technical complexity (*cf.* Figure 3.12). Other important features mentioned by the authors are low inventory levels achieved with the help of just-in-time production, high utilization of machinery, and continuous improvements. Since this type of manufacturing strategy is highly demanding in terms of appropriate management, strategies, and control systems, it is relatively rare (*cf.* Porter, 1996). According to Ward et al., successful lean competitors have typically spent many years building up capabilities in critical areas such as quality control, logistics etc. (*cf.* Womack et al., 1990).

Comparative Analysis of the Typologies of Manufacturing Strategy

As with many other typologies / taxonomies of manufacturing strategy, both Hayes and Wheelwright (1979a) and Ward et al. (1996) extensively discuss the external environment, especially the product offering and market position of the business unit. In our opinion, these dimensions are critical elements of every business strategy and thus an obvious starting point for the formulation of a manufacturing strategy. Consequently, achieving an external fit, that is, aligning the manufacturing process with the competitive arena, is of major importance; however, it does not follow that external fit can be considered as the manufacturing strategy. Rather, the manufacturing strategy largely concerns internal structures, the design of which is an important element of the manufacturing organization and its processes (internal fit) (*cf.* Bozarth and McDermott, 1998).

Two central concepts in this regard are technical flexibility and technical complexity. The former refers to flexibility in the use of machinery, flexibility in process, product flexibility, routing flexibility, flexibility of volume, flexibility of expansion and process-sequence flexibility (Kim and Lee, 1993). It is particularly important that manufacturing strategy be so designed that the different product variants resulting from the business strategy can be handled without production lead-times' exceeding the desired delivery time (Olhager and Rapp, 1985, 1996). Technical complexity concerns the degree of mechanization in the manufacturing process and of integration among the various steps in the process (Kim and Lee, 1993). Figure 3.13 shows how the two typologies of manufacturing strategy can be related to each other in regard to technical flexibility and technical complexity.

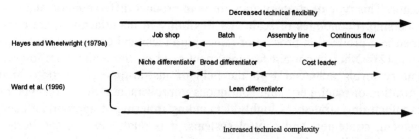

Fig. 3.13. The relationship between two typologies of manufacturing strategy

Figure 3.13 shows that there are clear and substantial similarities between the manufacturing-strategy typologies developed by Hayes and Wheelwright (1979a) and those of Ward et al. (1996). As noted in the preceding discussion, what Hayes and Wheelwright term a job-shop strategy is characterized by the manufacture of unique products in limited volumes. In order to manage rapid changes in volume effectively, a unit needs a manufacturing apparatus that is flexible but technically not very complex. Ward et al. use another term – niche differentiator – for units with this type of manufacturing strategy.

For business units with a more standardized product offering, a batch strategy is appropriate. According to Hayes and Wheelwright, the distinguishing feature of this strategy is that the products are manufactured in batches at different work stations. Units with this manufacturing strategy, which are called broad differentiators by Ward et al., require a manufacturing process that is technically somewhat more complex than for a niche differentiator (job-shop) strategy. With further standardization, it becomes possible to switch to an assembly-line strategy, and with highly standardized products in large volumes, a continuous-flow strategy. A cost leader is the term used by Ward et al. for units with strategies involving high technical complexity and limited possibilities of rapidly changing their manufacturing process. Ward et al. have also identified a fourth strategy, that of a so-called lean differentiator, which is focused on manufacturing relatively unique products at low cost. In this case, a relatively high degree of technical complexity is combined with a technical flexibility that permits some adaptation to customer requirements.

We have chosen to base our discussion on the typology of Hayes and Wheelwright (1979a), since the choice of manufacturing process and the internal operating conditions of the unit are crucial factors in a manufacturing strategy (*cf.* Bozarth and McDermott, 1998; Rudberg, 2002).[41] Ward et al. also discuss the internal and operating dimensions, but we find the typology of Hayes and Wheelwright to be better developed. In particular, the latter addresses more adequately such essential aspects of manufacturing strategy as the relationship between the degree of flexibility in manufacturing and technical complexity (*cf.* Kim and Lee, 1993). The typology also considers such important dimensions as lead-time in manufacturing, desired delivery time, and the possibility of manufacturing to stock (*cf.* Olhager and Rapp, 1985, 1996). Furthermore, Hayes and Wheelwright discuss in detail how to obtain a good fit between the manufacturing process and the product offering of the business unit. Ward et al. also treat this relationship, but without allowing for the possibility that several different manufacturing strategies may be feasible with a given business strategy.[42] Finally the typology of Hayes and Wheelwright is widely accepted among scholars and has also been tested empirically (Bozarth and McDermott, 1998). Hereafter, job-shop and batch strategies will be considered together in one single category, and assembly-line and continuous-flow strategies in another. This simplification is possible because of the substantial similarities between the manufacturing strategies concerned.

Summary

For a corporation to be a strong competitor, its management must possess a thorough understanding of the environments in which its business units operate, as well as extensive knowledge about ways to use the internal structures of the business units to position the product offering. Such understanding and knowledge will require strategic congruence, which in this chapter has been defined as consistency among corporate, business, and functional strategies. This means that the strategy at each organizational level is appropriate to the firm's competitive arena and overall strategic aims.

Basing corporate businesses on a common logic will ensure clarity about the mechanisms that create value. One major advantage of such focusing is that it permits integrated planning and follow-up, thus considerably facilitating co-ordination of the goals and strategies of the three organizational levels. Among additional other benefits, corporate management can ensure that synergies will be exploited and can also participate more effectively in the development of individual business units. Thus, strategic congruence improves the possibilities of matching strategies with the environment (external fit) and of establishing a control system that will support the implementation of these strategies (internal fit).

In this book we consider the three principal levels of strategy on the basis of a comparative analysis of well-known strategic typologies. These typologies are thoroughly discussed in regard to archetypes, features, and contributions within and outside the academic field concerned. At each level, we have selected one strategic typology which we have considered particularly appropriate for the purposes of the subsequent discussion and especially for the development of the tentative model in Chapter 5. At the corporate and business-unit levels, we have chosen Porter's (1980, 1987) typologies. These have been empirically tested, are internally consistent, and are widely accepted among scholars. At the functional level, we have chosen the manufacturing-strategy typology of Hays and Wheelwright (1979a) since it treats internal operating conditions in a clear fashion, is widely accepted among scholars, and has been tested empirically.

Notes

1. Skinner (1969, p. 139) summarizes the situation as follows: "They seek a kind of blending of low costs, high quality, and acceptable customer service. The view prevails that a plant with reasonably modern equipment, up-to-date methods and procedures, a co-operative workforce, a computerized information system, and an enlightened management will be a good plant and will perform efficiently. But what is a good plant? What is efficient performance?"

2. SWOT analysis (the assessment of Strengths and Weaknesses of the company in the light of the Opportunities and Threats in its environment) and the value chain are discussed in Chapter 2. These two instruments were developed by researchers of the so-called Design School and the Positioning School.

3. Synergies like skills sharing and activity sharing are discussed in detail in the next section, which treats typologies of corporate strategy.

4. However, Stobaugh and Telesio (1983), as well as Kotha and Orne (1989), also consider other internal structures such as appropriate organization of manufacturing.

5. In the type of corporation referred to by Rumelt (1974) as a single business, the degree of diversification is extremely low. The corporation is organized according to different functions. In such a corporation, corporate and business strategies coincide; thus, it can be said to compete directly on a product market.

6. Examples of other goals would be those for the development of the corporation's market positions and market shares. This type of goal can normally be related directly to business-unit operations and products. Compare Note 5 above, on corporations with an extremely low degree of diversification.

7. The vision is an important component of the corporate strategy. A vision should be based upon the overall corporate objectives. Normally, it also includes basic values as guidelines for decision-makers and employees.

8. The following corporations are among those included in the study: Du Pont, Exxon, General Electric, IBM, Procter & Gamble, Westinghouse, and Xerox.

9. Porter (1987) decided to choose 1950 as the base year in order to eliminate distortions caused by World War II.

10. According to Porter (1987) an industry is a subset of a field. An example taken from the article: insurance is an industry in the field of financial services.

11. To measure the success of diversification strategies, Porter (1987) calculated the percentage of entries made by 1975 and by 1980 that had been divested or closed down as of January 1987.

12. The figure describes pure forms of the four corporate strategies identified by Porter (1987). As indicated in this section, these strategies need not be mutually exclusive. For example, a restructuring strategy may also include elements of transfer of skills and/or activity sharing. It is also important to note that the positioning of the different strategies in the figure, and in the following figures, is only approximate.

13. Strategies of cost leadership and differentiation are discussed in the next section, which is on business strategies.

14. The difference was 2.9 percentage points.

15. In all, eight different corporate strategies were identified. Five of these (centralized, strategic programming, financial programming, strategic venturing, and holding company) were considered to lack the potential for sustainable success. See Goold and Campbell (1987a) for a detailed discussion.

16. As indicated in the preceding discussion, a corporate strategy can be based on several different types of value creation. We have indicated the type of value creation most common in the case of financial control, based on the reasoning of Goold et al. (1994).

17. The ability to make use of skills in various ways, and within a single firm, is particularly difficult to imitate. According to Prahalad and Hamel (1996), it requires a thorough knowledge and deep understanding of the internal structures that support the sharing of skills.

18. Nokia maintains that its own manufacture of mobile telephones is a core competence and one of the main reasons why the firm has been able to build up a strong competitive position and a high market share. SonyEricsson, by contrast, has chosen to "outsource" its production of mobile telephones to Flextronics. The following quote from Prahalad and Hamel (1996, p. 226) gives food for thought: "Outsourcing can provide a short-cut to a more competitive product, but it typically contributes little to building the people-embodied skills that are needed to sustain product leadership."

19. According to Prahalad and Hamel (1996), many corporations fail to develop core competencies precisely because they have treated their business units as autonomous firms. They argue that even units apparently unrelated may have a common core competence.

20. This figure, like the ones where business strategies (Figure 3.10) and functional strategies (Figure 3.13) are compared, is not claimed to show exactly how different typologies are interrelated. Rather, it should be viewed as a starting point for comparative analysis.

21. Porter (1985), too, strongly emphasizes the importance of internal fit and its interrelationship with external fit. The value chain, for example, is a tool launched by Porter to facilitate analysis of the firm's internal structures for the purpose of successfully positioning its products on the market. See Chapter 2 for a detailed discussion.

22. The corporate-strategy typology developed by Goold et al. (1994) is derived from the findings published in *Strategies and Styles* (Goold and Campbell, 1987a). As is apparent from the review of the literature in Chapter 2, this typology is based extensively on the manner in which corporate management designs and uses systems of planning and follow-up to control business units. This typology shows the need for strategic congruence to achieve integrated control – and vice versa. On the other hand, the authors do not appear to have had the ambition of clearly distinguishing strategic congruence and integrated control; this statement applies particularly to the development of their typology of corporate strategy. In our opinion, separate consideration of the two concepts is necessary for analyzing more thoroughly how external and internal fit affect competitive advantage and ultimately performance.

23. See Chapter 2 for a description of the value chain.

24. Production should be interpreted in a broad sense. In many manufacturing industries, value added consists largely of inputs of parts to the end product. Nevertheless, it is possible in most cases to identify a distinct process of refinement.

25. Other sources of data that Porter (1980) claims to have used include: statistical scholarly research, supervision of industry studies by teams of MBA students, and work with U.S. and international companies.

26. The study describes the business strategies of Japanese firms and the design and use of their management control (costing techniques).

27. Cooper (1996, p. 220) defines functionality as "the degree of success in designing the product to meet the specifications that customers desire."

28. The authors use the term Outpacing for this type of strategy.

29. Porter (1996, p. 41 ff), defines the productivity frontier as: "the sum of all existing best practices at any given time. Think of it as the maximum value that a company delivering a particular product or service can create at a given cost, using the best available technologies, skills, management techniques, and purchased inputs ... As companies move to the frontier, they can often improve on multiple dimensions of performance at the same time. For example, manufacturers that adopted the Japanese practice of rapid changeovers in the 1980s were able to lower costs and improve differentiation simultaneously. What were once believed to be real trade-offs – between defects and costs, for example – turned out to be illusions created by poor operational effectiveness. Managers have learned to reject such false trade-offs."

30. According to Anthony et al. (1992, p. 333), a business strategy is customarily separated into two dimensions: "(1) its mission ('what are its overall objectives?') and (2) its competitive advantage ('how should the business unit compete in its industry to accomplish its mission?')."

31. Gupta and Govindarajan (1984) chose to operationalize strategic mission as a continuous variable. They defend this choice on the ground that a transition from a "pure build" strategy at one end to a "pure harvest" strategy at the other is reflected both in the six strategic missions of Hofer and Schendel (1978) and in the eight strategic missions of MacMillan (1982).

32. Miles and Snow (1978) employ the term "organizational typology" rather than "business-strategy typology." Their reason is that they have also chosen to include structure and process as bases for their classification. As is apparent from the presentation, Miles and Snow attach importance to the interaction of external and internal fit. The typology developed reflects this choice (Venkatraman and Camillus, 1984).

33. Miles and Snow (1978) emphasize that when a firm achieves a good fit between environment, strategy, structure, and process, it may have difficulty in conducting the business outside of this setting.

34. The Strategy and Control section of Chapter 2 describes a number of studies on the relationship between business strategy and control systems. Although different typologies of business strategy have been used in these studies, many researchers in their subsequent analysis of the findings have equated prospectors and differentiators, for example. On such a basis, however, it is difficult to explain some of the findings – for example, in the study by Simons (1987) prospectors are found to use tight control, whereas Govindarajan's (1988) study shows that a strategy of differentiation leads to loose control. Kald et al. (2000) argues that these types of ambiguous findings can be explained only through detailed efforts to relate the business strategy typologies to one another.

35. Focusing will be excluded from further consideration since it is not an explicit strategy in itself but a choice within a strategy. According to Kald et al. (2000), this explains why focusing is not considered in the contingency studies on strategy and management control (see, the Strategy and Control section of Chapter 2).

36. Kald et al. (2000) cite the study by Simons (1987) as an example. Simons showed that prospectors featured tight control – an unexpected finding. On the basis of the hypotheses developed in the theoretical analysis by Kald et al., Simon's results may be interpreted instead to mean that he studied prospectors with a cost-leadership strategy emphasizing hold as the strategic mission. The analysis by Kald et al. is based on the assumption that cost leadership always leads to tight control whereas differentiation always leads to loose control.

37. Hayes and Wheelwright develop their reasoning further in an article published later that same year (Hayes and Wheelwright, 1979b). In this article, the authors describe how the process-product matrix can be

used to analyze which growth strategies can be appropriate given the firm's position in the product and process life cycle. Their typology of manufacturing strategy is also presented in the book *Restoring Our Competitive Edge: Competing Through Manufacturing* (Hayes and Wheelwright, 1984).

38. One manufacturing strategy that Hayes and Wheelwright (1979a) do not discuss is projects. According to Hill (1989), a project strategy is used for large-scale, unique, and complex products. With a project strategy, control differs in important respects from that used in other manufacturing strategies. We have therefore decided not to consider the project strategy in this book.

39. In certain situations, forecasts of individual products may be highly uncertain. According to the reasoning of Olhager and Rapp (1985, 1996), it may then be advantageous to separate manufacturing into two steps. In the first step, the product is refined without becoming entirely customer-specific. In the second step, customer-specific parts are manufactured and the final product is assembled. In the authors' view, the advantage of this "two-step" approach is that in the first step manufacturing may be entirely to stock (inventories of semi-manufactures).

40. Ward et al. (1996) used the so-called configuration approach to find linkages between business and manufacturing strategies as well as internal structures and the environment (*cf.* Miller and Mintzberg, 1988). According to Ward et al. (ibid, p. 598), this approach to the study of strategy can be termed as "identifying dominant gestalts of observable characteristics or behaviors which appear to lead to a particular outcome (such as success or failure)."

41. Hayes and Wheelwright (1984, p. 32) define manufacturing strategy in the following way: "It is critical that these decisions, made throughout the organization and at all levels, be consistent with the decisions made at other points in time and within other categories, and that their cumulative result over time is the desired manufacturing structure and infrastructure. Otherwise, unintended drifting will take place. It is this pattern of structural and infrastructural decisions that constitutes the 'manufacturing strategy' of a business unit." On page 33 they also state: "...the primary function of a manufacturing strategy is to guide the business in putting together the set of manufacturing capabilities that will enable it to pursue its chosen competitive strategy over the long term."

42. Compared with the typology of Hayes and Wheelwrights (1979a), that of Ward et al. (1996) is characterized by an indistinct boundary between business and manufacturing strategy. The explanation lies in the authors' ambition to link these two strategic levels. For our purposes, however, it is unfortunate from a pedagogical standpoint since we are seeking to make clear the differences between business and manufacturing strategies.

4 Integrated Control

A firm cannot become a strong competitor through strategic congruence alone – it is just as important to establish a system of integrated control. In this chapter the concept of integrated control is defined and related to other important concepts in the field of management control and manufacturing control. We shall initially show how research in these two areas has expanded to cover more organizational levels and more decision levels than before, a development stemming from a growing interest in integrated control. We shall then describe and discuss the concepts of management and manufacturing control, with special emphasis on procedures for planning and follow-up. We shall also identify a number of central dimensions in the design and use of management- and manufacturing-control systems. The purpose of this chapter is to provide a more thorough discussion of integrated control, especially those dimensions likely to affect the possibilities of establishing coherent strategic planning and follow-up. These dimensions are a fundamental point of departure in the tentative model.

Integrated Control Defined

Integrated control exists when strategic planning and follow-up at each organizational level are coherent throughout the firm. The purpose of integrated control is to facilitate the exchange of information between different organizational levels and decision-makers concerning strategic, tactical, and operating decisions. The use of similar concepts and principles of control throughout the corporation enhances the transparency of the planning and follow-up processes (Jansson et al., 2000). For example, it becomes easier to analyze the impact of activities in the value chain, together or separately, on the competitiveness and, ultimately, the performance of the business units and the corporation as a whole. In this way, it is possible to co-ordinate strategic planning and ongoing follow-up, thus improving the chances of achieving strategic congruence and of successfully implementing the strategies of the firm. To put it another way, integrated control facilitates the establishment of a high degree of internal fit, that is, of congruence between the strategies, internal structures, and expected performance of the firm.[1]

The example of the successful firms sometimes referred to as "world-class manufacturers" has shown that it is particularly important to achieve integration of management control and manufacturing control (Yoshikawa et al., 1994; Cooper, 1996). While these two control systems have often been viewed as separate areas of research, taken together they offer a vast potential for inducing behavior consistent with the objectives and strategies of the firm. To facilitate co-ordination of the manufacturing function with the goals and strategies of the business unit and the corporation, the same fundamental premises should apply to planning and follow-up. For example, a manufacturing-control system based on just-in-time (JIT) features a very strong focus on cost-effective production (Vollmann et al., 1992).[2] As a consequence, it is suitable to base management control on monetary information and high-intensity follow-up.[3] When management control and manufacturing control are similar in design and use, not only is co-ordination of the business simplified; an essential condition is also fulfilled for integration of the systems of control. In Chapter 5 we discuss how variations in the design and use of management control and manufacturing control can be assumed to affect the possibilities of achieving integrated control.

Although integrated control seems to make a difference for a firm's possibilities of being competitive, researchers in the areas of strategy and control have long shown rather limited interest in this subject. A plausible explanation is that these areas have been narrowly focused in regard to the organizational levels (corporate, business-unit, and operational[4] levels) and decision levels (strategic, tactical, and operational[5] levels) studied. Cases taken from actual practice, however, have demonstrated that the boundaries between management control and manufacturing control – formerly quite clear – are vanishing (see, for example, Howell and Soucy, 1987). As a consequence, research in management control and manufacturing control has been gradually broadened to include both more organizational levels and more decision levels.

As can be seen in Figure 4.1, research on control systems has shifted focus from two organizational levels to the interrelationship of control systems at all organizational levels. For a long time, research in the area of management control was concentrated on the design and use of the management-control system at the corporate and business-unit levels (Anthony et al., 1992), whereas the studies on manufacturing control were directed at the business-unit and operating levels (cf. Vollmann et al., 1992). According to Ittner and Larcker (2001), researchers in management control started

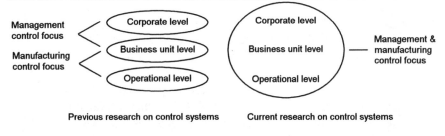

Fig. 4.1. Focus of research on control systems at different organizational levels

to show an interest in manufacturing control during the later part of the 1980's. Many of the empirical studies focused on describing manufacturing flows with the aid of performance-measurement systems (see, for example, Abernethy and Lillis, 1995; Perera et al., 1997). In contrast to studies in the area of manufacturing control, which often emphasized the design of planning procedures,[6] researchers in management control concentrated primarily on the impact of performance measures on human actions, and particularly whether those actions were consistent with the chosen manufacturing strategy (see, for example, Chenhall, 1997). Another area of considerable interest concerned new methods of product costing and how they could help to make manufacturing more efficient (Bromwich and Bhimani, 1994).[7] Activity-based costing (ABC) enabled management to analyze the cost structure of manufacturing at the activity level (Shank and Govindarajan, 1993).[8, 9] The possibilities of making the firm more competitive, by identifying which activities created value and which ones did not, were among the many benefits of installing such a costing-system.

Thus, researchers in management control have partially abandoned their previous focus on the corporate and business-unit levels and have begun to study the operating level as well. In the area of manufacturing control, the tendency seems less clear. As early as the 1960's, there were normative discussions – general, to be sure – on appropriate ways to control and organize manufacturing from a corporate point of view (Skinner, 1969). Even though these discussions showed that the question was highly relevant, comparatively few articles treating the link between manufacturing control and corporate strategy were published in the 1970's and 1980's (Kotha and Orne, 1989). One of these was an article in 1984 by Wheelwright which dealt with the difficulties in co-ordinating manufacturing strategies in highly diversified corporations, or conglomerates (cf. Wheelwright, 1984; Hayes and Wheelwright, 1984). In the 1990's, however, the corporate-strategy dimension appears to have attracted growing attention

(Rudberg, 2001). One explanation for this development is the strategic significance now attributed to the increasingly extensive integration between corporation and supplier. Network models of this type, in which collaboration can take the form of product development and JIT solutions,[10] for example, require co-ordination across producing business units (Womack and Jones, 1994; Cooper, 1996). Another explanation for the heightened interest in the corporate-strategy level is the need to exploit, develop and disseminate the knowledge generated within advanced manufacturing functions (Dent, 1996). In regard to both inter- and intraorganizational co-ordination, corporate management, and the nature of the corporate strategy are of pivotal significance, or, as Dent (ibid, p. 257) put it:

> The network model implies a fundamental reorientation of management approach, from hierarchical to lateral notions. Local subsidiaries no longer perform solely a local role, rather, under flexible specialisation,[11] they become part of a broader, global effort. Innovations are not owned by the units developing them, but are made available throughout the world. In short, the role of national subsidiaries calls for specialization and expertise, but their value is only realised in conjunction with others, through lateral communication in project teams and so forth. This requires a movement from fragmented functional analysis to a more systematic, synthetic approach. Moreover, the role of the centre becomes less to direct and control, and more to create conditions for integration, encouraging lateral linkages and reciprocal obligations, and rewarding results.

The extension of research on management control and manufacturing control to include additional organizational levels is tied to a corresponding expansion of the scope of research, which is now directed increasingly at different decision levels (*cf.* Figure 4.2). For a very long time, researchers in management control were heavily influenced by Anthony's (1965) frame of reference. According to Anthony and his normative reasoning,

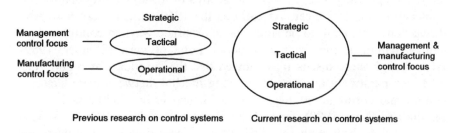

Fig. 4.2. Focus of research on control systems at different decision levels

management control is an activity that facilitates tactical decisions and influences behavior for the purpose of furthering the implementation of strategy.[12] In addition, Anthony maintains that given the unsystematic character of strategic decision-making and the focus of operational decision-making on individual transactions, there is a need for the kind of decision support that a management-control system cannot provide. Because of these two limitations, and as indicated in Figure 4.2, research on management control has focused on the tactical decision level (Otley, 1994).[13] Developments in the area of manufacturing have been similar; here there has been considerable interest in operational decision-making, whereas the link with the strategic and tactical levels has not received the same attention (cf. Kotha and Orne, 1989; Vollmann et al., 1992).

However, the tendency among leading companies has shown that a focus on one or two decision levels is much too narrow to explain the role of control systems in the process of creating a strong competitive advantage. A growing number of empirical studies suggest that the differences between strategic, tactical, and operational decisions are diminishing, thus improving the conditions for creating common frames of reference (see, for example, Nilsson and Rapp, 1999). The start of this development can be traced to the late 1970's, when Hayes and Abernathy (1980), among others, reported serious deficiencies in the planning and follow-up systems at US companies. One of the problems identified by the authors was that strategic planning in many companies was far too general. Another problem was that planning and follow-up at many US firms tended to focus on short-term financial measures like return on investment (ROI). Control at US companies thus differed from the design of planning and follow-up systems chosen by their Japanese competitors. In Japan, management realized at an early stage the importance of establishing integrated control, where the differences between strategic, tactical, and operative decisions were minor. How Japanese managers went about linking together the different decision levels is described by Wheelwright (1981, p. 70) as follows:

In each case, top management took seriously its responsibility for setting consistent long-term goals toward which even short-term operations decisions could be directed. And, as a result, in each case lower-echelon manufacturing managers clearly understood the strategic significance of their day-to-day concern with operational detail. In contrast, American companies usually separate production decisions that are strategic from those that are merely operational. In Japan, no such separation occurs, for Japanese managers treat virtually all operational issues as strategic.

In reaction to increasingly intense competition, particularly from Japanese companies, old organizational solutions and control models began to be questioned. As indicated in the introduction to this book, the 1980's and 1990's were characterized by efforts to make Western firms more flexible and adaptable. Many of the changes were organizational in nature, such as a stronger process orientation, a higher degree of decentralized decision-making, and changes in learning processes (Otley, 1994). These changes, in turn, led to a shift in interest from centralized strategic planning to a greater emphasis on the tactical and operating levels (Johnson, 1992; Dent, 1996).[14] As a consequence of this development, and as shown in Figure 4.2, there has been a tendency among researchers in management and manufacturing control to broaden the scope of their studies to include all decision levels. After previously maintaining that control systems at the strategic, tactical, and operating levels were based on different logics, and must therefore be designed differently, a growing number of researchers hold that these differences are decreasing. Otley (1999, p. 365) expressed this tendency as follows:

Although it may well have been sensible to concentrate initially on the core area of 'management control', it is now necessary to pay more attention to the neglected elements of strategy and operations. This is particularly important as contemporary organizations are themselves changing, illustrated by such developments as business process re-engineering and de-layering, where the same manager may well be responsible for some elements of strategy, management control and operational control.

Perhaps the principal explanation for this development is that far-reaching decentralization of decision-making to the operational level is accompanied by greater involvement in, and responsibility for, operations. In a case study of the control systems at Sandvik Bahco, Nilsson and Rapp (1999) showed that this type of development can result in a situation where personnel at the operational level tend to want more and more comprehensive information, and not just information from the manufacturing-control system. They may also begin to question the framework within which operations are conducted, thus altering the learning process at the operating level (cf. Argyris, 1977). However, according to Nilsson and Rapp, this does not mean that there are no differences in information needs at the various decision levels and that a common control system is most suitable. Rather, it is a question of using a common frame of reference to create a meaningful dialogue between the three different decision levels (cf. Jönsson and Grönlund, 1988). The purpose of integrated control is to facilitate such a dialogue and to make it easier both to choose a suitable strategy and to implement it.

In summary, the discussion above shows that practice and research in management control and manufacturing control have been extended to more organizational levels and more decision levels than before. As an example of this twofold extension, many companies have begun to use their management-control systems to follow up certain aspects of manufacturing (*cf.* Dixon et al., 1990; McNair et al., 1990). Another consequence is that selected areas of planning and follow-up, which formerly were included in management control, are being decentralized to the operating level (Nilsson and Rapp, 1999). These two cases show that the extension of management control and manufacturing control has increased the number of points of contact between these two control systems and thus made it easier to achieve integrated planning and follow-up. In view of the rather limited number of empirical studies in this area, however, it is necessary to discuss integrated control in greater depth. In other words, even though the range of research has expanded to include more organizational levels and decision levels, there are still few studies that discuss how to match a control system at a higher level with a control system at a lower level. To assist us in this discussion, we need a common frame of reference for the two concepts of management control and manufacturing control. In the following two sections, we shall review these concepts on the basis of generally accepted definitions. We shall also identify a number of central dimensions in the design and use of management- and manufacturing-control systems. These dimensions are important as a foundation for the subsequent discussion on the possibilities of establishing integrated control systems.

Management Control

By management control we mean the formalized, information-based routines, structures and processes used by management to formulate strategies and to implement them by influencing employee behavior (*cf.* Simons, 1995, p. 5; Anthony and Govindarajan, 2004, p. 4). This definition, which emphasizes the formal control of the firm, has an important role to fill in both the formulation and the implementation of strategies. Since we have chosen to regard strategy formulation as a deliberate and conscious process of thought, it is natural to focus on ways in which formalized control can support this process. We would like to emphasize, however, that informal control, through the corporate culture, for example, can also affect which strategies are considered and the possibilities of implementing them successfully (*cf.* Roberts, 1990). Thus, the formal control system cannot be designed or used in a manner totally at odds with the norms and values prevailing within the firm (*cf.* Jones, 1983).

In the process of strategy, the principal function of the control system, according to the older definitions, like that of Anthony (1965), is typically to compare the outcome for a period against stated goals and strategies. A control system designed and used in this way is termed by Simons (1995) as a diagnostic control system, in other words, a system used to "motivate, monitor, and reward achievement of specified goals (ibid, p. 7)." Our definition emphasizes, in addition, what Simons would call an interactive control system - that is, a system used to "stimulate organizational learning and the emergence of new ideas and strategies (ibid)." Using an example from the consumer-goods industry, Simons (1995, p. 5) describes how the control system can be used to maintain or alter patterns in organizational activities. From this example, it is apparent that a well-functioning control system must be both interactive and diagnostic.[15, 16]

Desirable patterns include not only goal-oriented activities – ensuring that new stores open on schedule – but also patterns of unanticipated innovation – discovering that branch employees' experiments with the layout of a store have doubled expected sales figures. Employees can surprise, and management control systems must accommodate intended strategies as well as strategies that emerge from local experimentation and independent employee initiatives.

Simons (1995) contends that whether a control system should be considered diagnostic[17] or interactive[18] depends primarily on its use. Typical diagnostic uses are implementation of strategy, responsibility accounting, and financial reporting to outside parties. Interactive use focuses the attention of management and other employees on areas of strategic uncertainty with the aim of establishing a dialogue about these areas. This assumption means that employees at operational levels will participate in the development of strategy. Simons' discussion of interactive and diagnostic use has proven fruitful in studies of the relationship between strategy and management control. This set of concepts has been used frequently, not only by Simons himself (1990, 1991, 1994, 1995), but also in case studies (see, for example, Berglund, 2002) as well as survey-based studies (see, for example, Nilsson and Kald, 2002). As noted previously, Simons focuses on strategy formulation (interactive use) and strategy implementation (diagnostic use). In the discussion to follow, the use of the control system will therefore be considered primarily on the basis of its role in the formulation and implementation of strategies. These two concepts will also be used in the subsequent sections and chapters. The reason is that the concepts of formulation and implementation are well established in the fields of strategy, management control, and manufacturing control. A uniform set of concepts is an advantage in a discussion of the prerequisites for establishing an integrated control system and of its effects on the creation of competitive advantage.

Simons (1995) maintains that it is particularly important to study the use of the control system since the design of the system tends to be relatively unaffected by the strategy chosen. However, the empirical support for this viewpoint is quite limited – for example, in a considerable proportion of the questionnaire-based studies that could show a relationship between strategy and control, the focus has been on the design dimension.[19] In light of this fact, we have chosen to consider the design of the management-control system as well, in other words, the way in which control reports and models reflect the business of the firm. For instance, the design of the control systems is affected by such factors as the chart of accounts, the way in which the budget is prepared, and the key numbers used in ongoing follow-up. Furthermore, we have chosen to discuss design in the dimensions of structure and process. By structure we mean the specific components of the management-control system such as planning instructions, budget forms, and calculation models. By process we mean the routines associated with these structures and required for them to be usable in decision-making. Examples include procedures for budgeting and follow-up (Nilsson, 1997, p. 14 f).

Given the focus of the book, and the evolution of research in management and manufacturing control as described in previous sections, we have included not only tactical control, but also strategic and operational control (cf. Otley, 1994). From the foregoing description, it is also apparent that one must study the design and use of the management-control system at all of the principal organizational levels – corporate, business-unit, and operational – in order to analyze the effects of coherent planning and follow-up. On the other hand, in choosing appropriate subsystems on which to focus, we have limited our discussion to strategic planning (including budgeting) and follow-up. The reason is that these two subsystems constitute the core of the management-control system in most firms. Examples of other subsystems of management control are investment control, product-cost estimates, and transfer prices. Unlike more comprehensive planning and follow-up, these procedures are focused on certain very specific types of decision situations (cf. Anthony and Govindarajan, 1995).

The basic elements of a typical planning and follow-up procedure, and the relationship of these elements to each other, are shown in Figure 4.3. This figure illustrates the "core" around which all management-control systems are built and is central to the subsequent discussion. As can be seen in the figure, the management-control process begins with long-range activities that include the setting of goals, the formulation of guiding principles, and the choice of strategies for reaching the goals. The strategy of the firm should be based, if possible, on analyses of threats and opportunities in the firm's environment. Similarly, the firm must be given an internal appraisal in which its strengths and weaknesses are identified. According to Learned et al. (1965), the purpose is to achieve a "fit" between the firm's environment, its capabilities, and its competencies.[20]

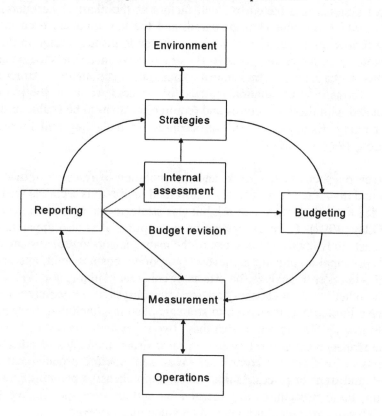

Fig. 4.3. Phases of planning and follow-up – management control. Source: Anthony RN, Dearden J, Bedford NM. 1989. *Management Control Systems,* p. 27 (modified)

The next step is to translate the strategic plan into a budget for one fiscal year; this step entails estimating revenues and costs for all activities and responsibility centers covered in the strategy. The budget is commonly accompanied by a set of monetary and non-monetary key numbers, sometimes in the form of a Balanced Scorecard (Olve et al., 1999; Olve et al., 2003).[21] In these cases the planning process also includes the choice of appropriate key numbers and numerical targets for the coming period. Once the budget has been prepared and numerical targets have been set, the process of follow-up begins. This process involves the collection of both monetary and non-monetary information on the current progress of the business (Goold et al., 1994). One central aspect of follow-up is to provide managers at all levels – in most cases once a month – with reports that compare the current situation with strategy and the budget. This feedback can lead to revision of the budget (Anthony et al., 1989). According to the review of the literature in Chapter 2, three dimensions of particular importance are customarily employed in describing and analyzing the design and use of planning and follow-up procedures: tight and loose control, monetary and non-monetary control, and time horizon. In the following three subsections, these dimensions will be described in detail in order to provide a foundation for the development of the tentative model in Chapter 5.

Tight and Loose Control

The concept of tight versus loose control has interested researchers in management control for several decades (see, for example, Hopwood, 1972; Otley, 1978; Bruggeman and Van der Stede, 1993). The difference between tight and loose control lies in the way in which management chooses to plan the business and to follow up business performance (Simons, 1987). According to Anthony et al. (1992, p. 580 ff), if management monitors the activities of business units frequently, it is said to exercise tight control. Another feature mentioned by the authors is that goals are often short-term and very specific. It is also stressed that profit targets which have been decided – and normally expressed in a budget – are considered a binding contract. Follow-up is detailed, and deviations from approved plans are generally not considered acceptable (Goold et al., 1994, p. 415).

Loose control, on the other hand, is characterized by more limited management involvement in day-to-day operations. Anthony et al. (ibid) maintain that in these circumstances the budget is regarded primarily as an instrument of communication and planning rather than a binding contract. Follow-up is less frequent and less detailed than with tight control. Another major difference from tight control, mentioned by Goold et al. (1994, p. 412 ff), is that failure to meet objectives seldom carries the same serious consequences.

Anthony et al. (1992, p. 581 f) emphasize two benefits of tight control. First, tight control is considered to prevent inefficiency and wasteful practices in general. Second, advocates of tight control maintain that difficult budget targets will force managers to seek new and innovative ways to improve the efficiency of the business. As for the drawbacks of tight control, the authors discuss four particularly serious dysfunctional effects. First, overly difficult profit targets may lead managers to reach shortsighted decisions that jeopardize long-term strategy. Second, managers may be tempted to avoid major investments with no positive short-term impact on profits. Third, excessive focus on profits may induce managers to negotiate for targets that they find easy to accomplish. Finally, tight control may lead managers to make changes in the accounting system in order to present a better profit than was actually achieved during the period.[22]

The danger of data manipulation in the case of tight control was also pointed out in an empirical study by Hopwood (1972). According to the analysis of Anthony et al. (1992, p. 582), the study by Hopwood showed that a strong emphasis on budget targets can interfere with communication between different organizational levels and create job-related tensions. Otley (1978), on the other hand, reached a different conclusion in his empirical study. He showed that under certain conditions tight control can help to motivate management and employees to achieve better financial performance than they would have with loose control. Govindarajan (1984) concluded from these conflicting findings, and a study of 58 business units, that whether tight or loose control is preferable depends on the situation.

As is apparent from our review of the literature in Chapter 2, the environment is a situational variable of great importance in the current context. At the business-unit level, for example, difficulties in predicting demand are a feature of a turbulent environment, in which a differentiation strategy is particularly suitable. These difficulties create uncertainty and make future revenues difficult to forecast, thus limiting the importance of the budget – i.e., a situation appropriate for loose control (Govindarajan, 1988). As discussed in previous sections, however, the various business units and functions of a corporation are not exposed to exactly the same degree of uncertainty (cf. Lawrence and Lorsch, 1967). Not infrequently, they operate in different sub-environments and follow different strategies.

Consequently, the position on a tight/loose continuum may vary from one business unit or function to another (*cf.* Simons, 1995).[23] At the corporate level, by contrast, there are reasons to believe that this position is dependent on synergy potential, which is a central dimension of corporate strategy (Nilsson, 2002).[24] When the circumstances described above lead to overly large differences in planning and follow-up procedure at each organizational level, it may be more difficult to establish integrated control.

Monetary and Non-monetary Control

A frequent point of departure in defining the concept of management control is that planning and follow-up involve financial, or monetary, targets (Frenckner, 1983, p. 68). However, with the tendency described previously, where the differences between strategic, tactical, and operational decisions are continually diminishing, new information needs have emerged (Otley, 1994). At the operating level, one development has been that far-reaching decentralization of decision-making has created a clear need for strategic and tactical information (*cf.* Nilsson and Rapp, 1999). At the same time, the importance of manufacturing to a strong competitor– as manifested in such concepts as "World Class Manufacturing" – has led to a demand from management at the strategic and tactical levels for information directly related to operations (Nanni et al., 1992; Bromwich and Bhimani, 1994). Measures previously used only in operating control, such as those showing the physical flow in manufacturing and the company's progress in quality enhancement, are now, to a large extent, treated by the management-control system. The greater importance of the management-control system in both strategic planning and operating control explains why some scholars are talking about "expanded management control." "Strategic management" is another concept frequently used to emphasize that traditional monetary management control has changed to include non-monetary information as well (Lindvall, 2001; Nilsson and Olve, 2001). Although we share this view, we will continue to use the well-established concept of "management control."[25]

The fact that non-monetary information is now an essential element of management control is particularly evident, for example, from the impact of the Balanced Scorecard (Kald and Nilsson, 2000; Olve et al., 2003). In this model – developed by Kaplan and Norton (1992, 1993, 1996a, 1996b, 2001, 2004) – the company's long-term strategy is linked with its day-to-day operations. Measures are provided for different perspectives, each of which represents an important dimension of the company's business. The perspectives reflect how well the firm is doing in creating value for its owners, how relationships are managed, the efficiency of internal business processes, and how the firm manages learning and innovation (ibid).[26] Since the four perspectives are equally important in the long run, they should be balanced against each other; that is, no one perspective should be allowed to predominate over the others. One purpose of a balanced scorecard is to link financial results with the conduct of the business at the operational level. These cause-and-effect relationships are hypotheses; an example would be the statement that with motivated and knowledgeable employees, financial performance will improve (see Figure 4.4). As indicated by the figure, both monetary and non-monetary information is required for on-going follow-up to ensure that what is being done in regard to customers, processes, and learning is consistent with strategies and goals.

The Balanced Scorecard is not the first management-control model in which non-monetary information plays a significant role in planning and follow-up. For example, a French model, the Tableaux de Bord (Lebas and Chiapello, 1996; Epstein and Manzoni, 1998), has been used since the early 1940's. Another illustration is the Performance Pyramid, which was developed by McNair, Lynch and Cross (McNair et al., 1990). The introduction of these new models reflects a growing interest in the firm's effectiveness: that is, the extent to which the firm is doing the right things (*cf.* Lindvall, 2001, p. 47 f).

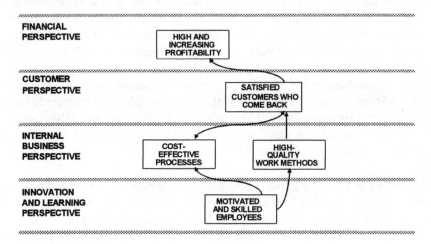

Fig. 4.4. Example of cause–and-effect relationships in a balanced scorecard

According to Lindvall (ibid), traditional management control, with its strong orientation toward monetary information, has a different focus: that is, on efficiency. Despite a general trend in which non-monetary information is gaining importance, there are substantial differences from company to company. Whether a firm chooses to emphasize monetary or non-monetary information is determined by the situation. Our review of the literature shows that regardless of organizational level, strategy is a central situational variable. At the corporate level, the choice of strategy is largely linked to synergy potential, whereas the environment has a more direct affect on strategy at the business-unit and functional levels. In cases where these situational variables lead to the use of the same type of information at each organizational level, it is easier to establish integrated control. If this congruence is not present, there must be some way of translating non-monetary information into monetary terms. There have been endeavours to find such solutions; one of them has been designated "Value Modeling." [27]

Time Horizon

Another dimension in defining the concept of management control is the time horizon for planning and follow-up. One contribution in this area is that of Johnson and Kaplan (1987), who hold that at American companies the time horizon is generally too short and there is excessive focus on monetary information. Their criticism can be summarized in the following excerpt (Johnson and Kaplan, 1987, p. 195):

> There is no doubt that ROI control and the profit center form of organization were not only greatly useful but likely necessary for the growth and prosperity of large, hierarchical organizations during the past sixty years. Nevertheless, despite the successes, problems associated with short-term performance measures such as ROI[28] have become painfully evident in recent years. The problems likely arise from an excessive focus on achieving short-term financial performance. Many articles and books have criticized U.S. executives for their narrow, short-term outlook and their overreliance on financial transactions to achieve immediate profitability objectives.

We have previously mentioned one of the articles referred to by Johnson and Kaplan (1987) in the excerpt above: "Managing Our Way to Economic Decline," by Hayes and Abernathy (1980). Like Johnson and Kaplan, the authors maintain that far-reaching decentralization, where the profit center is the primary unit of managerial responsibility, leads to heavier reliance on monetary measures like ROI in evaluations of individual managers and management groups. Since senior executives at US corporations often have financial and accounting backgrounds, they lack detailed familiarity with business operations. According to Hays and Abernathy, if there is greater distance between those entrusted with positioning the business unit on the market and those who evaluate the performance of these managers, quantifiable criteria will be used.[29] The overall consequence of these circumstances will be strategic planning with many shortcomings.

... we believe that during the past two decades American managers have increasingly relied on principles which prize analytical detachment and methodological elegance over insight, based on experience, into the subtleties and complexities of strategic decisions. As a result, maximum short-term financial returns have become the overriding criteria for many companies (Hayes and Abernathy, 1980, p. 70).

The short-term behavior long typical of many US firms has increasingly spread to other continents. Hamel (2000) provides numerous examples in which this so-called "quarterly capitalism" leads to deferment of long-term investments, often in research and development. Instead of focusing on laying a foundation for future profits, executive management increasingly spend their time on various financial transactions to improve total shareholder return. De-mergers, spin-offs, share buybacks, and other techniques are employed if they will yield shareholder value (ibid, p. 40).[30] Although short-term behavior is a general tendency, empirical studies indicate the presence of substantial differences between individual companies in this regard. One manifestation of these differences is in the way that individual companies, or groups of companies, design and use their management control systems (see, for example, Roberts, 1990).

Our review of the literature shows that differences in time horizon tend to follow from the objectives and strategies chosen by the firm, and that they influence the degree to which quick monetary results are given priority. For example, with a corporate strategy based on low synergy potential, a so-called portfolio-management strategy, business units will operate as independent firms. The absence of interdependence means that short-term profit maximization will probably be given priority and that units that fail to achieve the required rate of return may be quickly divested (Porter, 1985; Espeland and Hirsch, 1990). Consequently, at the corporate level, the time horizon, as manifested in the design and use of management control, tend to be linked to synergy potential and to the corporate strategy related to this potential. At the business-unit and functional levels, the environment, and the strategy chosen for matching external demands and internal resources, will be critical situational variables, according to the literature review. Establishing integrated control will be easier if the situational variables lead each organizational level to conduct its activities on the basis of roughly similar time horizons. Through such control the corporation will be given a clear common focus in which the time horizon in itself need not have a substantial impact on the firm's competitiveness. An example of such a situation is provided by Goold et al. (1994), who show how short-term actions can bring success in mature industries where low manufacturing costs are the principal means of competition.

Manufacturing Control

Manufacturing control refers to the formalized, information-based routines, structures and processes used by management to formulate strategies and to implement them by controlling manufacturing processes, including materials, machinery, employees, and suppliers (cf. Vollmann et al., 1992, p. 2; Olhager and Rapp, 1995, p. 31). As in our definition of management control, we have chosen to highlight the role of the manufacturing-control system in the formulation and implementation of strategies. This choice is based on the previously noted expansion of research in manufacturing control in regard both to the organizational levels and to the decision levels studied. As mentioned earlier, the reason for this expansion is that activities at the operating level have been linked more closely to those at the business-unit and corporate levels. One consequence has been that many decisions that were formerly considered strategic or tactical have now been decentralized to the operational decision level (Johnson, 1992; Otley, 1994). In light of this development, we have chosen not only to discuss the operational decision level, but also to highlight the connection between manufacturing control and the strategic and tactical levels. In order to place manufacturing control in a tactical and strategic context, we consider all organizational levels: that is, not only the business-unit and operational levels, but also the corporate level. We have thus sought to bring our definition into line with the latest developments in this field of research. However, the link to strategy formulation and implementation can still be made more explicit in many definitions of the concept of manufacturing control. It will probably take some time before the expanded scope of research is fully reflected in concepts and definitions.[31]

As in our definition of management control, design and use are central dimensions of a manufacturing-control system. We have chosen to focus on the same aspects of design and use as in the discussion on the concept of management control. The reason is that the dimensions are substantially generic and can therefore be used to describe and analyze almost all formalized and cybernetic control systems.[32] By use we mean the work to "motivate, monitor, and reward achievement of specified goals" (Simons, 1995, p. 7). The use of the manufacturing-control system, however, is not limited to following up goals that have already been set, but should also – through organizational learning – contribute to the formulation of new goals. This process should take place in a strategic dialogue between senior executive management and subordinates at the operational levels. Simons (1995, p. 5) argues that such a dialogue should involve an exchange of information: "(1) to signal the domain in which subordinates should search for opportunities, (2) to communicate plans and goals, (3) to monitor the achievement of plans and goals, and (4) to keep informed and inform others of emerging developments."

A well-functioning strategic dialogue also requires that the manufacturing-control system be designed to support the formulation and implementation of strategies. As with a management-control system, the design of a manufacturing-control system can be separated into a structural and a process dimension. The former dimension concerns specific tools and models such as instructions and forms for preparing a purchasing plan. The latter dimension relates to the procedures and processes in which these structures are used, for example, vendor and supply management. In the subsequent discussion, these planning and follow-up procedures will be treated in some detail. It may be noted that planning procedures are of greater importance in manufacturing control than in a typical management-control system. Another difference, also evident from the literature review, is that manufacturing control is more focused on quite specific techniques to improve planning and follow-up.

Figure 4.5 is a diagram of planning and follow-up procedures in a typical manufacturing-control system (cf. Hill, 1989; Vollmann et al., 1992). As is shown in the figure, these procedures can be classified under vendor and supply management, resource management, and customer and delivery management. The figure also shows that planning and follow-up have a distinctly hierarchical structure. The highest level consists of activities involved in general production planning. The information used is therefore aggregated and has a long time horizon. The planning process begins with co-ordination of goals and strategies for the manufacturing function with business-unit and corporate strategies (Skinner, 1969).[34] In the next step, manufacturing strategy, which has a time horizon of 3-5 years, is broken down into a capacity strategy and a sales and operations plan.[35] In this step, demand management provides an input in the form of a short-term forecast of production volume.[36]

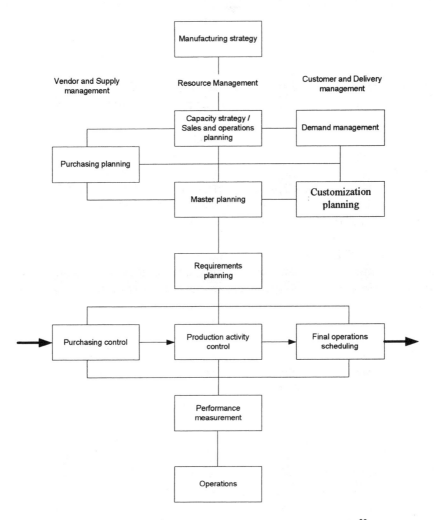

Fig. 4.5. Phases of planning and follow-up – manufacturing control.[33] Source: Olhager J, Rapp B. 1995. *Operations Research Techniques in Manufacturing and
Control Systems.* p. 32 (modified)

Sales and operations planning must also be co-ordinated with purchasing planning, which includes long-term purchasing agreements. The final
step is the preparation of a master plan in which materials and capacity
planning are integrated and customers are given estimated delivery times.
In cases where products are offered in different varieties, end-product configurations must also be established through customized planning before a
master plan can be prepared (Olhager and Rapp, 1985).

At lower levels, planning and follow-up are intended to support decision-making at the operating level; thus, the information here is more detailed. The master schedule feeds directly into the requirements planning, where estimates are made of the necessary labor and machine capacity for manufacturing the products in question. The requirements plan then serves as the basis for purchasing control, production-activity control, and final operations scheduling (Olhager and Rapp, 1995). Purchasing control ensures that input goods for production arrive at the right time and meet agreed standards of quality. One important task is to optimize the amount of inventory, that is, to limit inventory as much as possible without jeopardizing on-time delivery. Production-activity control is focused primarily on the manufacture of standardized products and semi-finished products to stock. Performance measurement therefore emphasizes follow-up of inventory levels and the master plan. In cases where the firm offers different varieties of its products, or wholly unique products, a final-operations schedule is used. This plan is co-ordinated with production-activity control in order to ensure that there will be adequate production of semi-finished goods.[37] Since customized products are not kept in stock to the same extent as standardized products, performance measurement is focused on following up on-time delivery (Olhager and Rapp, 1996).

Although manufacturing control is subdivided into a clear hierarchy, decisions at different levels cannot be taken in isolation; on the contrary, the various procedures of manufacturing control must be linked together. According to the review of the literature in Chapter 2, three central dimensions in this kind of integrated planning and follow-up are capacity and planning strategy, customer-order decoupling point, and control concept. These dimensions, which are described in detail in the following three subsections, serve as the basis for developing the tentative model presented in Chapter 5. The discussion of control classified by type of information used – monetary or non-monetary control – can be found in the section "Management Control."

Capacity and Planning Strategy[38]

Capacity strategy has a planning horizon of 1-5 years and is focused primarily on the timing of capacity changes. According to Olhager et al. (2001), these changes affect the manufacturing infrastructure and come in large, discrete steps. Planning strategy, on the other hand, is used to balance sales and production in a short-term perspective. In the literature, capacity strategy is often regarded as the starting-point for the development of planning-strategy. Olhager et al. (2001) agree in principle with this

categorization but argue that the two strategies are intimately intercon-
nected and must consequently be integrated. The authors contend, for example, that investment in new capacity can be avoided with a well-
considered planning strategy. We agree and have also chosen to discuss
capacity and planning strategy in conjunction.

In decisions affecting capacity, management should have a clear conception of the desirable balance between the demand for capacity and the supply of capacity. The two principal alternatives available are termed by Olhager et al. (2001) as capacity-demand surplus and capacity-supply
surplus. The former alternative entails high utilization of the firm's machinery and equipment capacity, thus contributing to low costs. The risk,
however, is that it will be difficult to maintain on-time delivery. The authors characterize the latter alternative as one with idle production capacity, which in turn permits high flexibility and favors on-time delivery. The
drawback, however, is that cost effectiveness suffers since the production
apparatus is not used as efficiently as with capacity-demand surplus. On
the basis of these two alternatives, the authors identified three types of capacity strategies: lag, lead, and track. As shown in Figure 4.6, the distinguishing feature of a lag strategy is that new production capacity is acquired after an increase in demand has been noted (capacity-demand
surplus). With a lead strategy, manufacturing capacity is adjusted before
the changes in demand occur (capacity-supply surplus). A tracking strategy combines the two other alternatives.

With a given manufacturing capacity (i.e. capacity strategy), the planning of manufacturing (Sales and Operations Planning) can modify supply
– according to Olhager et al. (2001) – with one of the following planning
strategies: level, chase, and mix. With a strategy of leveled production, a
previously set volume of production is maintained for the whole period,
contributing to low costs. With a chase strategy, the volume of production
should be adjusted according to sales for the period, thus attaining a high
degree of flexibility. As the term implies, a mix strategy combines a level
strategy and a chase strategy.

As previously noted, the choice of appropriate capacity and planning
strategies should be co-ordinated since these are interdependent. By deductive reasoning, Olhager et al. (2001) conclude that there are two combina-

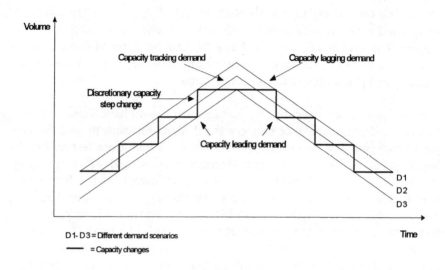

Fig. 4.6. The timing of long-term changes in capacity. Source: based on three separate tables in Olhager J, Rudberg M, Wikner J. 2001. *Long-term Capacity Management: Linking the Perspectives from Manufacturing Strategy and Sales and Operations Planning*

tions where a good fit may be presumed to exist between capacity and planning strategy. The first combination is intended to achieve high capacity utilization and consists of lag and level strategies. The other combination – lead and chase – focuses on resource availability and flexibility. According to the authors, the purpose of this combination is not to achieve low production costs; rather, the focus is on high quality and similar features.

As indicated in the review of the literature in Chapter 2, manufacturing strategy, and particularly technical flexibility, is an important situational variable in the choice of capacity and planning strategy. The research by Olhager et al. (2001) indicates that in a turbulent environment where a high degree of technical flexibility is required, a combination of lead and chase is particularly appropriate. Lag and level are a suitable combination in situations of stable demand and a low degree of technical flexibility. In cases where integrated control is desired, where manufacturing strategies are formulated and implemented in the context of corporate and business strategies, capacity and planning strategies should be governed by the same principles. Without such co-ordination, there is a risk that the long-

and short-range planning of production functions will be based on entirely different time horizons, thus making it considerably more difficult to co-ordinate manufacturing and the work of exploiting synergies through activity sharing.

Customer Order Decoupling Point

Closely tied to capacity and planning strategy is the customer-order de-coupling point (CODP), defined as the point in time when the product is designated for a specific customer. Olhager and Rapp (1985, 1996) hold that the CODP is the divider between customer-driven and forecast-driven planning and control. Activities that are upstream in relation to the CODP must be based on forecasts, whereas activities downstream from the CODP are based on actual customer orders. On this basis – that is, the critical point in time when product and customer are linked together – it is possible to distinguish four manufacturing situations: manufacturing to a stock of finished goods (MTS), assembly to customer order (ATO), manufacturing entirely to customer order (MTO), or engineering to order (ETO). Figure 4.7 describes these situations and shows how they can be related to the CODP as well as the estimated delivery lead-time.

According to Olhager and Rapp (1985, 1996), MTS is found in the manufacture of standardized products and can be used when the desired delivery time is shorter than the production lead-time. As can be seen in Figure 4.7, the CODP is then located outside the production process. Since delivery can be made directly from inventory, delivery lead-time is limited to the time required for shipment. It is essential, however, that demand be stable and that reliable sales forecasts can be made. Furthermore, given the dependence on forecasts, actual sales must be monitored so that the accuracy of the forecasts can be verified (Vollman et al., 1992, p. 361). In cases where the firm offers different varieties of the final product, the latter is assembled to customer order (ATO). Olhager and Rapp (1985) contend that this type of partially standardized products permits dividing production into two steps.[39] In the first step the standardized parts of the product are manufactured entirely to stock. The second step consists of manufacturing customer-specific parts and assembly of the product (i.e. CODP after procurement and fabrication activities). Delivery lead-time can thereby be limited to the time required for final assembly and shipment. However, the division of manufacturing into two steps can entail considerable problems. Olhager and Rapp (ibid) argue that different types of planning methods are used to cope with this situation. One example is modulization –

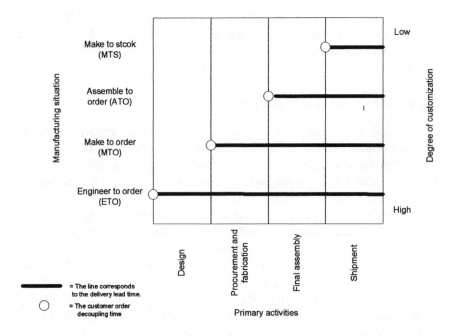

Fig. 4.7. Customer order decoupling points. Source: Based on Olhager J, Rapp B. 1996. On the Design of Computer-aided Manufacturing Planning and Control Systems. p. 3

in other words, separation of the products into modules, for example, standard modules and customer-specific modules. According to the authors (ibid), the advantage of this division is that the modules are related to different time horizons and are thus easier to survey.

With MTO products are highly customized, i.e., extensively adapted to customer requirements. The CODP precedes procurement and fabrication activities since manufacturing is determined by a pre-existing design (*cf.* Figure 4.7). Planning and promised delivery times are governed by existing orders and the estimated production lead-time for each individual product (Vollmann et al., 1992, p. 360). A primary objective of production planning is to ensure that production lead-time does not exceed a reasonable and desired delivery time (Olhager and Rapp, 1985). With the requirement of a reasonable delivery time, in combination with limited stability of volume and product specifications, production must be flexible (Hayes and Wheelwright, 1979a). When the product is engineered to order (ETO), production must be even more flexible and adaptable. The reason is that both the volume of production and product specifications are extremely difficult, if not impossible, to forecast (Olhager et al., 2001). Production planning and control may thus be characterized as customer-driven, and the CODP precedes designing. Production lead-time is calculated on the basis of order backlog as well as estimates for each individual product (*cf.* Vollmann et al., 1992, p. 359 f).

On the basis of the review above, and the previously presented summary of the literature, it is clear that the position of the customer-order decoupling point is dependent on the situation. MTS and ATO are appropriate when products are standardized and demand is stable, that is, when manufacturing strategy features a limited need for technical flexibility. MTO and ETO are used primarily when products are highly customized. With such a manufacturing strategy, there is considerable uncertainty, and a high degree of technical flexibility is required (*cf.* Vollmann et al., 1992, p. 359 ff). Where the situational variables above lead to excessive differences in planning and follow-up at each organizational level, it is difficult to establish integrated control. As previously mentioned, the design and use of planning procedures appropriate for MTS, for example, are quite different from those suitable for ETO. In the former case, precise forecasts are important; in the latter, flexible planning should be given priority.

Control Concept

In short-term planning and follow-up, an important element is the control concept – or, as some writers have chosen to call it – the shop-floor system (Vollmann et al., 1997). Two commonly used methods based on different concepts of control are materials-requirements planning (MRP) and just-in-time (JIT). The MRP-based approach to shop-floor scheduling is very flexible and can cope with large variations both in volume of production and in product mix. According to Vollmann et al. (1992, p. 370 ff) MRP is an appropriate method of control when the unit operates in turbulent competitive arenas, in other words, on markets characterized by a high rate of new product introduction, sudden changes in demand, etc. Typically, products are customized to a large degree and manufactured in relatively low volumes.

Hill (1991) maintains that MRP is based on the fact that the demand for all subassemblies, components, and raw materials is dependent upon the demand for the final product. To minimize change-over costs resulting from the relatively low volumes of each product, complex centralized

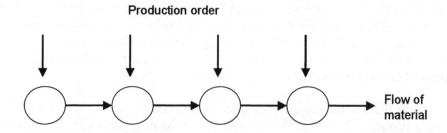

Fig. 4.8. The push principle. Source: Olhager J, Rapp B. 1985. *Effektiv MPS: Referenssystem för datorbaserad material- och produktionsstyrning* (In Swedish, *Efficient MPS: Reference Systems for Computer Based Materials and Manufacturing Control*), p. 31

planning is called for. Production starts at the lowest level; when the article has been completely processed at that level, it is transferred to the next level for further processing. In this way, raw materials, subassemblies and components are "pushed" through production to meet due-date requirements (Olhager and Rapp, 1985). [40, 41] The "push" principle is described in Figure 4.8.

As for the JIT method, it is found in a number of variants; the examples most commonly cited are taken from firms like Toyota, with high-volume, repetitive manufacturing methods (ibid, p. 70 f). Hill (1991, p. 219) characterizes JIT "…as a system based upon the concept of producing small quantities just in time as opposed to many current philosophies which are based on making inventory 'just in case' it is required." In other words, JIT implies that all materials should be in active use within the manufacturing process in order to avoid "unnecessary" costs. Consequently a central aim is to achieve extremely cost-effective production with short lead-times. Thus, JIT can be characterized as both a manufacturing concept and a control concept (*cf.* Askenäs, 2000). As indicated at the outset of this section, the latter has been chosen as the basis for our discussion of JIT.

From this standpoint we may note that JIT as a method of control does not offer the same extensive flexibility as MRP for handling variations in production volume and product mix. [42] According to Vollmann et al. (1992, p. 373) a JIT approach to shop-floor scheduling is designed to provide support for standardized products manufactured in high volumes. In order to offer short customer lead-times, a production strategy with high

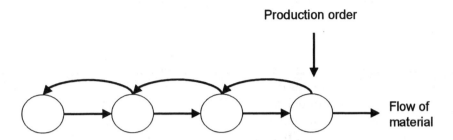

Fig. 4.9. The pull principle. Source: Olhager J, Rapp B. 1985. Effektiv MPS: Referenssystem för datorbaserad material- och produktionsstyrning (In Swedish, *Efficient MPS: Reference Systems for Computer Based Materials and Manufacturing Control*), p. 31

technical flexibility is most appropriate, such as an assembly line. The strong process orientation makes it easier, as well as necessary, to allocate costs at the activity level and thus to eliminate activities which do not create value (*cf.* Sillince and Sykes, 1995). JIT can also help to improve cost effectiveness by minimizing inventories (Kato, 1993). More generally, JIT facilitates detailed follow-up – for example by determining the effect of quality improvements on costs of reworking, guarantees, etc. (Bromwich and Bhimani, 1994, p. 47 f).

Given the importance of cost-effective production, JIT focuses on a continuous flow of articles that pass sequentially through processing activities. As shown in Figure 4.9, the demand at the finished-product level is transferred to the immediately preceding production level, where it gives rise to a demand for inputs at that level. In this way raw materials, subassemblies, and components are successively "pulled" through production (the "pull" principle) (Olhager and Rapp, 1985).

A control principle designed on this basis, however, will require fixed production schedules. According to Hill (1991) the workload must be the same each day, and the sequence of items to be assembled must be nearly identical for a long period of time. One important reason for this is the high cost of changes in production scheduling and capacity (Vollmann et al., 1997).[43]

In light of the above, we can state that JIT – unlike MRP – is a particularly appropriate control concept in stable environments, where a long planning horizon is possible and limited technical flexibility is required. Consequently, the choice of control concept, like the choice of capacity and planning strategy as well as customer-order decoupling point, is dependent on the situation. As shown in previous sections, manufacturing strategy, and particularly the degree of technical flexibility, is a principal situational variable in this context. Thus, in a corporation where there are different manufacturing strategies, different control concepts will also be found. The significant differences in the design and intended use of shop-floor systems, however, make it more difficult to establish a coherent system of planning and follow-up.

Summary

In this chapter integrated control is defined as control in which strategic planning and follow-up at each organizational level are coherent throughout the firm. The purpose is to facilitate the exchange of information between different organizational levels and decision-makers concerning strategic, tactical, and operational decisions. In this way strategic planning and ongoing follow-up can be co-ordinated, thus increasing the chances of achieving strategic congruence and of successfully implementing the strategies of the firm. To put it another way, integrated control makes it easier to establish a high degree of internal fit, that is, congruence between the strategies and the internal structures of the firm. This congruence – or internal fit – is essential if the firm is to be highly competitive and, ultimately, if it is to yield a good financial return to its owners.

We have chosen to focus on management-control systems and manufacturing-control systems since integration of these two systems may be considered particularly important to the firm's capacity for creating competitive advantage. Despite the numerous benefits of integrated control, previous research on control systems has largely focused on only two organizational levels and a limited number of decision situations. Examples from practice, however, have shown that the boundaries between management control and manufacturing control, which were once quite clear, are now disappearing. As a consequence, research in management control and manufacturing control is gradually expanding to include both more organizational levels and more decision levels. In this book, therefore, we have chosen to discuss how the systems of control are interlinked at the corporate, business-unit, and operational levels and how they can be used in situations of strategic, tactical, and operational decision-making.

We decided to focus on planning and follow-up procedures since these constitute the "core" around which all systems are built. Furthermore, on the basis of the literature review, we identified a number of central dimensions in the design and use of management and manufacturing control. These dimensions are used in Chapter 5 for discussing the circumstances under which it can be assumed possible to achieve integrated control. Planning and follow-up in management-control systems are considered in the dimensions of tight and loose control, monetary and non-monetary control, and time horizon. Planning and follow-up in manufacturing-control systems are considered in the dimensions of capacity and planning strategy, customer-order decoupling point, and control concept. Since it is reasonable to assume that both management- and manufacturing-control systems are influenced by the nature of the strategy chosen, it is not meaningful to discuss the possibilities of achieving integrated control without also treating the conditions for strategic congruence. This interdependence emerges clearly in the next chapter.

Notes

1. It has been shown in previous chapters that there is interdependence between strategic congruence and integrated control. In Chapter 2, in the section "Toward a More Complex Theory," we discuss how the establishment of integrated control is facilitated in cases where there is already a high degree of strategic congruence. In corporations where business units operate in similar environments, it is considerably easier to design planning and follow-up procedures that suit all business units than where this is not the case.

2. Just-in-time (JIT) is subsequently described in detail under the heading of "Manufacturing Control."

3. In Chapter 2, in the section "Strategy and Control," we use a number of empirical studies as a basis for discussing how requirements of cost effectiveness influence the design and use of management control.

4. "Functional level" is another term.

5. Anthony (1965) prefers to use the concept of task control.

6. One important question in these studies is how planning systems should be designed according to the manufacturing strategy chosen, particularly in regard to requirements of technical flexibility.

7. In our review of the literature, we do not describe the studies that concern the relationship between strategy and the design and use of product costing. The reason is that we have limited the discussion in the tentative model (see Chapter 5) to strategic planning (including budgeting) and follow-up. For the reasons why this limitation was adopted, see the "Management Control" and "Manufacturing Control" sections in the present chapter.

8. In Activity Based Costing the basic principle is that indirect costs are to be allocated according to the origin of the cost. In an ABC calculation, the allocation key is termed the cost driver.

9. Lindvall (2001, p. 197) emphasizes that Scandinavian scholars (for example, Frenckner, 1991) like their colleagues elsewhere in Europe (for

example, Bhimani, 1996), have made considerable efforts to determine whether the method differs from ones previously introduced. Among other things, it has been maintained that the idea of replacing standardized additional amounts by linking the cost to a variability factor was previously advanced by Törnqvist (1929) for trade and by Madsen (1958) for manufacturing (Frenckner and Olve, 1992, p. 189).

10. In this case, JIT (just-in-time) means that input goods are delivered continuously to the firm at the time when they are to be used in production. In this book, however, JIT will subsequently be viewed as a control concept rather than a manufacturing policy. A more thorough discussion is provided later in this chapter under the heading of "Manufacturing Control."

11. According to Dent (1996, p. 256), the purpose of "flexible specialisation" is to avoid overlapping and duplication of activities. Dent maintains that this can be done by focusing production on specific components, products and/or processes.

12. Anthony (1965) defines management control as follows: "Management control is the process by which managers assure that resources are obtained and used effectively and efficiently in the accomplishment of the organization's objectives." In later editions presenting the conceptual framework, the definition was modified in order to highlight even more clearly the role of the control system in implementing strategy. In Anthony and Govindarajan (2004, p. 7), the following definition is used: "Management control is the process by which managers influence other members of the organization to implement the organization's strategies."

13. Anthony et al. (1992, p. 9 f) presents the difference between strategic planning, management control, and task control as follows: "As will be seen, management control fits between the other two activities in several respects. Strategic planning occurs at the top management levels, task control occurs at the lowest levels in the organization, and management control is in between. Strategic planning is the least systematic, task control is the most systematic, and management control is in between. Strategic planning focuses on the long run, task control focuses on short-run operating activities, and management control is in between. Strategic planning uses rough approximations of the future, task control uses accurate current data, and management control is in between. Each activity involves both planning and control; but the

planning process is much more important in strategic planning, the control process is much more important in task control, and planning and control are of approximately equal importance in management control." In Anthony and Govindarajan (2004, p. 6) the term "strategy formulation" is used instead of "strategic planning."

14. As indicated in the general background discussion in Chapter 1, far-reaching decentralization is not solely beneficial. In cases where the focus on planning and follow-up has been carried too far, there is a danger that corporate activities will be inadequately co-ordinated. It is thus a major challenge to grant business units sufficient freedom in tactical and operational decision-making while maintaining well-functioning overall co-ordination of different corporate activities.

15. Simons (1995, p. 5) defines management control as follows: "Management control systems are the formal, information-based routines and procedures managers use to maintain or alter patterns in organizational activities."

16. In his presentation of the conceptual framework, Simons (1995, p. 7) highlights two additional dimensions of a control system – aside from interactive and diagnostic control. One dimension is belief systems (core values). The other dimension is boundary systems (risks to be avoided). In the subsequent discussion, as indicated in Chapter 2, only the dimensions of diagnostic and interactive control will be used. The reason is that Simons has clearly illustrated how these two dimensions can be linked to the design and use of the firm's planning and follow-up procedures.

17. Simon's (1995, p. 59) definition of diagnostic control is as follows: "Diagnostic control systems are the formal information systems that managers use to monitor organizational outcomes and correct deviations from preset standards of performance."

18. Simons (1995, p. 95) defines interactive control as "…formal information systems managers use to involve themselves regularly and personally in the decision activities of subordinates."

19. For a detailed description of these studies, see the section "Strategy and Control" in Chapter 2.

20. For a detailed description of the strategic-planning process and its methods, see the section "Strategic Management" in Chapter 2.

21. The Balanced Scorecard is described in greater detail in this chapter in a later subsection under the heading of "Monetary and Non-monetary Control."

22. According to Anthony et al. (1992, p. 582), data can be manipulated in a number of different ways. One of them is to borrow from future earnings. Another is to falsify data.

23. According to Simons (1995, p. 161), researchers have generally treated "tightness of controls" as a unitary concept. His criticism of this viewpoint is expressed in the following quotation, where situational adaptation is taken to an extreme: "In any organization, at any point in time, and at any level, managers will report varying degrees of 'tightness' in respect to belief systems, boundary systems, diagnostic control systems, and interactive control systems" (ibid). What Simons means is that one particular subsystem can be used for tight control, while another subsystem can be used for loose control. It is important, however, to ensure that the sub-systems in conjunction are designed and used – in terms of tight and loose control – in a manner appropriate to strategy (*cf.* Kald et al., 2000). Otherwise, the desired behavioral effect may be lost – for example, by combining a tight budgeting procedure with loose follow-up.

24. Tendencies of how synergy potential affects the firm's position on the tight/loose continuum is described in Chapter 2 in the section "Strategy and Control."

25. Our agreement with this expanded definition of management control does not mean that non-monetary information is always used in planning and follow-up. One limitation is that information must be distributed within the framework of the formal planning and follow-up procedures. Thus, the information must be available to the accounting department.

26. The original four perspectives used by Kaplan and Norton (1992) were (1) the financial perspective, (2) the customer perspective, (3) the internal business-process perspective, and (4) the innovation and learning perspective. As shown in empirical studies in the Nordic countries

and elsewhere, it is common to add other perspectives – such as an employee perspective – as a complement (Ewing, 1995).

27. The purpose of Value Modeling is to understand in detail and to communicate how the firm creates value (Donovan et al., 1998). Value Modeling picks up where the Balanced Scorecard leaves off; in other words, causal relationships of the type described in Figure 4.4 are developed further. The aim is to determine how a change at the operating level affects financial results and ultimately the creation of shareholder value. The example used in the figure – the assumption that with motivated, knowledgeable employees profitability will increase – shows that many causal relationships may be difficult, if not impossible, to verify. It should be noted that in Kaplan and Norton's latest book – *Strategy Maps* – the authors focus on causal relationships (Kaplan and Norton, 2004).

28. Return on investment (ROI) is a ratio where the numerator is business profit as reported in the income statement. The denominator is total assets, or sometimes capital employed, items which are found in the balance sheet.

29. According to Johnson and Kaplan (1987, p. 200 f), measures of this kind encourage managers to try to generate earnings through creative financial transactions. The authors provide many examples of such transactions: creative re-arrangement of ownership claims through mergers and acquisitions, divestures and spin-offs etc. For examples of data manipulation, see Note 22.

30. Hamel (2000, p. 40) makes an interesting observation on the concept of "unlocking" shareholder wealth: "It is fashionable today to talk of 'unlocking' shareholder wealth. The metaphor is telling. The assumption is that wealth is already there – it's already been created – and with a little creative engineering it can be set free."

31. Not in the area of management control, either, has the scope of research fully expanded to include several decision levels and organizational levels. This is apparent, for example, in a newly published edition of the textbook *Management Control Systems*, by Anthony and Govindarajan (2004, p. 6 ff). Here the authors still distinguish between strategic, tactical, and operating decisions and hold that management control only covers tactical decisions.

32. Note that in our definition of management control and manufacturing control we emphasize the importance of double-loop learning. By this we mean that the control system is not to be used only for implementing strategies, but also to aid in the process in formulating new strategies. Morgan (1986, p. 88) expresses this idea as follows: "Single-loop learning rests in an ability to detect and correct error in relation to a given set of operating norms. Double-loop learning depends on being able to take a 'double look' at the situation by questioning the relevance of operating norms." Compare Robert N. Anthony's (1965) definition of management control, which is heavily influenced by the idea that the control systems should be used primarily for implementation of strategy; see Footnote 12.

33. The elements of manufacturing and capacity strategy have been added to the original figure. It may be noted that sales and operations planning is normally regarded as the planning level with the longest time horizon in a system of manufacturing planning and control. However, we have chosen to include manufacturing strategy as well to make clear its connection with the design and use of the control system. The inclusion of capacity strategy is discussed in Footnote 38. Some other minor modifications to the original figure are discussed in Olhager and Rapp (1996).

34. The co-ordination of corporate, business, and manufacturing strategies is described in the section "Strategic Congruence Defined" in Chapter 3.

35. Sometimes the term production planning is used instead of sales and operations planning (Olhager et al., 2001).

36. According to Olhager et al. (2001), the purpose of demand management is not only to forecast demand. Another important task is to seek to influence demand through various activities such as campaigns, pricing, etc.

37. For a discussion on ways to organize the manufacture of unique products, see Chapter 3, Footnote 39.

38. Planning strategy is another designation for sales and operations planning and is considered to be part of the manufacturing-control system (*cf.* Figure 4.5) – roughly as a budget is a part of the management-control system (*cf.* Figure 4.3). As for capacity strategy, the definition

of this concept is not as clear. Some scholars hold that capacity strategy is a part of overall manufacturing strategy (for an overview, see Olhager et al., 2001). In our view, however, capacity strategy could also be included in the manufacturing-control system. The reason is the close link to sales and operations planning highlighted by Olhager et al., among others. We discuss this link in detail in the following section.

39. See Chapter 3, Footnote 39, for a more through discussion.

40. According to Hill (1991), the sub-assemblies, components, and raw materials have dependent demands.

41. According to Hill (1991), it may be argued that this is in fact a pulling action.

42. A method of production-activity control that is a hybrid of MRP and JIT can enhance the firm's capacity to cope with variations in the volume of production and the product mix. For a more detailed description, see Vollmann et al. (1992, p. 380 ff).

43. According to Hill (1991), production rates in JIT are set in such a manner as to ensure uniform daily demand. Consequently, changes would be expensive to implement.

5 A Tentative Model

The purpose of this chapter is to integrate into a tentative model the concepts developed in the three preceding chapters. We begin by discussing the principal variables and relationships in this model. Special emphasis is placed on the interplay between the corporate, business-unit, and functional levels, where strategies and control systems are to be adapted to each other and to the business environment. On the basis of the units' business strategies and manufacturing strategies, we identify four distinct positions and one intermediate position. For each position, the requirements for creating strategic congruence and integrated control are discussed in detail. In the next and final sections of the chapter, our discussion is enlarged to include two distinct strategic positions at the corporate level. By expanding the analysis to include an additional organizational level, we show clearly how a misfit between strategies and control systems can make it more difficult for a firm to be a strong competitor.

Principal Variables and Relationships

Based on the theoretical foundations of the book, a model summarizing the principal variables and relationships was presented in Chapter 2. In the following section, the model is further developed to reinforce the message of the book: that all organizational levels must be considered when strategies and control systems are to be adapted to each other and to the environment (*cf.* Figure 5.1). As shown in the discussion in previous chapters, this means, for example, that strategic congruence may be difficult to achieve in corporations where the business units operate in environments with different degrees of uncertainty. When the differences in the subenvironments[1] of units and functions are too great, it is difficult to establish a common business logic with similar critical success factors. Consequently, to achieve a match between environment and strategies – an external fit – management needs an in-depth knowledge of the markets and industries that fit the corporate business.

Figure 5.1 shows that this essential knowledge is not only about the potential adaptability of corporate and business-unit subenvironments[2] and

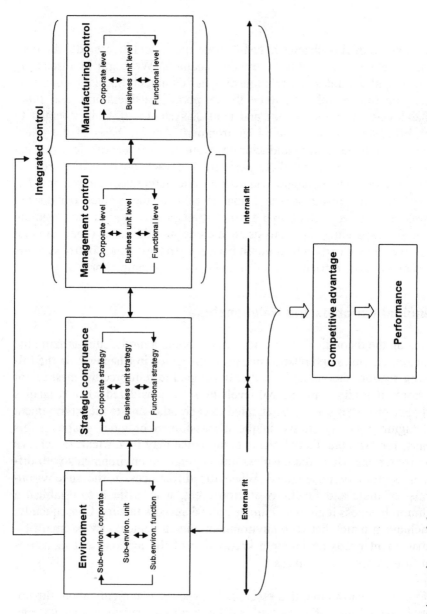

Fig. 5.1. A tentative model

strategies to each other. Equally important are the functions of the units, particularly the subenvironment for manufacturing. For example, a manufacturing strategy developed in a stable environment can prove disastrous for a unit with a new business strategy that calls for highly flexible manufacturing (cf. Kotha and Orne, 1989). To avoid this kind of misalignment between different strategic levels, it is essential that management view the business in a holistic perspective. This means that considerable attention must be paid to the interaction of the corporation, businesses, and functions with the environment and with each other in the effort to be highly competitive. Thus, planning based on mechanical analysis of goals and strategies tends to focus excessively on placing all activities within a given framework (cf. Mintzberg et al., 1998). In this situation, there is a danger that the strategies formulated, particularly at lower organizational levels, will be inappropriate to the prevailing environment.

In previous chapters we discussed how some financially successful firms have been able to achieve a high degree of strategic congruence while avoiding many of the problems identified above.[3] These firms seem to operate in subenvironments where the degree of uncertainty, and the decision situations faced by management, are similar in nature.[4] The advantage of such focusing is that the control systems of the firm can be designed and used in a more uniform manner than in cases where strategies are not mutually consistent (cf. Nilsson, 2002). In the latter instance, there is a considerable risk that the differences between corporate, business, and functional strategies will result in highly disparate information needs at different organizational levels, thus subjecting the control systems to incompatible demands. In the former case, by contrast, the information needs will likely be congruent, so that the control systems can be based on similar principles (cf. Argyris, 1977). It follows that with high degree of strategic congruence, the control systems can be adapted to the strategy followed at each level without jeopardizing the establishment of an integrated control system. As shown in Figure 5.1, when a coherent system of strategic planning and follow-up is to be created, congruent strategies can be expected to facilitate integration of the critical control systems: management control and manufacturing control. An internal fit – that is, a match between strategies and internal structures – requires such integration.

Just as integrated control is difficult to achieve without strategic congruence, the opposite is also true. With a control system that does not provide uniform and transparent information on all organizational levels, it will probably be much more difficult to formulate and implement mutually consistent strategies. This interdependence of environment, strategies, and internal structures is shown by the arrows in the tentative model. The model also illustrates how these dependencies affect the firm's potential for being a powerful competitor – a recurring theme in our book.

In the following two sections, we discuss in greater depth the variables and relationships identified in the tentative model. We place considerable emphasis on discussing thoroughly and in detail the conditions for simultaneously establishing strategic congruence and integrated control. In this discussion the strategic typologies chosen in Chapter 3 are used. We also refer to a number of highly important dimensions – treated in Chapter 4 – in the design and use of a control system.[5] For readers interested in a detailed presentation of the studies used in the model, we consequently refer to the introductory chapter of the book. In the first section, strategic congruence and integrated control are discussed at the business-unit and functional levels. The reason why we begin with these two organizational levels is that being a strong competitor is heavily dependent on the success of the business unit in positioning its product offering on the market. From the previous discussion, we can also assume that the creation of competitive advantage is influenced by the manner in which business-unit strategies, functional strategies and control systems are adapted to conditions at the corporate level. This subject is discussed in the second section.

Strategic Congruence and Integrated Control at the Business Unit and Functional Levels

Up to this point, the discussion has made clear that being strongly competitive requires both strategic congruence and integrated control at the same time. Figure 5.2 – which is based on this necessity – shows how different combinations of business and manufacturing strategies can be assumed to affect the possibilities of achieving a high degree of strategic congruence and a high degree of integrated control. Such a situation is characterized by mutual accommodation of strategies and control systems and by their adaptation to the environment. The firm will then operate at a higher level of efficiency, and thus be more competitive, than otherwise (*cf.* Hrebiniak et al., 1989). This competitive strength is manifested in the creation of value above the minimum required by the firm's stakeholders.

Where a good fit can be expected between the business and manufacturing strategies of a unit (a high degree of strategic congruence), with favorable conditions for integrating the systems of management control and manufacturing control (a high degree of integrated control), the expression

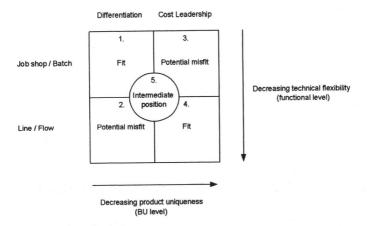

Fig. 5.2. Possibilities of achieving strategic congruence and integrated control

"fit" is used in Figure 5.2. Where a poor fit can be assumed between the business and manufacturing strategies of a unit (a low degree of strategic congruence), with limited possibilities of integrating the systems of management control and manufacturing control (low degree of integrated control), the expression "potential misfit" is used in the figure. The concept of "intermediate position" is used to designate combinations of business and manufacturing strategies that are mixed – i. e., not purely of one kind or another. To achieve strategic congruence and integrated control in these cases, it is important that management understand how the business units can consistently create competitive advantage and a strong market position.

An analysis of the potential for creating congruence and integrated control is based on the dimensions that can be assumed to be especially important for establishing a "fit." These dimensions were identified in Chapter 2 and elaborated in the two subsequent chapters.[6] There we showed that at the business-unit level the degree of product uniqueness is an important dimension of business strategy. At the functional level, the degree of technical flexibility is of major significance for the choice of manufacturing strategy.[7] As for the design and use of management control, it can be described on the basis of intensity of monitoring (loose or tight control), type of information used (nonmonetary or monetary control), and time perspective (short-term or long-term).[8] The principal dimensions in a manufacturing-control system are type of information used (nonmonetary or monetary control), capacity and planning strategy (lead / chase or lag / level), customer-order decoupling point (make-to-order or make-to-stock), and control concept (materials-requirement planning or just-in- time).[9]

Figure 5.3 illustrates the chosen dimensions and their expected effect on the establishment of strategic congruence and integrated control. Where the extent of product uniqueness and the requirements of technical flexibility coincide, the figure shows that the conditions for achieving a high degree of strategic congruence should be favorable. For example, it is appropriate to combine a cost-leadership strategy, where products are standardized and demand can be readily forecast (the dimension of "product uniqueness"), with a manufacturing strategy based on a stable mix and volume of production (the dimension of "technical flexibility"). Furthermore, integrated control requires that management control and manufacturing control be based on uniform principles of control – that is, a common basis for the contribution of planning and follow-up to the creation of value by the firm. These principles should be reflected in the dimensions shown by the figure to be important in each control system. For example, management control with a strong monetary focus is difficult to integrate with manufacturing control that emphasizes nonmonetary information directly related to operations (the dimension of "Type of information used"). Another example: tight financial control with frequent follow-up (the dimension of "Intensity of monitoring") facilitates integration when used together with a manufacturing-control system based on just-in-time (the dimension of "Control concept").[10] The explanation is that the objectives and aim of just-in-time are the same as those of tight management control: to achieve extremely cost-effective production.

This type of analysis is essential to the discussion that follows; it also indicates the way in which this discussion is organized. As previously mentioned, the analysis is based largely on the empirical studies with a contingency-theory approach that were reported in the review of the literature. It may be noted, however, that research on management control and manufacturing control, despite its extension to several organizational levels, has not yet noted all relevant relationships between strategy and control systems. For example, very few studies clearly link the choice of corporate strategy to the design and use of the manufacturing-control system.[11] In our view, though, many of the relationships identified at a specific organizational level are valid at other levels as well. The arguments and reasoning in support of this assumption are presented in the sections immediately to follow.

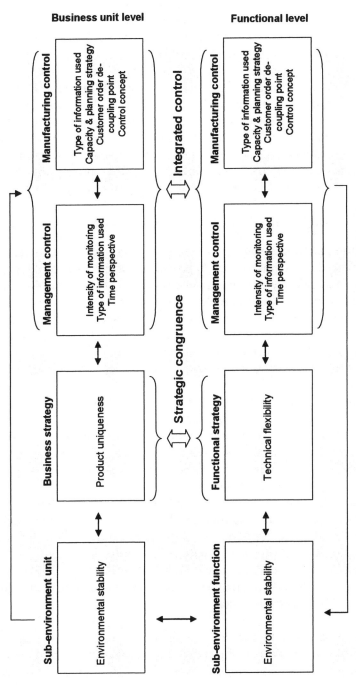

Fig. 5.3. Strategic congruence and integrated control at the business-unit and functional level

Finally, it may be noted that the ensuing discussion is not intended to present in detail the factors that determine whether strategic congruence and integrated control can be achieved. Rather, the purpose is to describe a number of tendencies in regard to the fit between different strategic levels (corporate, business and functional) and the role of control systems in this respect.[12] As we would also like to stress, although this book focuses on fit, we can expect that successful firms will continually be changing their strategies and control systems. Consequently, periods with a high degree of strategic congruence and integrated control will often be followed by periods of instability and disequilibrium. The anticipated effects of such a situation on strategies and control systems will be briefly discussed in Chapter 6. We shall now review each of the positions in Figure 5.2.

Position 1: Differentiation and Job-Shop/Batch

With a differentiation strategy, business-unit management seeks to establish a strong market position with product offerings that are perceived throughout the industry as being unique (Porter, 1985, p. 14). The chosen business strategy specifies those elements of the sub-environment, such as customers and suppliers, with which the unit interacts – also referred to as the domain (cf. Ford et al., 1988).[13, 14] The choice of a differentiation strategy means that the unit interacts primarily with elements typical of a turbulent environment with a high degree of uncertainty (Miller, 1987, 1988). For example, it is difficult to learn about the preferences of purchasers of differentiated products, and thus to forecast demand. One reason is that the product features considered unique by customers can change as a result of actions by competitors (Shank and Govindarajan, 1993, p. 105). According to the authors, this situation also creates uncertainty about the appropriate focus of the unit's efforts to develop new products. The uncertainty is related primarily to the product attributes that customers will regard as exclusive and unique in the future (Biggadike, 1979; Miller, 1986). Finally Govindarajan (1988) has identified another source of turbulence and uncertainty. Referring to Hambrick (1983) and Chandler (1962) he claims that in the effort to achieve uniqueness, a differentiation strategy leads to a broad product range with consequent high costs of inventory, distribution, and marketing. A broad product range is associated with uncertainty due to the complex business environment.

It is apparent from Figure 5.4 that the unit's business and functional strategies must be co-ordinated if a high degree of strategic congruence is to be achieved. To be sure, so-called protective buffers partially protect the

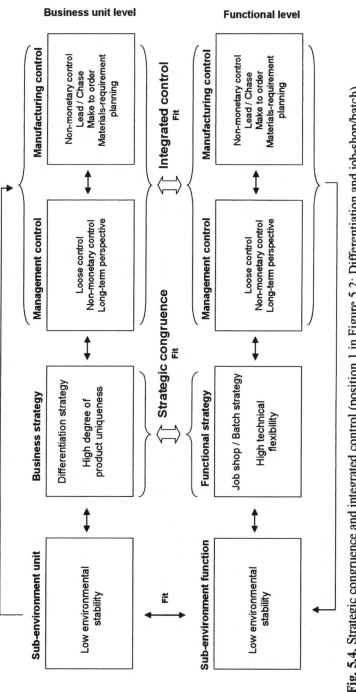

Fig. 5.4. Strategic congruence and integrated control (position 1 in Figure 5.2: Differentiation and job-shop/batch)

manufacturing function from harmful environmental influences (Thompson, 1967).[15] For example, the purchasing department should seek to maintain a constant flow of materials in order to avoid disrupting production (ibid). Yet despite protective buffers, it is reasonable to assume that a turbulent environment almost always affects the business-unit level in the form of an unstable subenvironment for manufacturing. Since a differentiation strategy is accompanied by uncertainty and thus difficulty in planning operations, manufacturing strategy must focus on the capacity to cope rapidly with change – and especially – flexibility in regard to changes in volume, to changes in product specifications, and also to the introduction of completely new products (Stobaugh and Telesio, 1983; Bartezzaghi, 1999). Therefore, manufacturing strategy should emphasize technical flexibility – that is, variables like flexibility in the use of machinery, product flexibility, flexibility in processes, and flexibility of volume (Kim and Lee, 1993).

A high degree of technical flexibility means that both machinery and employees must be capable of meeting unique and varying product specifications with production lead-times that do not exceed a desired reasonable delivery time (Olhager and Rapp, 1985). Here, a low degree of technical complexity is most suitable – in other words, limited mechanization and limited integration of different steps in the manufacturing process (cf. Kotha and Orne, 1989). In these circumstances both a job-shop strategy and a batch strategy may be considered appropriate for achieving a high degree of strategic congruence (cf. Parthasarthy and Sethi, 1992). The former strategy is well adapted to the manufacture of products that are completely unique and subject to rigorous quality standards – in other words, attributes typical of a differentiated product. The latter strategy is particularly suitable when the product offering must meet high quality standards but is somewhat more standardized, and processing in batches is desired (Hayes and Wheelwright, 1979a). Furthermore, it may be noted that the technical flexibility, while somewhat less with a batch strategy than with a job-shop strategy, is adequate for managing the kind of uncertainty typically found with a differentiation strategy (Kim and Lee, 1993; Ward et al., 1996). Both types of manufacturing strategy are thus appropriate with a business strategy focused on a high degree of product uniqueness.

The congruence between a differentiation and a job-shop/batch strategy means that the degree of uncertainty for the business unit and the manufacturing function converge. In the theoretical frame of reference, it has been emphasized that such convergence is a pre-condition for establishing integrated control (cf. Figure 5.4). To achieve an internal fit in this specific case, management control and manufacturing control must therefore be adapted to the high degree of uncertainty involved in the chosen business and manufacturing strategies. As for management control, several studies have shown that loose and nonmonetary control, combined with a long-term perspective, is appropriate when the chosen strategies entail uncertainty (Kald et al., 2000).[16] This uncertainty, which is due to factors like changing customer preferences, makes planning difficult at the unit and functional level. For example, the difficulties in predicting demand complicate the preparation of reliable forecasts and a credible strategic plan (cf. Mintzberg et al., 1998). Another and closely related problem is that future revenues and costs are difficult to estimate. The rapidly changing assumptions on which the budget is prepared reduce the role of the budget as an indicator of the performance level (Govindarajan, 1988). Consequently, plans and budgets should not be taken as binding contracts or as a basis for frequent and detailed follow-up (i.e. tight control). Anthony et al. (1992, p. 580 ff) indicate that suitable uses for plans and budgets in this type of situation are as decision support and as an aid in communication (i.e. loose control).

In a management-control system used dynamically to stimulate desired action, there will typically be an emphasis on information that is directly related to operations and thus operationally oriented. When the criteria for good financial performance are unclear, the focus shifts from following up the output of the refinement process to the way in which this output is created (cf. Govindarajan, 1988). Particularly when differentiation and job-shop/batch strategies are combined, nonmonetary information will be especially appropriate in planning and follow-up. The reason is that the success of these strategies is determined by product dimensions such as high quality and reliable delivery, which are difficult to control with traditional monetary measures (Kaplan and Norton, 1992). The strong link of nonmonetary information both to strategies and to operational activities also facilitates analysis and discussion of central cause-and-effect relationships (Donovan et al., 1998). Such a "strategic dialogue" between business-unit management and decision-makers at the functional level is a significant element in the process of formulating new strategies (Simons, 1995). An additional reason why nonmonetary information is suitable is the long-term perspective typical of a differentiation strategy, with its clear focus on innovation and product renewal (Miller, 1987, 1988; Kald et al., 2000). Govindarajan and Gupta (1985) have shown that the use of subjective (non-formal) and long-run criteria[17] helps to improve efficiency in businesses where many of the products are in the early stages of their life cycles. In summary, planning and follow-up with these features are consistent with management control where flexibility is important – at both the business-unit level and the functional level.

An uncertain subenvironment at the business and functional levels also affects the design and use of manufacturing control. In this connection, it is important to respond rapidly to changes in the volume and mix of production. The technical flexibility required to cope with the uncertain demand situation of a differentiation strategy is achieved, as previously mentioned, through a job-shop/batch strategy. However, if these strategies are to be successfully implemented, and flexible production is to be supported, much is required of planning at both the business-unit and functional levels (Vollmann et al., 1992). According to Olhager et al. (2001), this situation calls for a capacity and planning strategy in which manufacturing capacity is adjusted before demand changes (lead) and the volume of production with a given capacity ceiling is adapted to the sales of the period (chase). The authors argue that this will create a capacity surplus which allows for higher flexibility, favors on-time delivery, and positively affects product quality. As noted in previous discussions, these attributes are very important for implementing both a differentiation and a job-shop/batch strategy. The drawback, however, is that there will be idle production capacity, which will have a negative impact on cost effectiveness (ibid).

With a high degree of technical flexibility, moreover, planning can be based on a customer-order decoupling point early in the production chain. In this situation the product is usually manufactured to customer order (MTO). With MTO, products are highly customized, i.e. extensively adapted to customer requirements (Olhager and Rapp, 1985, 1996). Here, conditions thus favor the efficient manufacture of products with a high degree of uniqueness, meeting rigorous requirements of product differentiation.[18] As for short-term planning and follow-up, materials-requirement planning is a good choice when a differentiation strategy and a job-shop/batch strategy are combined. Unlike just-in-time, MRP can cope with numerous product variations and time-discrete demand (Vollmann et al., 1992, p. 370 ff). According to Hill (1991), lead-times, volume of production, and levels of inventory can be specified with relatively little advance preparation. This method of planning and follow-up is thus particularly appropriate to the requirements of manufacturing batches at different work stations. In following up important dimensions of the chosen business and manufacturing strategies – such as quality levels, reliable delivery, and lead times – primarily nonmonetary information is used. Perera et al. (1997) have shown that this kind of information is especially common with manufacturing strategies in which flexibility and customer focus are major dimensions (*cf.* Abernethy and Lillis, 1995).[19]

In summary, manufacturing control designed and used in this way is intended to manage uncertainty through flexible routines rather than by achieving high capacity utilization and eliminating activities that do not create value. A manufacturing-control system with this focus resembles in many ways the management control suitable for a situation where differentiation and job-shop/batch strategies are combined. For example, the difficulties of forecasting mean that the budget can be expected to function as a framework for the focus of operations. In production planning, this framework can serve as a rough starting point, with the focus on creating scope for rapid adjustment to new patterns of demand. Another example is that in management control and manufacturing control, it may be assumed that nonmonetary information will be emphasized. Follow-up will thus reflect the focus of strategy on unique products and the long-term time frame characteristic of the business. With a common basis for management control and manufacturing control, in the form of mutually consistent strategies, transparency in the planning and follow-up processes will be enhanced. The congruence of unit and functional planning horizons, and similar criteria for follow-up, are essential if the two control systems are to provide clear indications of intended strategies and plans as well as progress in achieving them. In addition, the discussion as to whether goals and strategies should be modified – the so-called strategic dialogue – is facilitated if the system is based on a uniform set of concepts (*cf.* Argyris, 1977).[20] In light of the discussion so far, the conditions for establishing this type of coherent planning and follow-up should be favorable in this specific instance.

Position 2: Differentiation and Line/Flow

Compared to Position 1 in Figure 5.2, the combination of a differentiation and a line/flow strategy[21] may be assumed to offer limited possibilities for establishing a high degree of strategic congruence (*cf.* Figure 5.5). From the analysis in the preceding section, it is apparent that a unit with a differentiation strategy typically operates in a turbulent sub-environment with considerable uncertainty. Since the business strategy is based on product uniqueness, and adaptation to customer requirements is an important dimension, manufacturing strategy should focus on attaining a high degree of flexibility in regard to volume of production and product mix. A line/flow strategy, by contrast, is focused on achieving short lead-times

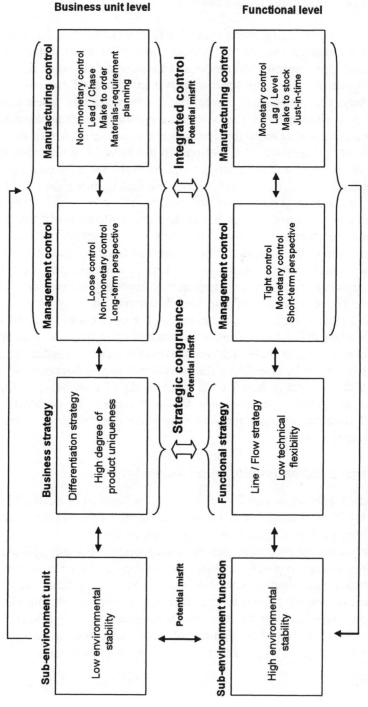

Fig. 5.5. Strategic congruence and integrated control (position 2 in Figure 5.2: Differentiation and line/flow)

and low manufacturing costs through standardized products in high volumes (Hayes and Wheelwright, 1979a). For these goals to be within reach, high technical complexity is unavoidable; in other words, extensive mechanization and the integration of different steps in the process are required (Kotha and Orne, 1989). In addition, the machinery used is often advanced and highly specialized, and the employees generally have a narrow competence profile. The disadvantage of a line/flow strategy is illustrated by Figure 5.5, which shows that technical flexibility is limited – in other words, changing the volume of production and the product mix is both difficult and costly (Kim and Lee, 1993).

According to Hayes and Wheelwright (1979a), a line strategy is an appropriate choice when the competitiveness of the business unit is dependent on a highly cost-effective production apparatus. A flow strategy is designed to cope with situations where the products of the business unit are generally standardized and manufactured in extremely large volumes. With both strategies, desired delivery lead-time is shorter than production lead-time, so that manufacturing to stock is necessary (Olhager and Rapp, 1985, 1996). In addition, long production runs are essential for the capital-intensive production apparatus to be used efficiently. Therefore, to benefit from the advantages of a line/flow strategy, it must be possible to plan both production volume and product mix in detail. This presupposes a stable subenvironment and a limited degree of uncertainty – a situation that may be hard to achieve for a business unit with a differentiation strategy (*cf.* Hayes and Wheelwright, 1979a; Kim and Lee, 1993). In light of our previous analysis, buffers can probably isolate manufacturing only in part from the effects of the difficulties of predicting demand – a consequence of the chosen business strategy.

The difficulty of combining a differentiation and a line/flow strategy can also be expected to impact management control and manufacturing control. In view of the substantial differences in the goals and focus of these strategies, there are disparate information needs at the business-unit and functional levels, respectively. As previously discussed, a management-control system suitable for a business unit with a differentiation strategy should emphasize loose control and nonmonetary information, and it should reflect a long-term perspective. At the functional level, a line/flow strategy, with its focus on large-scale, cost-effective production, implies quite different requirements in regard to the design and use of management control. For example, it is hard to achieve favorable conditions for long production runs without comprehensive, well-established procedures for planning and budgeting. Since there is an additional cost of changing the focus of manufacturing, it may be assumed that plans and budgets will be regarded as commitments – a characteristic of tight management control (*cf.* Hopwood, 1972; Otley, 1978; Bruggeman and Van der Stede, 1993).

Another typical feature of tight control is frequent and detailed budget follow-up (Anthony et al., 1992). With the chosen manufacturing strategy and its emphasis on cost effectiveness, it is appropriate in designing follow-up procedures at the functional level (*cf.* Nilsson and Rapp, 1999). Furthermore, Abernethy and Lillis (1995) have shown that with a manufacturing strategy based on mass production and standard product lines, measures of efficiency play a major part in the control of this function.[22] However, with the use of such monetary information, and a constant search for activities that create no value, there is a risk that planning and follow-up will be given a short-term focus (Johnson and Kaplan, 1987). This would directly conflict with the long-term perspective reflected in the design and use of the control system at the business-unit level. Fundamental differences in the intensity of monitoring at the business and functional levels are an example of yet another problem. In addition, as has been previously stressed, there are the difficulties of isolating the manufacturing function from the turbulent, uncertain environment of the business unit. Substantial and frequent shifts in the focus of manufacturing would soon give rise to problems in a highly formalized control system based on stable planning conditions.

A turbulent subenvironment at the functional level could also entail problems with the kind of manufacturing control appropriate to a line/flow strategy (*cf.* Figure 5.5), for in manufacturing control, as in management control, planning would be based on the possibility of preparing reasonably reliable forecasts. In line with the analysis of Olhager et al., (2001), to achieve effective utilization of the capital-intensive production apparatus, it is thus important to avoid acquiring new production capacity before an increase in demand has been noted (i.e. a lag capacity strategy). Within the limits of existing capacity, management can be expected to establish a situation where a previously set volume of production is maintained during the period (i.e. leveled planning strategy). According to Olhager et al. (2001), the danger with a combination of lag/level strategies is that it may be difficult to maintain on-time delivery, with dissatisfied customers as a consequence. Large and rapid shifts in customer preferences are particularly difficult to manage satisfactorily with this combination of capacity and planning strategies.

Stable conditions for planning are also necessary if a customer order is to be placed near the end of the production chain, with manufacture to the stock of finished goods (MTS). MTS is often found in the manufacture of standardized products and is thus a frequent customer-order decoupling point with a line/flow strategy. It is primarily used in situations where desired delivery time is shorter than production lead-time (Olhager and Rapp, 1985, 1996).[23] As for the control concept, just-in time (JIT) is suitable because of the rather limited number of product variations with a typical line/flow strategy, the rate-based demand, and the strong focus on extremely cost-effective production (Vollmann et al., 1992, p. 370 ff). With JIT there is little tolerance for deviations from plan, since there is no stock of semi-finished goods, and production is continuous. Thus, according to Hill (1991) the workload must be the same, and the production sequence must be nearly identical for a long period of time. The method also allows detailed follow-up of activities that do not create value. For the most part, monetary information is used in this type of follow-up – for example by calculating the costs of reworking, guarantees etc. (Bromwich and Bhimani, 1994, p. 47 f).

In summary, there are substantial differences between the design and use of the manufacturing control appropriate at the business-unit and functional levels, respectively. As shown in Figure 5.5, a manufacturing-control system intended to implement a differentiation strategy should emphasize nonmonetary control, lead/chase, make-to-order, and materials-requirement planning. By contrast, at the functional level – where a line/flow strategy is followed – the emphasis should be on monetary control, lag/level, make to stock, and just-in-time. On these premises, there are limited possibilities of establishing manufacturing control with coherent planning and follow-up at the business-unit level and functional levels. As for management control, the problems are similar, with wholly different information requirements at the two organizational levels. This means that the conditions for establishing an integrated control system are not present.

Position 3: Cost Leadership and Job-Shop/Batch

Business units with a cost-leadership strategy typically seek to achieve the lowest costs in their industry through a standardized product offering manufactured in high volumes According to Porter (1980, p. 35), however, such a strategy does not mean that quality, product image, and bases for differentiation can be ignored, but only that they are not the primary strategic goal. Given the choice of a cost-leadership strategy, the business unit interacts primarily with elements typical of a stable environment (Miller,

1987, 1988). An example of such an element is found where customer demand is easier to predict than with a differentiation strategy. By competing solely through low manufacturing costs, rather than product uniqueness, the business unit focuses on a dimension where customer behavior is predictable with a relatively high degree of certainty (Shank and Govindarajan, 1993, p. 105). Shank and Govindarajan also maintain that low-cost units try to keep their product offerings stable, thus eliminating the uncertainty involved in a comprehensive research and development program (Biggadike, 1979; Miller, 1986). Referring to Chandler (1962) and Hambrick (1983), Govindarajan (1988) claims that the degree of uncertainty is lower because of the narrow product lines commonly found with a cost-leadership strategy. He argues that since sales volume is not spread over several product variants inventory-carrying costs can be lowered and production runs made longer.

Since a cost-leadership strategy is typically found where demand is stable, with few variations in product mix and product offering, a job-shop/batch strategy is probably inappropriate (Kim and Lee, 1993; Ward et al., 1996). As indicated previously, the purpose of such a manufacturing strategy is to provide the technical flexibility to cope with unique and varying product specifications (i.e. a turbulent subenvironment). In view of the stable environment typically found with a cost-leadership strategy, the benefit of high technical flexibility is limited and probably not reasonably proportionate to the cost. In all likelihood, it is neither desirable – nor perhaps even possible – to establish a situation where both business and functional strategies are appropriate to the firm's competitive arena. As can be seen in Figure 5.6, this lack of strategic congruence between a cost-leadership strategy and a job-shop/batch strategy can also be expected to have implications for the control systems. As with the situation shown by Position 2 in Figure 5.2, the differences in strategic focus at the business-unit and functional levels, respectively, mean that quite disparate information needs may be assumed to exist. This situation complicates the exchange of information between different organizational levels and decision-makers concerning strategic, tactical, and operating decisions. The absence of shared concepts and principles also makes the planning and follow-up process less transparent. The causes of these problems become clear when management control and manufacturing control are analyzed in detail at the respective organizational levels.

As shown in Figure 5.6, we can expect management control at the business-unit level to be affected by the high degree of environmental stability

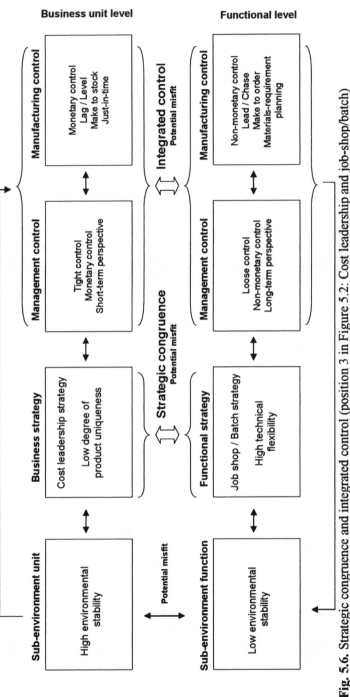

Fig. 5.6. Strategic congruence and integrated control (position 3 in Figure 5.2: Cost leadership and job-shop/batch)

associated with the choice of a cost-leadership strategy. One feature of a business based on stable conditions is that reliable plans and forecasts are possible (Mintzberg et al., 1998). Given the limited variation in the conditions prevailing when plans are prepared, it is appropriate to use budget variances as performance indicators (Govindarajan, 1988). In these circumstances, it is therefore common to regard the strategic plan and the budget as binding contracts and as the basis for frequent and detailed follow-up (i.e. tight control). According to the reasoning of Anthony et al. (1992, p. 584), the emphasis should be on outcomes in relation to plans and budgets, meaning that the focus of follow-up is on the output of the refinement process – rather than on the way in which this result is accomplished. The reason is that under such stable conditions, the central cause-and-effect relationships will probably be known.

Given the strong emphasis on result rather than process, in combination with rigorous standards of cost effectiveness, monetary information predominates both in planning and in follow-up (cf. Nilsson, 2002). Another reason for this predominance is that a cost-leadership strategy is common in mature industries where the business is managed with a short-term perspective and high-risk investments are avoided (cf. Miller, 1986, 1987; Goold et al., 1994, p. 420 ff). In situations where the products of the unit are mature and in the later stages of their product life cycles, short-term and objective (formula-based) criteria are normally used for evaluation (Govindarajan and Gupta, 1985).[24] In summary, a management-control system designed and used in this manner bears little similarity to the planning and control appropriate for a job-shop/batch strategy. In previous sections, loose control, nonmonetary control, and a long-term perspective characterized a management-control system suitable for a manufacturing strategy with this focus.

As for manufacturing control, and in line with the reasoning of Olhager et al. (2001), the stable subenvironment at the business-unit level makes it feasible to acquire new production capacity after an increase in demand has been noted (i.e., a lag capacity strategy). With reliable sales forecasts, it is also easier for management to maintain a previously set volume of production within the limits of a given manufacturing capacity (i.e. leveled planning strategy). According to the authors, this combination of lag and level strategies is intended to permit high capacity utilization and cost-effective production – two critical success factors with a cost-leadership strategy (Porter, 1985). When products are standardized, the possibility of manufacturing to stock (MTS) provides yet another way of achieving steady high capacity utilization (Olhager and Rapp, 1985, 1996). Instead of varying the volume of production, the volume of inventory is adjusted according to current demand. It may be noted, however, that this adjustment is often marginal because of a relatively stable demand pattern (cf. Hill, 1991). Another benefit of MTS, is that delivery times can be kept shorter than production lead-time (Olhager and Rapp, 1985, 1996).

With a constant workload, as well as a limited number of product variants, just-in-time is a control concept suitable for a cost-leadership strategy. By simplifying shop-floor procedures and minimizing changeover costs and work-in-progress, it is possible to lower manufacturing costs radically (Vollmann et al., 1992, p. 373). Another instrument in the incessant search for cost effectiveness is detailed and comprehensive monetary follow-up (Abernethy and Lillis, 1995). As shown in previous sections, it is difficult to combine just-in-time with the planning and follow-up appropriate to a job-shop/batch strategy. Admittedly, there are examples of companies that have integrated just-in-time and materials-requirement planning to achieve efficient manufacture of customized products (Vollmann et al., 1992, p. 380 ff). But in cases where the competitiveness of the unit is wholly dependent on its cost effectiveness, manufacturing control should be focused exclusively on achieving high volumes, short lead-times, low changeover costs, etc. This means that planning and follow-up at both business and functional levels must have a common basis; i.e., it must be possible to establish a high degree of integrated control. However, such is not the case if manufacturing control at the functional level is appropriate to a job-shop/batch strategy whereas planning and follow-up at the business-unit level are suitable for a cost-leadership strategy. Figure 5.6 shows that the former strategy may be assumed to entail manufacturing control emphasizing nonmonetary control, lead/chase, make-to-order, and materials-requirement planning. A strategy of the latter kind, according to our reasoning, has quite different features: monetary control, lag/level, make-to-stock, and just-in-time.

Position 4: Cost Leadership and Line/Flow

Compared to Position 3 in Figure 5.2, a combination of a cost-leadership and a line/flow strategy may be assumed to offer much better possibilities for achieving a high degree of strategic congruence (cf. Figure 5.7). As has already been indicated, the aim of a cost-leadership strategy is to create competitive advantage by being the low-cost manufacturer on the market. High cost effectiveness in relation to other competitors calls for a standardized product offering manufactured in large volumes (Porter, 1980, 1985;

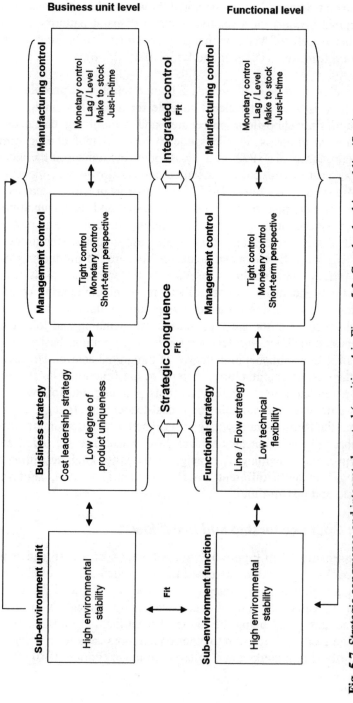

Fig. 5.7. Strategic congruence and integrated control (position 4 in Figure 5.2: Cost leadership and line/flow)

Parthasarthy and Sethi, 1992). Substantial economies of scale require a heavily mechanized and integrated manufacturing process typically associated with a line strategy. When the products are extremely standardized and in the nature of raw materials, such as refined oil, a flow strategy is more appropriate (Hayes and Wheelwright, 1979a). Both of these manufacturing strategies entail a high degree of technical complexity and a low degree of technical flexibility (cf. Kotha and Orne, 1989). This is particularly true of a flow strategy, where manufacturing plants are extremely specialized and capital-intensive (Kim and Lee, 1993). As previously noted, given the substantial cost of changing the volume and mix of production, a line/flow strategy clearly requires a high degree of certainty in plans and forecasts. The stable environment associated with a cost-leadership strategy makes it easier to meet this requirement, one reason being the favorable conditions for predicting customer demand (Shank and Govindarajan, 1993, p. 105).

The chosen business and manufacturing strategies, and the accompanying environmental stability, also affect management control and manufacturing control. In the area of management control, studies have shown that managers of businesses with low uncertainty generally view formalized instruments for planning and follow-up as important (Langfield-Smith, 1997; Kald et al., 2000). The possibility of estimating future revenues and costs with a reasonable degree of certainty tends to give the budget a significant role at the business-unit level (Govindarajan, 1988). As previously mentioned, budgets in this type of situation are commonly regarded as binding contracts, and budget follow-up is both frequent and detailed (i.e. tight control). Another characteristic is that the focus is on the results of the business unit and the function rather than the manner in which these results are achieved (Anthony et al., 1992, p. 580 ff). With this type of output control, in combination with an emphasis on cost effectiveness and a short-term time perspective, monetary information can be assumed to dominate planning and follow-up (Nilsson, 2002). In summary, this should lead to tight monetary control with a short-term focus at both the business-unit and functional levels.

Management control designed and used in this way is quite similar to the type of manufacturing control that is suitable when both a cost leadership and a line/flow strategy are followed. For example, stable conditions for planning at the business and functional levels make it possible to combine a lag capacity strategy and a leveled planning strategy. A situation of capacity-demand surplus and high capacity utilization can thus be established, while on-time delivery is maintained (Olhager et al., 2001). Reliable delivery is also made possible by the limited degree of customization and the fact that that the customer-order decoupling point can be located near the end of the production chain. As previously noted, some form of manufacturing to stock is necessary with standardized products since the production lead-time is normally longer than the desired delivery time (Olhager and Rapp, 1985, 1996). Moreover, given the strong focus of the chosen strategies on short lead-times and cost-effective manufacturing, just-in-time is an appropriate control concept. The favorable conditions for maintaining a constant workload make it especially likely that the benefits of just-in-time will be exploited; these include, for example, a continuous flow, very high capacity utilization, and minimization of change-over costs and work-in-progress (Vollmann et al., 1992, p. 371 ff).

One of the main reasons why conditions favor the establishment of a coherent system of planning and follow-up is that both a cost-leadership strategy and a line/flow strategy serve the same goal: for the firm to be a strong competitor through manufacturing standardized goods at the lowest cost on the market. In cases where management control and manufacturing control are designed and used on the basis of these two mutually consistent strategies, procedures, plans, reports, etc. will reflect this common goal. Thus, the control systems can be expected to provide not only a fairly consistent picture of intended strategies and plans, but also information about progress in achieving these strategies. The evaluation of the strategies and discussions on possible changes in them should thereby be facilitated. Moreover, congruent business and manufacturing strategies mean that the degree of turbulence and uncertainty coincides at the business-unit and functional levels. The result, as shown in our previous discussion, is that the same conditions apply to plans and reports. For example, a budget developed under highly uncertain conditions will have nowhere near the same credibility and relevance as one prepared in a stable environment. The former kind of budget is even difficult to use as a basis for the type of production planning designed to achieve extremely high capacity utilization since it calls for planning well in advance. In summary, we can thus conclude that the introduction of an integrated control system is considerably easier if business and manufacturing strategies are congruent. Moreover, such congruence means that the degree of uncertainty will converge at the business-unit and functional levels. In this specific case – where a cost-leadership strategy and a line/flow strategy are combined – both these criteria are met.

Position 5: An Intermediate Position

Porter (1985) holds that in most cases a differentiation strategy and a cost-leadership strategy are mutually exclusive. According to other scholars, being highly competitive requires companies to resort to low prices as well as differentiated product offerings (Johnson, 1992). In our previous review of various business-strategy typologies, we find empirical support both for Porter's view (see, for example, Hall, 1980) and for the position represented by Johnson (see, for example, Cooper, 1996). Toyota, Nissan and Sony are often mentioned as examples supporting the position that a strategy combining differentiation and cost leadership can be successfully implemented (Kato, 1993). A distinguishing feature of firms like these is that they use advanced production technology, for example, numerically controlled multi-task machines (CNC), flexible manufacturing systems (FMS), and computer-aided design and manufacturing (CAD/CAM) (Kim and Lee, 1993; McDermott et al., 1997). New technology and management methods have made it possible to provide product variety and customization through flexibility (Kotha, 1995; Jazayeri and Hopper, 1999). According to McDermott et al. (1997), these findings are an important complement to the product / process matrix developed by Hayes and Wheelwright (1979a). In addition, these companies have spent many years building up capabilities in such critical areas as quality control and logistics (Ward et al., 1996). Thus, combining strategies of differentiation and cost leadership, a so-called intermediate position (*cf.* Figure 5.2), entails major investments in tangible and intangible assets and also calls for skillful management (Kotha, 1995). These factors may explain why only a few firms with a strategy based on an intermediate position have succeeded in becoming strong competitors with a good performance record.

Another probable reason is that many companies have been unable to establish strategic congruence and integrated control. It is a formidable challenge to design and implement a manufacturing strategy that meets the requirements of cost effectiveness and is also capable of responding to rapid changes in demand. Ward et al. (1996) argue that in many cases the business unit follows a line/flow strategy at the functional level in order to limit manufacturing costs. They take marketing and value-adding service activities as examples of ways in which the unit then seeks to create a differentiated product offering. The problem with this solution is that it can be very difficult to respond fast enough to changes in the volume and mix of production. For in practice an intermediate position means that the

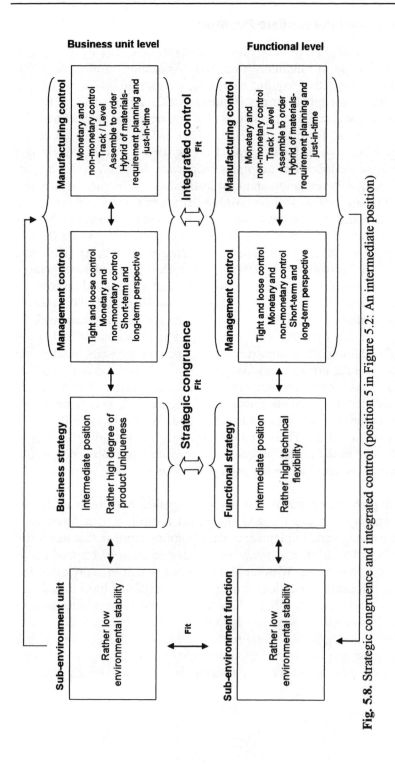

Fig. 5.8. Strategic congruence and integrated control (position 5 in Figure 5.2: An intermediate position)

business unit competes by offering products that are differentiated but manufactured at a low cost. As with a differentiation strategy, the unit interacts with elements characteristic of a relatively turbulent and uncertain environment (*cf.* Figure 5.8). As shown in previous sections, this means, among other things, that customer preferences as to which product attributes are unique and thus worth a premium price are difficult to forecast (Shank and Govindarajan, 1993). This type of uncertainty and turbulence at the business-unit level is difficult to eliminate; therefore, it almost always creates an unstable subenvironment for production.[25] To achieve strategic congruence, manufacturing strategy should focus on maintaining a rather high level of technical flexibility (*cf.* Figure 5.8).

As noted previously, however, combining a high degree of technical flexibility with cost-effective production entails considerable difficulties and substantial investments (*cf.* Kotha, 1995; Ward et al., 1996). To enhance flexibility at least to some degree, different variants of the manufacturing strategies originally identified by Hayes and Wheelwright (1979a) have been developed. One example is the type of manufacturing strategy based on group technology, in which the advantages of a batch strategy and a line strategy are achieved simultaneously. According to Hill (2000, p. 134 ff) this is possible by modifying the processes and/or the functional organization suitable for a batch strategy to a type of production layout normally found with a line strategy. Another example by the author (ibid, p. 138) is a mixed mode assembly line – basically a process line developed to produce a relatively wide range of products. A manufacturing strategy with this focus permits the manufacture of a given range of products without stopping the process to adjust the machinery.

There are also other examples of manufacturing strategies that improve the possibilities of cost-effectively manufacturing short runs of different products. According to Kim and Lee (1993) these types of manufacturing strategies feature high technical complexity with extensive mechanization and far-reaching integration of the different steps in the manufacturing process. Such strategies are often based on so-called Flexible Manufacturing Systems (FMS).[26] Vollmann et al. (1992, p. 559) hold that FMS are very flexible and at the same time permit many of the efficiencies of large-scale, integrated manufacturing systems. Examples of benefits identified by the authors are reduced machine-setup times, substantially shorter production lead times and smaller inventories of work in progress. According to Hill (2000, p. 133 f) a typical FMS is built up around a number of machining centers that in turn consist of numerically controlled multi-task machines with built-in tool-changing capability. Computer programs are used to control these machines – so-called computer-aided design and manufacturing. The cells are connected by automated transport (Hill, 1989). A number of scholars argue that this type of advanced technology is a critical element of a manufacturing strategy suitable for a combined differentiation and cost-leadership strategy (see, for example, Kotha and Orne, 1989; Kim and Lee, 1993; Kotha, 1995).

A good fit between business and manufacturing strategy is often essential for establishing an integrated control system. Figure 5.8 shows that in such a situation the business unit and the function typically operate in subenvironments with a similar degree of turbulence and uncertainty. Thus, the information needs at the respective organizational levels can be expected to coincide, with similar design and use of management control and manufacturing control as a consequence. An intermediate position, however, means that the control systems cannot be so clearly categorized as in cases where single-type business and manufacturing strategies are combined. In light of our previous discussion, management control at both business-unit and functional levels may need to strike a balance between loose and tight control and between monetary and nonmonetary control, as well as reflect both a short-term and a long-term perspective (*cf.* Figure 5.8). For example, the relatively high degree of turbulence makes it difficult to prepare reliable plans of future revenues and costs (*cf.* Mintzberg et al., 1998). At the same time, detailed follow-up of cost is necessary to eliminate activities that create no value. In the budget, costs can therefore be expected to play a major part in both planning and follow-up, whereas less attention will be paid to revenue. The focus is thus probably shifted from financial performance to follow-up for the purpose of ensuring that costs are held at a constant low level.

This type of on-going follow-up, however, has certain limitations in regard to potential for improving cost effectiveness. The reason is that product costs over the life cycle are incurred to a substantial extent right on the drawing board (Berliner and Brimson, 1988). Especially when differentiation and cost-leadership strategies are combined, it is vital to take advantage of all opportunities to find "smart" and "inexpensive" solutions.[27] Cooper (1996) maintains that methods like target costing and value engineering can be used to control life-cycle costs right at the planning stage. To prevent tight cost control from jeopardizing quality, many firms strive for constant quality enhancement in accordance with total quality management (TQM). Chenhall (1997) is one researcher who has found a positive correlation between employing TQM and using non-financial measures for evaluating managers. These findings are consistent with the studies that have shown non-monetary information to be especially appropriate with manufacturing strategies focused on flexibility and adaptation to customer requirements (Abernethy and Lillis, 1995; Perera et al., 1997). In addition, given the capital-intensity of modern manufacturing technology, a long-term perspective must be taken in investment decisions (i.e. strategic planning and budgeting). Since these investments are intended to improve quality, delivery time, flexibility, etc., nonmonetary information is often needed as a complement to traditional investment calculations in monetary terms (Kaplan, 1986; Bhimani and Bromwich, 1989; Lee, 1996). This long-term view provides a counterweight to the short-term perspective reflected in relatively tight and continual cost follow-up to eliminate all activities that create no value.

As with management control, the design and use of manufacturing control should reflect the mixed character of strategy (cf. Figure 5.8). This means that planning and follow-up at the business-unit and functional levels is assumed to meet the requirements of a product offering where competition is on the basis of both differentiation and cost effectiveness. As mentioned previously, a manufacturing strategy based on FMS supports such a business-strategic positioning. A comprehensive review of the literature by Young and Selto (1991), "New Manufacturing Practices and Cost Management," shows that both monetary and nonmonetary information is used in manufacturing control (FMS). For example, there are various performance and cost measures related to quality as well as measures of operating performance related to usage, downtime, and flexibility. We can also assume that the balance between monetary and nonmonetary information can be influenced by the type of control concept considered appropriate for the implementation of chosen strategies (cf. Bromwich and Bhimani, 1994).

Regarding the choice of control concept, some guidance can be found in the experience of business units with a manufacturing strategy based on cellular manufacturing. Among the companies using this technique – which bears at least some similarities to FMS[28] – there are many examples of units that combine materials-requirement planning (MRP) and just-in-time (JIT). According to Vollmann et al. (1992, p. 380 ff) the unit in question has often first installed MRP and then implemented some parts of JIT. One reason why cellular manufacturing supports the integration of MRP and JIT is that control of a cell is relatively uncomplicated. Vollmann et al. (ibid, p. 382) emphasize, among other things, the possibility of performing several routing steps in only one step. According to the authors, that allows the shop floor to be scheduled at the level of part numbers.

It is also important that planning procedures facilitate adjustment of long-term manufacturing capacity at the same rate as changes in demand occur (track). However, it is inappropriate to attempt adjusting production volume for the period entirely to sales (chase), even when the products are assembled to fill a customer order (ATO). The reason is that fairly stable conditions for planning are required if the benefits of JIT – primarily a continuous flow with short lead-times (Hill, 1989) – are to be realized. Planning should therefore be focused on maintaining a predetermined volume of production during the period (level) (*cf.* Olhager et al., 2001).

In summary, the purpose of designing and using manufacturing control in this way is to achieve a balance between flexibility and stability in planning and follow-up. There are many similarities to the management-control system appropriate for a combination of differentiation and cost-leadership strategies. It may be assumed, for example, that follow-up within the framework of management and manufacturing control has both a monetary and a nonmonetary focus. The former is intended to ensure a high degree of cost effectiveness, whereas the latter is aimed above all at following up areas of importance for product differentiation. Another example of similarities is that planning at both the business-unit and functional levels is complicated by rather limited environmental stability. Concededly, the need for planning stability is less with FMS than with a manufacturing strategy based on line/flow technology, but fairly steady use of machinery and equipment is required if the possibilities for cost-effective manufacturing are to be fully exploited. Therefore, despite some turbulence and uncertainty, considerable effort should be devoted to forecasting the volume of production and the product mix in the short run. The budget, with its 12-month perspective, should be used only as an approximate starting point in this connection. These examples, as well as the discussion in other respects, show that the design and use of the two control systems are based on similar planning horizons and performance criteria. Consequently the possibilities of achieving integrated control should be rather favorable, provided management has a clear conception of the way in which the dimensions of the control systems should be balanced.

Strategic Congruence and Integrated Control at the Corporate Level

In this section we expand the discussion to include the effects of conditions at the corporate level on business-unit strategies and control systems. Our purpose is to show how different combinations of corporate, business, and manufacturing strategies may be assumed to affect the possibilities of achieving a high degree of strategic congruence and integrated control. One basis for our analysis is Figure 5.2, where five different positions of business and manufacturing strategy are identified. In Figure 5.9 these positions are combined with two different corporate strategies: portfolio management and activity sharing.[29] Where we can assume that there is a good fit between corporate, business, and manufacturing strategies (a high degree of strategic congruence), with favorable conditions for integrating the systems of management control and manufacturing control (a high degree of integrated control), the expression "fit" is used in Figure 5.9. Where we can assume that there is a poor fit between corporate, business, and manufacturing strategies (a low degree of strategic congruence), with limited possibilities of integrating the systems of management control and manufacturing control (low degree of integrated control), the expression "potential misfit" is used in the figure. Finally, with certain combinations of strategies and control systems, both a fit and a potential misfit can be considered possible. In Figure 5.9 the designation "fit/potential misfit" is used for these cases. The concept of "intermediate position" is used to designate combinations with mixed business and manufacturing strategies.

The analysis of the possibilities of establishing strategic congruence and integrated control at the corporate level is based on Figure 5.10 and the discussion in previous sections. As can be seen in the figure, the dimension of synergy potential (high or low) has been added now that the analysis has been expanded to the corporate level. This dimension, which was identified in Chapter 2, is of great significance for the chosen corporate strategy. On the other hand, there has been no change in the dimensions that describe business and manufacturing strategy, or the design and use of management control and manufacturing control (cf. Figure 5.3). We shall now discuss the various combinations of corporate, business, and functional strategies identified in Figure 5.9. For each corporate strategy, we shall first consider the combination or combinations where we may expect favorable conditions for establishing strategic congruence and integrated control. We shall then review the other combinations, i.e., those where a fit/potential misfit – or a potential misfit – is probable.

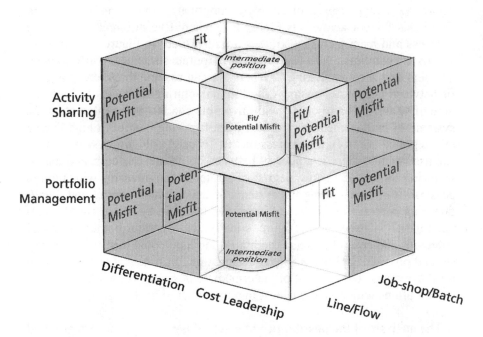

Figure 5.9. Possibilities of achieving strategic congruence and integrated control

Combination of Portfolio Management, Cost Leadership, and Line/Flow

A portfolio-management strategy is distinguished by a high degree of diversification; in other words, the firm operates in a large number of unrelated industries. The low synergy potential, which according to Figure 5.11 follows from the chosen corporate strategy, means that shareholder value is created primarily through contributing capital and professional management techniques. According to Porter's reasoning (1987), the need for co-ordination within the corporation is thus limited, so that the different business units can be operated largely as if they were separate companies. Furthermore, the absence of interdependencies among business units mak-

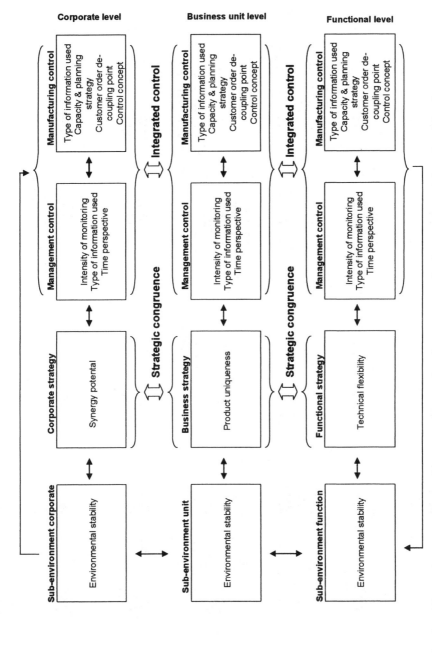

Fig. 5.10. Strategic congruence and integrated control at the corporate-, business unit, and functional levels

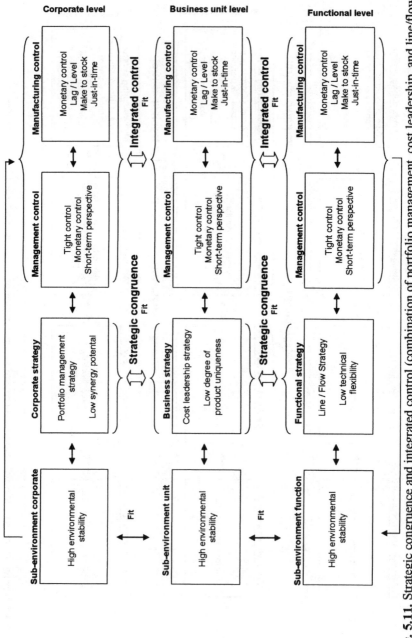

Fig. 5.11. Strategic congruence and integrated control (combination of portfolio management, cost leadership, and line/flow)

es rapid restructuring possible when profitability problems arise in individual business units (cf. Porter, 1985, p. 381). Consequently, units failing to achieve the rate of return required by the corporation can be quickly divested, an option desired in portfolio-management strategies, where rapid monetary results are usually emphasized and a distinctly short-term perspective is applied (Espeland and Hirsch, 1990; Goold et al., 1994; Hitt et al., 1996). By contrast, when there are strong interrelationships among corporate units, as with an activity-sharing strategy, for example, management must evaluate the contribution of the business unit to overall operations, rather than focus only on the financial results of that particular unit (cf. Porter, 1985, p. 381).[30]

The risk of a portfolio-management strategy, where the interrelationships between the units are limited, is that corporate management will not develop a common business logic – referred to by Goold et al. (1994) as Parenting Advantage.[31] The corporation will then consist of business units operating in quite different kinds of subenvironments and with substantial diversity of strategic focus. In corporations of this disparate character, the potential for achieving a high degree of strategic congruence is limited. This may also explain why many conglomerates have reported anemic financial returns, thus giving the portfolio-management strategy a bad reputation among some practitioners and scholars (cf. Porter, 1987).[32] At the same time, however, studies have shown that corporate groups with extensive diversification can achieve high profit levels (Goold and Campbell, 1987a; Johnson and Thomas, 1987; Nilsson 2000).[33] Research results of this type have probably contributed to the interest in corporate management and its role in the creation of competitive advantage. Not that the concept of synergy has been abandoned – rather, it is a question of emphasizing the role of corporate management in identifying which types of business and functional strategies are most compatible with a chosen corporate strategy. As a result of this development, strategic congruence is now considered quite important for creating a strong competitive advantage, not only at corporations with possibilities of activity sharing, but also at those with low synergy potential.

The studies by Goold et al. (1994) and Nilsson (2002) indicate that a business strategy appropriate to a portfolio-management strategy is focused on high cost effectiveness. A cost-leadership strategy is often found in mature and stable industries where the business operates with a short-term perspective and risky investments are avoided (cf. Miller, 1986, 1987 Goold et al., 1994, 420 ff). This type of business strategy, as previously noted, is particularly appropriate to combine with large-scale, cost-effective production – a typical situation for a line/flow manufacturing strategy. In a stable environment, where many of the products are in the final phase of their life cycle, the degree of uncertainty is low, and the conditions for planning operations in detail are favorable (*cf.* Govindarajan, 1984; Kald et al., 2000). The potential for maximizing the volume and minimizing the cost of production is therefore particularly high (Vollmann et al., 1992). Given this very strong emphasis on cost effectiveness, the business unit can generate a large cash flow for the corporation without endangering its own long-term survival (Goold and Campbell, 1987a; Goold et al., 1994). Thus, a cost-leadership and line/flow strategy resembles a portfolio-management strategy in a number of ways – primarily in the search for activities that do not create value. The high degree of strategic congruence is also reflected by the fact that the corporation, business units, and functions operate in similar environments and are thereby exposed to the same degree of uncertainty (*cf.* Figure 5.11).

The good fit between a strategy of portfolio management, cost leadership, and line/ flow should also be reflected in the design and use of the systems of control. On the basis of the above, a company with a portfolio-management strategy may be expected to let its business units operate on a more autonomous basis (*cf.* Porter, 1987). Since the synergies are primarily financial, the need for co-ordination is limited, and the corporate control systems are therefore focused on maximizing the profit of each business unit (Espeland and Hirsch, 1990; Hitt et al., 1996). Consequently, we can expect that procedures for strategic planning and budgeting will be less extensive and will have a strong monetary emphasis. Goold and Campbell (1987a) have shown that such a planning process, where the business units are given substantial freedom to prepare their business plans and budgets, is usually combined with extensive and financially focused reporting procedures. The reason is that the plans approved by corporate management are regarded as contracts, with little tolerance for deviations – so-called tight control (Anthony et al., 1992). The emphasis on short-term financial performance also means that the use of monetary information is stressed in the key ratios used by the corporation (Nilsson, 2002). As shown in Figure 5.11, and the discussion in previous sections, management control designed and used in this manner bears many similarities to the planning and follow-up appropriate to a cost-leadership and line/flow strategy.

As for the design and use of manufacturing control, the chosen corporate strategy means that there is little need for far-reaching co-ordination of business-unit manufacturing. Such co-ordination need not be considered unless there is substantial synergy potential – in other words, with a corporate strategy based on activity sharing (Jones, 1983; Porter, 1987). With a portfolio-management strategy, corporate management is instead expected to create value by developing the operations of individual business units. A frequently used way of enhancing business-unit competitiveness, as previously mentioned, is to provide functional leadership through professional management techniques (Goold et al., 1994, p. 78). This means, for example, that corporate management seeks to establish the kind of manufacturing control which can be assumed will further improve business-unit performance. For such a uniform system to be feasible, the corporation must focus on certain markets and industries; in other words, a high degree of strategic congruence[34] is necessary. As noted in previous sections, the corporate, business, and functional strategies of the firm are mutually consistent in this case, with the strategy at each organizational level appropriate to the firm's overall strategic aims (cf. Figure 5.11). Since all business units and their functions operate in environments with a similar degree of uncertainty, information needs can be expected to converge. In these circumstances, the conditions for establishing a common system of manufacturing control may be considered favorable.

Since a portfolio-management strategy emphasizes short-term financial performance, corporate management will probably design manufacturing control with such a focus. Planning and follow-up based on monetary control is particularly appropriate because the corporation operates in stable, mature industries where cost effectiveness is essential to being competitive (cf. Porter, 1980). In addition, the stable environment is conducive to reliable forecasting of the future mix and volume of production. Thus, the conditions are highly favorable for effectively utilizing the capital-intensive production apparatus typically associated with a cost-leadership and line/flow strategy. For example, it is practical in this case to avoid acquiring new manufacturing capacity until an increase in demand has been noted (i.e. lag capacity strategy). Another example is that the volume of production can be maintained at a stable level during the planning period, thus helping to minimize changeover costs (i.e., leveled planning strategy) (Olhager et al., 2001). Yet another aspect is that a steady high level of capacity utilization can be achieved by manufacturing directly to stock (MTS) (Olhager and Rapp, 1985, 1996). Finally, the stable planning conditions make it possible to base the corporate control concept on just-in-time (JIT) (Vollmann et al., 1997). As previously discussed, JIT is a method developed for the specific purpose of shortening lead times and minimizing production costs (Hill, 2000).

In summary, the conditions for establishing a corporate-wide system of manufacturing control will probably be favorable. Planning and follow-up procedures designed and used as described above are also quite appropriate for the strategies followed at the business-unit and functional levels (*cf.* Figure 5.10). With manufacturing control based on a limited number of similar success factors, corporate management can participate in the development of individual business units. It is also necessary that management control be substantially similar to manufacturing control if an integrated control system is to be established. In both control systems, the focus is on short-term financial performance and a constant search for activities that do not create value. The case studies by Goold et al. (1994, p. 420 ff) indicate that management control systems designed and used in this way are appropriate when a strong focus on short-term profit does not lead to negative development for the business unit. Porter (1980) goes even further, holding that successful implementation of strategies emphasizing cost effectiveness calls for control systems strongly focused on low costs:

Cost leadership requires aggressive construction of efficient-scale facilities, vigorous pursuit of cost reductions from experience, tight cost and overhead control, avoidance of marginal customer accounts, and cost minimization in areas like R&D, service, sales force, advertising, and so on. A great deal of managerial attention to cost control is necessary to achieve these aims. Low cost relative to competitors becomes the theme running through the entire strategy, though quality, service and other areas cannot be ignored (Porter, 1980, p. 35).

Portfolio Management – Combinations of Misfit

Figure 5.9 shows that other combinations of corporate, business-unit, and manufacturing strategies, based on a portfolio-management strategy, can be expected to produce a potential misfit.[35] In two of these combinations business strategy is based on product differentiation. As noted previously, this type of business strategy is intended to make the firm strongly competitive through the uniqueness of its products. The environment is turbulent, with a high degree of uncertainty in regard to future demand patterns and in other respects. At the same time, the unit is heavily dependent on innovative and successful product development. It is therefore necessary to manage the business with a long-term perspective rather than a focus on current performance (Kald et al., 2000). From previous sections, it is apparent that a portfolio-management strategy, with its limited synergy potential, features a distinctly short-term perspective. According to Goold et al. (1994, p. 420), there is a risk that emphasis on short-term performance will lead to avoidance of long-term investments and to a lack of interest in finding joint projects with other business units. Consequently, the appropriateness of this short-term focus and the possibilities of establishing a high degree of strategic congruence at the corporate level are limited. In cases where a differentiation strategy and a line/flow strategy are combined (Position 2 in Figure 5.2), there is also a poor fit between business and manufacturing strategies.

The difficulties of combining a portfolio-management strategy and a differentiation strategy will probably affect planning and follow-up as well. As previously discussed, a management-control system suited to a portfolio-management strategy tends to emphasize tight and monetary control, and reflect a short-term perspective. As for manufacturing control, the corporate management of a portfolio-managing firm may be assumed to favor planning and follow-up focused on short lead-times and cost effectiveness. Manufacturing control will then be based on a capacity and planning strategy combining lag and level, manufacturing to the stock of finished goods, and just-in-time as the control concept. With a differentiation strategy, where the business features a high degree of uncertainty, we can expect quite different information needs in regard to planning and follow-up. In previous sections it was shown that management control appropriate to such a strategy would be based on a long-term perspective, and control would be loose and nonmonetary. Moreover, given the uncertainty at the business-unit level, with the consequent requirement of high technical flexibility, manufacturing control could be expected to emphasize non-monetary control, lead/chase, make-to-order, and materials-requirement planning. Taken together, these factors allow little possibility of establishing coherent strategic planning and follow up throughout the firm.

In Figure 5.9 there is also a combination of portfolio managers where the business units follow a cost-leadership strategy and the manufacturing strategy is based on job-shop/batch production. In this case, too, the possibilities of establishing strategic congruence and integrated control are probably limited. The reason is that a job-shop/batch strategy is intended to provide technical flexibility to cope with unique and varying product specifications. As shown in the discussion in previous sections, such a manufacturing strategy is less appropriate in a stable environment where large-scale, cost-effective production has the highest priority. The management control and manufacturing control that support a job-shop/batch strategy are also markedly different from the planning and follow-up characteristic of a portfolio-management strategy and a cost-leadership strategy. The former is adapted to a situation of high uncertainty, where a long-term perspective and flexibility are essential. The latter is based on stable planning conditions, a constant search for activities that do not create value, and the requirement of rapid monetary results. This makes it difficult to establish coherent planning and follow-up throughout the firm. The conditions for achieving an integrated control system are probably better when a line/flow strategy, focused on standardized products in high volumes, is combined with a portfolio-management and cost-leadership strategy (*cf.* Figure 5.9).[36]

The final combination in Figure 5.9, where a portfolio-management strategy is the point of departure, consists of units without a distinct business or manufacturing strategy of a single kind. As previously mentioned, a characteristic feature of this so-called intermediate position is that the business unit seeks to attain a strong competitive position by offering both low prices and differentiated products. Firms that have successfully implemented such a strategy are distinguished by excelling in at least two important areas. First, there has been substantial investment in advanced new production technology, such as flexible manufacturing systems (FMS) (Kim and Lee, 1993). Second, management has focused for a long time on building up a strong competence in production technology (*cf.* Womack et al., 1990). Consequently, major investments are a prerequisite if a combined differentiation and cost-leadership strategy is to be successfully implemented. However, there are reasons to believe that this type of long-term, high-risk investment is often avoided by corporations with a portfolio-management strategy. Instead, according to the reasoning of Goold et al., (1994, p. 420), they tend to seek a good return through small and low-risk investments. Thus, a portfolio-management strategy and business and manufacturing strategies based on an intermediate position are not congruent.

The heavy emphasis of a portfolio-management strategy on short-term performance can also be expected to affect the design and use of planning and follow-up procedures. In our previous discussion, we have shown that with portfolio managers both management control and manufacturing control are typically focused on constant improvement of cost effectiveness. Control systems designed and used in this manner are to some degree consistent with the information needs of a strategy combining product differentiation and cost effectiveness. For instance, they meet the need for on-going follow-up to maintain costs at a constant low level. Another example is a marked emphasis on plans and forecasts to prepare for long production runs and thus achieve steady utilization of the production apparatus. The problem, however, is that this continual tight follow-up of costs can be taken too far, thus undermining the aspect of strategy based on product differentiation. As previously noted, non-monetary information, for example, must be used to monitor quality, delivery time, flexibility, and other important dimensions of a differentiation strategy. Researchers like Bhimani and Bromwich (1989) even question whether traditional monetary management control can provide adequate support for decision-making in advanced manufacturing environments. Corporations with a portfolio-management strategy, particularly those with a record of conservative management control, are unlikely to take the lead in designing control systems appropriate to such environments. Thus, it is probably difficult to achieve coherent planning and follow-up which suit the firm's needs at the corporate, business-unit, and functional levels.

Combination of Activity Sharing, Differentiation, and Job-Shop/Batch

A corporation with a strategy of activity sharing does business in a single industry or several closely related industries; in other words, the degree of diversification is low (Porter, 1987). Given the substantial similarities in the operations of the business units, the conditions for co-ordination are favorable. The high synergy potential, which as shown in Figure 5.12 results from the chosen corporate strategy, is reflected in the sharing of certain activities by the business units. For example, by co-ordination of manufacturing to achieve longer production runs, it is possible to improve cost effectiveness (ibid). If this kind of initiative is to succeed, however, comprehensive, detailed co-ordination of business-unit activities is required – often in the form of far-reaching operational integration. As previously emphasized, this interdependence of the units in the firm means that the whole, rather than the parts, must be in focus. The financial performance of each business unit in isolation is thus not very interesting; instead, the unit is evaluated on the basis of its contribution to the business as a whole. Therefore, quick action affecting the structure of the firm is often inappropriate for solving profitability problems of individual business units (*cf.* Porter, 1985, p. 381). In summary, this means that an activity-sharing strategy must be conducted from a longer-term perspective than a portfolio-management strategy (*cf.* Espeland and Hirsch, 1990; Goold et al., 1994; Hitt et al., 1996).

The long-term perspective characteristic of an activity-sharing strategy is also very important when a differentiation and job-shop/batch strategy is to be implemented. One of the reasons is the dependence on innovative and successful product development characteristic of a differentiation strategy (*cf.* Miller, 1987, 1988; Kald et al., 2000). At the same time, as has been emphasized in previous sections, the environment is turbulent, with considerable uncertainty about which products will be in demand *(cf.* Figure 5.12). One consequence is that investment in new products, new technologies, market development, etc. becomes riskier. Corporate management must not only view such investments in a long-term perspective, but must also be sufficiently knowledgeable about the businesses of the units (Nilsson, 2000). Particularly with an activity-sharing strategy, where there is often a clear core competence, corporate management and staff personnel can be expected to participate actively in the development of the units. According to Goold et al. (1994, p. 419), this involvement can take a number of forms, such as thorough analysis and review of business plans, investment proposals etc. According to the authors, however, perhaps the primary task of corporate management in this situation is to co-ordinate activities and decisions of business units in order to ensure that the firm capitalizes on synergies. In these circumstances, it would appear especially appropriate to combine an activity-sharing strategy with a differentiation and job-shop/batch strategy.

The favorable conditions for achieving a high degree of strategic congruence are also reflected in the probable convergence of information needs at the corporate, business-unit, and functional levels. One of the main reasons is that the corporation has chosen to focus on business units with a certain specific strategy.[37] As shown in Figure 5.12, the units – and their functions – are supposed to be facing the same degree of uncertainty because of this focus, since they interact with similar environmental elements *(cf.* Ford et al., 1988). In a corporation where the business units compete on the basis of differentiated products, with a flexible production apparatus for manufacturing, the environment can be assumed to be rapidly changing, competitive, and fast-growing *(cf.* Porter, 1980; Miller, 1986). To ensure that the competitiveness of the business units develops in a positive direction in this environment, corporate management is deeply involved in strategic planning and budgeting. With this kind of active management, the emphasis is likely to shift from financial information to non-monetary information for monitoring, controlling, and co-ordinating activities (Goold et al., 1994, p. 412 ff). The reason why non-monetary information more directly related to operations will be called for is that corporate management is probably familiar with the business and its critical success factors. In addition, active participation by corporate management in planning means that follow-up will be less comprehensive and more informal (i.e. loose control) (Anthony and Govindarajan, 2004, p. 636 ff). In summary, de-emphasis of financial performance can be assumed to be typical of control systems at corporations where business units

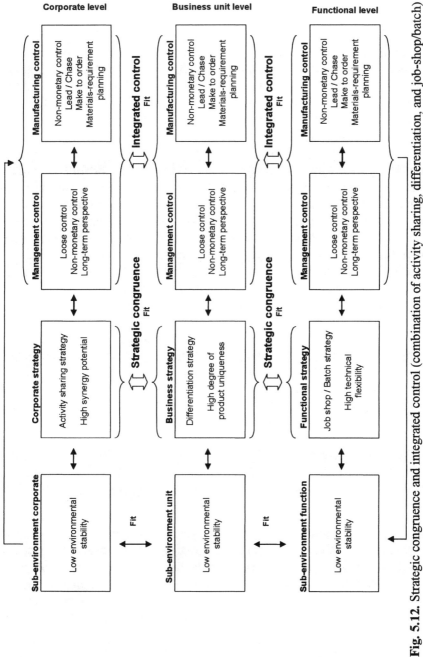

Fig. 5.12. Strategic congruence and integrated control (combination of activity sharing, differentiation, and job-shop/batch)

are mutually dependent and operations are viewed in a long-term perspective. As the discussion in previous sections has shown, management control designed and used in this way is similar to the kind of planning and follow-up appropriate to a differentiation and job-shop/batch strategy.

The turbulent environment, where shifts in customer demand are difficult to predict, also has a strong impact on the design and use of manufacturing control. With frequent changes in the volume and mix of production, it is difficult to achieve long production runs (Ward et al., 1996; Hill, 2000). This does not mean, however, that activity sharing among the production functions of the various business units is impossible or ruled out for other reasons. According to Porter (1987) there are numerous cases where sharing of production activities can reduce the cost of differentiation. But perhaps more important is the vast potential for further product differentiation – through activity sharing – in other functions such as marketing, research and development etc. (ibid).[38] In the latter situation, corporate-wide manufacturing control that gives priority to large-scale operations and cost effectiveness is not very suitable. The reason is that these kinds of decision-making routines and processes are too complicated and expensive for this type of situation (Goold et al., 1994, p. 424). Instead, corporate management can be expected to establish coherent planning and follow-up appropriate to the high degree of uncertainty typical of a differentiation and job-shop/batch strategy. In several previous sections of this chapter, it has been emphasized that this kind of manufacturing control has the following features: nonmonetary control, a capacity and planning strategy based on lead and chase, manufacturing to customer order, and materials-requirement planning as the control concept. These procedures for planning and follow-up also bear a strong resemblance to the kind of management control appropriate to the chosen corporate, business, and manufacturing strategies; i.e., conditions should favor the establishment of an integrated control system.

Combination of Activity Sharing, Cost Leadership, and Line/Flow

According to Porter (1987), an activity-sharing strategy can be appropriately combined with a cost-leadership strategy.[39] At the functional level, a line/flow strategy, with its efficient production apparatus, is probably necessary if manufacturing costs are to be the lowest in the industry (Hayes and Wheelwright, 1979a; Kim and Lee, 1993) – a central goal of a cost-leadership strategy (Porter, 1985). Through sharing activities within functions such as purchasing, production, and sales, the cost per unit produced can be lowered further. As has been noted previously, it is therefore particularly important with an activity-sharing strategy that corporate management create conditions that will facilitate the exploitation of synergies (*cf.* Goold and Campbell, 1987c). Business units should therefore be encouraged to co-operate. To ensure that this co-ordination functions satisfactorily, thus helping to reduce unit costs, corporate management often has support units and different staff functions at its disposal. According to Goold et al. (1994, p. 412 ff), such units are also intended to assist in the development of unit businesses, for example by evaluating business plans and investment proposals.[40, 41] The authors (ibid) also emphasize that sharing resources or service departments in such areas as marketing, engineering, and R&D can improve cost effectiveness at both corporate and business-unit levels.

Although an activity-sharing strategy and a cost-leadership and line/flow strategy appear mutually consistent, it is not self-evident that a high degree of strategic congruence can be achieved. The principal explanation is that short-term profitability is not equally important with these different strategies. From the discussion in previous sections, it is obvious that a cost-leadership strategy is based on meticulous cost control and that cash flow and profits are to be maximized in the short run. With an activity-sharing strategy, by contrast, being a strong competitor depends on the use of shared human and structural capital, and the business is managed with a longer-term perspective. According to Goold et al. (1994, p. 419 f) and Nilsson (2000), this long-term approach entails a danger that mediocre financial performance will be tolerated year after year. Such a tendency can be harmful to the business units and their functions. One consequence, for example, may be that the need for constantly improving efficiency is not sufficiently stressed. Instead of trying to eliminate all activities that do not create value, business-unit management may be tempted to undertake high-risk investments with a long pay-back period. Since the chosen business and manufacturing strategies require an intense focus on cost-minimization, this type of risky initiative may tend to erode the unit's competitive strength.

The need for well-developed cost control at the business-unit and functional levels should also impact the design and use of management control. From Figure 5.13 and the reasoning in previous sections, it is apparent that a cost-leadership and line/flow strategy is appropriately accompanied by tight monetary control, reflecting a short-term perspective. As for manufacturing control, it can be expected to have the following characteristics: monetary control, a capacity and planning strategy of lag and level, make-to-stock as the customer-order decoupling point, and finally, just-in-time as the control concept. At the corporate level, however, the chosen strategy of activity sharing will probably result in planning and follow-up that are differently designed and used. As previously emphasized, one feature typical of this strategy is that management control and manufacturing control are focused on nonmonetary information. Thus, there are certain differences in information needs between corporate management, on the one hand, and managers at the business-unit and functional levels, on the other. For this reason, there will be difficulties in establishing integrated control.

To summarize, in the situation described above, there is a poor fit between the corporate strategy, on one hand, and the business and manufacturing strategies, on the other, with limited possibilities of integrating the systems of management and manufacturing control. At the same time, however, empirical studies have shown that a relatively good match between strategies and control systems can also be achieved in this type of combination (Nilsson, 2002). With a low degree of diversification, and strategies with the same focus, there will be considerable similarities between the businesses of the units. For example, in a forest-products corporation, only limited differences can be expected from one mill to another in regard to organizational structure, critical success factors, etc. In manufacturing, it is not unusual, either, to find highly focused corporations, with largely identical business units, where the principal difference is that they serve different geographic markets. For natural reasons, it is easier to achieve a clear, common business logic in this type of firm than in a conglomerate, where the businesses of the units are often quite dissimilar (Goold and Campbell, 1987a).[42] As previously mentioned, the existence of numerous common features means that corporate management can be expected to participate very actively in the development of the units.

Close interaction between business-unit and corporate managements will contribute to an understanding of the information needs at the business-unit level. Since it is the business units that compete on the market, it is particularly important that the corporate control systems not hamper desired developments at the unit and functional levels. This realization can be the first step in the gradual adjustment of the corporate-wide manage-

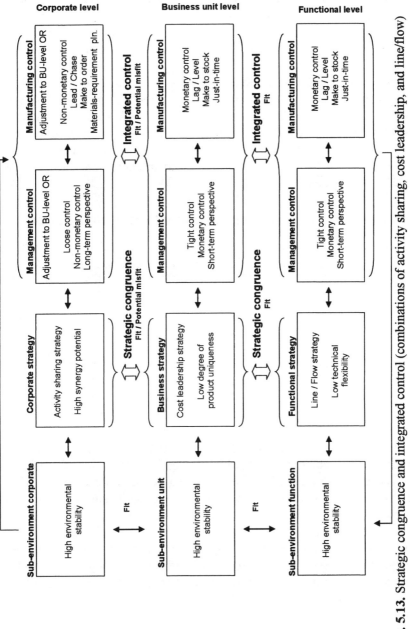

Fig. 5.13. Strategic congruence and integrated control (combinations of activity sharing, cost leadership, and line/flow)

ment-control system toward desired coherence in planning and follow-up. For example, the importance of extremely high cost effectiveness can lead corporate management to step up the frequency and detail of financial reporting. Another possible development is that corporate management will actively support corporate-wide manufacturing control that benefits from the stable planning conditions of the business units. As we have previously emphasized, one effect of a stable environment is that manufacturing control can be based on just-in-time, making it possible to increase the capacity utilization of machinery and equipment (cf. Vollmann et al., 1992). Focusing corporate-wide control more on cost effectiveness should probably affect the interpretation of corporate strategy as well. As a consequence of this adjustment, there will likely be more emphasis on short-term results and elimination of activities that do not create value, thus enhancing congruence between the respective strategies at the corporate, business-unit, and functional levels.

Combination of Activity Sharing and Intermediate Position

We have previously discussed the difficulties of combining a portfolio-management strategy with a business and functional strategy based on an intermediate position. At the root of these difficulties lies the short-term perspective of the portfolio-management strategy, which can be a hindrance to necessary investments (Espeland and Hirsch, 1990; Hitt et al., 1996). For example, substantial sums must often be invested in advanced production technology if the unit is going to succeed in combining product differentiation and cost leadership (cf. Womack et al., 1990; Kotha, 1995). Moreover, these kinds of very long-term, high-risk investments require thorough evaluation, with inputs from corporate staff. Firms with a portfolio-management strategy often lack the absolute, cutting-edge competence needed to analyze complex investment proposals entailing a high degree of uncertainty. At firms with an activity-sharing strategy, on the other hand, corporate management will often be thoroughly familiar with the business, with recourse to a large staff of specialists (Goold et al., 1994, p. 412 ff), and thus be in a good position to assess the actual business utility of the investments involved, with a business and functional strategy based on an intermediate position. As emphasized in several other sections, management will then apply a definite long-term perspective view to their businesses. In these circumstances, we may assume that a business unit seeking competitive advantage by offering differentiated products at low prices can prosper from belonging to a corporation with an activity-sharing strategy, this in view of the relatively favorable conditions there for establishing strategic congruence.

As for the control that we can assume will accompany an activity-sharing strategy, it is appropriate in certain respects for a business and manufacturing strategy based on an intermediate position. Figure 5.14 shows that planning and follow-up primarily support those aspects of strategy that are important for creating product uniqueness and technical flexibility. Non-monetary control can be cited as an example of the former (Nilsson and Rapp, 1999), while a control concept of materials-requirement planning is an example of the latter (Hill, 2000). However, corporate-wide management and manufacturing control designed and used in this manner will provide only limited support for large-scale, cost-effective production. If integrated control is to be achieved, corporate planning and follow-up must therefore focus much more strongly on constantly improving efficiency and on eliminating all activities that do not create value (*cf.* Figure 5.8). As mentioned in previous sections, this means that management control may need to strike a balance between loose and tight control, and monetary and nonmonetary control, as well as reflect both a short-term and long-term perspective. Manufacturing control must also be more mixed and appropriate for a product offering that competes through both differentiation and cost effectiveness. Figure 5.14 shows that such an intermediate position probably calls for manufacturing control with the following features: monetary and nonmonetary control, track and level as capacity and planning strategies, assemble-to-order as the customer-order decoupling point, and a hybrid of materials-requirement planning and just-in-time as the control concept.

To change corporate-wide planning and follow-up, making it more consistent with the information needs at lower organizational levels, is a complex and time-consuming process. With an activity-sharing strategy, however, the conditions for successively adapting management control and manufacturing control are particularly favorable. As we have previously emphasized, one of the main reasons is that an activity-sharing strategy will lead to close interaction between corporate and business-unit management. The interaction is part of a learning process that includes not only ways to improve the day-to-day management of the firm, but also the development of internal structures to facilitate this work. It is thereby possible to create an understanding of business-unit information needs and the kind of control that is most favorable to the development of unit competitiveness. In the next phase of this learning process, it can also aid in the

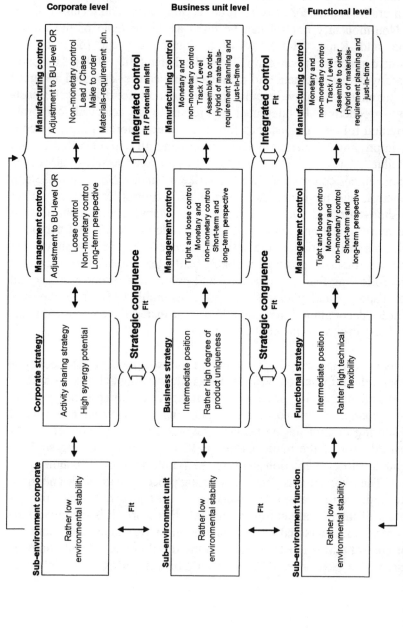

Fig. 5.14. Strategic congruence and integrated control (combination of activity sharing and intermediate position)

development of corporate-wide control for the purpose of establishing an integrated control system. For example, Nilsson (2002) has shown how an activity sharer changed parts of its overall system of management control to focus more on following up cost effectiveness at the business-unit level. It was thus possible to achieve a coherent system of planning and follow-up despite an initial potential misfit between strategies and control systems.

Activity Sharing – Combinations of Misfits

Figure 5.9 shows that other combinations of corporate, business, and functional strategies, based on an activity-sharing strategy, can be expected to result in a potential misfit. In the first combination, where the conditions for matching strategies and control systems are not very favorable, the business strategy is based on product differentiation. The manufacturing strategy is line/flow and is thus aimed at managing situations where business-unit products are highly standardized and manufactured in large volumes (Hayes and Wheelwright, 1979a). We can assume that such a manufacturing strategy would be very difficult to combine successfully with a differentiation strategy (cf. Figure 5.5). The reason is that a line/flow strategy requires stable planning conditions, a situation not easily achievable when the business unit competes through product differentiation (Kim and Lee, 1993; Shank and Govindarajan, 1993). The discussion in the initial sections of this chapter has shown, in addition, that a differentiation and line/flow strategy is a combination that makes it harder to establish integrated control. The former type of strategy calls for control systems adapted to planning and follow-up in a situation characterized by uncertainty. There, flexibility and a long-term approach, as well as the possibility of capturing a broad spectrum of critical success factors, are important. With the latter type of strategy, on the other hand, the appropriate focus of planning and follow-up would be on high cost effectiveness.

The next combination, which according to Figure 5.9 may lead to a potential misfit, consists of activity sharers where the business units follow a cost-leadership strategy and manufacturing strategy is based on job-shop/batch production. Like the situation described in the previous section, this combination can be assumed to entail difficulties in achieving a fit between strategies and control systems – particularly at the business-unit and functional levels. A job-shop/batch strategy features a high degree of technical flexibility and is thus particularly appropriate for small-scale manufacture of customized products (Hayes and Wheelwright, 1979a). On the other hand, it does not meet the need of a cost-leadership strategy for low production costs (*cf.* Hill, 1989). Nor is the kind of management control and manufacturing control suitable for a job-shop/batch strategy consistent with the type of planning and follow-up desired by business-unit management (*cf.* Figure 5.6). The substantial differences in information needs shown in Figure 5.6, and ultimately the uncertainty faced by each organizational unit, are the principal reasons why integrated control is difficult to establish with this set of strategies.

Summary

In this chapter we combine the concepts of strategic congruence and integrated control in a tentative model. We discuss the importance of these two variables for creating competitive advantage, and ultimately high performance, at the business-unit level as well as at the corporate level. At the business-unit level, we can expect that a differentiation strategy and a job-shop/batch strategy will lead to strategic congruence, thus favoring the establishment of integrated control. We can also expect a fit between strategies and control systems when a cost-leadership strategy and a line/flow strategy are combined. In these two combinations, the business unit and its functions typically operate in similar subenvironments, and the degree of uncertainty converges. Consequently, the same conditions prevail for preparing plans and reports, thus facilitating the establishment of an integrated control system. For example, a budget that has been prepared under high uncertainty does not have nearly the same relevance as one prepared in a stable environment. The congruence of business-unit and functional planning horizons enhances the transparency of the planning and follow-up processes.

When the analysis is expanded to the corporate level, the dimension of synergy potential (high or low) is introduced. Synergy potential affects, among other things, the degree to which the value chains of the business units must be co-ordinated. It thus also impacts the degree to which corporate management participates actively in the planning and follow-up of unit businesses. The possibilities of undertaking immediate structural measures, and the degree to which rapid monetary results are emphasized, are further aspects in which synergy potential can be assumed to affect strategies and control systems. On this basis, we can expect a fit between strategies and control systems when a corporate strategy of portfolio-management is combined with a cost-leadership strategy, provided, however, that a line/flow manufacturing strategy is followed. It is also possible to achieve a high degree of strategic congruence and integrated control when an activity-sharing strategy and a differentiation strategy are combined. Manufacturing strategy will then be job-shop/batch. By mutual adaptation of the corporate control systems and business-unit needs, it is also possible to achieve a fit when an activity-sharing strategy is combined with a cost-leadership and line/flow strategy. For such an accommodation to be possible, the corporation must have a low degree of diversity and the business units must have similar strategies.

In addition to these "pure," or unmixed, strategic combinations, we have also discussed a number of cases where the business units seek to compete by offering differentiated products manufactured at low cost. This so-called intermediate position requires substantial investment in tangible and intangible assets, and highly skilled management as well. One major difficulty is in designing planning and follow-up procedures appropriate for business and functional strategies that emphasize both product differentiation and cost-effective production. Our analysis shows that an activity-sharing strategy is most likely to result in strategic congruence and integrated control at a unit with a mixed business and manufacturing strategy. For example, the control systems typical of a business and manufacturing strategy with this focus are similar in design and use to the planning and follow-up typical of an activity sharer.

Notes

1. We have chosen to use the concept of "subenvironment" to make clear that the corporation and its units and functions often operate in different environments. Consequently, in this context the term "subenvironment" is used synonymously with "environment."

2. In previous chapters, corporate synergy potential has been regarded as an important situational variable. It has also been emphasized that it is the corporation's business units, not the corporation as such, that compete on the market. The meaning of the concept of "environment" is thus less clear for a corporation than for a business unit or function. However, with a so-called single business – that is, in cases where the degree of diversification is extremely low and the business is functionally organized, the corporation can be said to compete directly on a market (compare Chapter 3, Footnote 5). To cover cases like these, and for the logical cogency of our conceptual apparatus, we have therefore chosen to apply the term "subenvironment" to corporations as well.

3. For a more detailed discussion, see the section "Toward a More Complex Theory" in Chapter 2.

4. Goold et al. (1994) use the concept of "Heartland Business" to designated corporations where there is a common business logic. See also Chapter 1, Footnote 12.

5. As mentioned previously, our model is based on the research cited in the introductory chapters of this book. In many cases, the relationships treated in the model have been tested empirically and / or are based on theoretical reasoning. One example is the relationship between business and manufacturing strategies, which has been explored by such scholars as Hayes and Wheelwright (1979a), Kotha and Orne (1989), Kim and Lee (1993) and Ward et al. (1996). In this connection, however, it should be noted that we review the literature in three major and well-established fields of research. In the Introduction to this book, we emphasized that we thus could not undertake an exhaustive study of the literature. To our knowledge, however, few researchers have discussed how strategic congruence and integrated control together affect the creation of competitive strength.

6. See the section "Strategy and Control" in Chapter 2.

7. As shown in the foregoing discussion, technical flexibility refers to the degree to which the firm's production apparatus can rapidly cope with changes in the mix of products to be manufactured and to changes in volume. Technical flexibility is a very important aspect of a typical manufacturing strategy and is closely related to the degree of uncertainty and turbulence in the subenvironment of the production function.

8. For a summary of the research findings that describe the relationship between the dimensions of intensity of monitoring, type of information used, and time perspective, on the one hand, and the chosen business strategy, on the other, see Chapter 2, Table 2.2.

9. For a summary of the research findings that describe the relationship between the dimensions of information used, capacity and planning strategy, customer-order decoupling point, and control concept, on the one hand, and the chosen manufacturing strategy, on the other, see Chapter 2, Table 2.3.

10. Just-in-time (JIT) is described in the section "Manufacturing Control" in Chapter 4.

11. Much of the research that considers the relationship between strategy and control from a holistic perspective is focused on showing that manufacturing and management control must include all relevant organizational levels (in principle, the corporate, business, and functional levels) and decision levels (in principle, the strategic, tactical, and operational levels). Even though the scope of research has been broadened to include these levels, our knowledge is limited in regard to certain relationships between basic strategy and the design and use of control systems. In this respect, research, especially in the form of large-scale empirical studies, is still to a large extent focused on further study of "old" and well-established organizational levels and decision levels. For a detailed discussion of this research, see the section "Strategy and Control" in Chapter 2 and the section "Integrated Control Defined" in Chapter 4.

12. In this book we have chosen to discuss only a few combinations of strategies and control systems. Since there exist different degrees of fit (*cf.* Donaldson, 2001), it may be assumed that there are many more possible combinations of strategies and control systems with a reasonable degree of strategic congruence and integrated control. See also Chapter 6, the section "Summary and Conclusions."

13. Environmental elements are discussed in the section "Toward a More Complex Theory" in Chapter 2.

14. The concepts of "domain" and "subenvironment" are both used to designate the part of the environment with which a specific organizational unit has chosen to interact. Thus, the two terms are treated as synonymous.

15. Protective buffers are discussed in the section "Contingency Theory" in Chapter 2.

16. From the review of the literature, it can be seen that most of these studies were conducted at the business-unit level. Since some of the studies relate their findings both to strategy and to the degree of uncertainty, it is possible to apply findings reached at one organizational level to another level. For example, findings where business strategy and the degree of uncertainty are related to the design and use of the business unit's budget could be considered valid at the functional level as well, provided, however, that the degree of uncertainty is similar. We thus regard strategy as an intermediate variable between the environment – with its associated degree of uncertainty – and the internal structures of the firm. See also Footnote 11.

17. Two examples of long-run criteria are new-product development and market development. See also Chapter 2, Footnote 20.

18. Engineer to order (ETO) is common with customized products. However, we have chosen not to discuss this type of customer-order decoupling point since our focus is on products manufactured in series. See also the section "Manufacturing Control" in Chapter 4.

19. Perera et al. (1997) also study the cost and dependability dimensions of manufacturing strategy. For a more detailed discussion, see the section "Strategy and Control" in Chapter 2.

20. How an integrated control system can simplify or complicate the strategic dialogue – for example, in regard to gathering information about emerging threats and opportunities (*cf.* Simons, 1995) – is discussed in Chapter 6.

21. Hayes and Wheelwright (1979a) also use the terms "assembly-line strategy" and "continuous flow", respectively.

22. By efficiency-based measures Abernethy and Lillis (1995) mean monetary measures focused on cost effectiveness.

23. In cases where the firm offers different variants of the final product, the latter is assembled to customer order (ATO). For a description of ATO, see the section "Manufacturing Control" in Chapter 4.

24. Two examples of short-term criteria are operating profits and return on investment. See also Chapter 2, Footnote 20.

25. Buffers partially protect the production function from harmful environmental influences. See also the section "Contingency Theory" in Chapter 2.

26. According to Hill (1989), the first FMS was developed in the 1960s.

27. An intermediate position is assumed to be characterized by low unit costs achieved through highly efficient production. At the same time, there are areas where product differentiation entails additional costs, such as R&D, marketing, and service, for example. Consequently, an intermediate position does not offer the same possibilities as a pure cost-leadership strategy for achieving the lowest costs on the market. Therefore, there is a need to exploit all opportunities to enhance cost effectiveness, as long as doing so does not negatively affect the perception of the product as differentiated.

28. According to Vollmann et al. (1992, p. 70) cellular manufacturing takes place when a group of machines produce certain specific parts. The machines are manned by employees with a broad range of competence and thus capable of operating several machines.

29. Some empirical studies indicate that a corporate strategy of purely one kind provides the most favorable conditions for creating competitive advantage and providing a good return to shareholders. Corporations that have tried a strategy combining portfolio management and activity sharing do not seem to attain equally strong market positions, and consequently they earn a lower return (cf. Goold and Campbell, 1987a). One explanation is the difficulty in finding strategic features and critical success factors common to most of the business units (Goold et al., 1993b). We have therefore chosen not to discuss mixed corporate strategies further. See also Nilsson (2000).

30. This discussion is amplified in the subsection "Combination of Activity Sharing, Differentiation, and Job-Shop/Batch."

31. For a discussion of the concept of "Parenting Advantage," see the section "Corporate Strategy" in Chapter 3.

32. A conglomerate is another term for a corporation with a portfolio-management strategy.

33. The studies by Goold and Campbell (1987a) and Nilsson (2000) are described in detail in the section "Strategy and Control" in Chapter 2. The corporate-strategy typology developed by Goold et al. (1994), based on their empirical findings, is described in the section "Corporate Strategy" in Chapter 3.

34. Instead, Goold et al. (1994) use the closely related concept of "Heartland." See, for example, Chapter 1, Footnote 12.

35. Figure 5.10 provides a basis for the discussion of the combinations involving a portfolio-management strategy where there is a potential misfit. However, we do not develop a special figure for each combination, but only discuss these cases in principle on the basis of previous sections. The reason is the large number of combinations where there is a potential misfit (see Figure 5.9).

36. For a more thorough explanation, see the subsection "Combination of Portfolio Management, Cost Leadership and Line/Flow."

37. Additional examples are found in the section "Corporate Strategy" in Chapter 3.

38. See the section "Corporate Strategy" in Chapter 3.

39. Porter (1987) holds that a differentiation strategy is also appropriate for combination with an activity-sharing strategy. See the discussion in previous sections.

40. In a couple of recent articles Goold and Campbell discuss the difficult-ties of establishing the right amount of hierarchy, control and proc-essses. See Chapter 1, Footnote 13.

41. Goold et al. (1994) do not explicitly discuss activity sharers. Instead, they use the term "Strategic Planning Style" in their book. As can be seen from our discussion in Chapter 3 in the section "Corporate Strategy," strategic planning bears many similarities to an activity-sharing strategy.

42. It should be underscored that it is not impossible to establish a common business logic in a conglomerate. For further discussion, see the section "Combination of Portfolio Management, Cost Leadership, and Line/Flow."

6 Conclusions and Implications

The purpose of this chapter is to present the central conclusions reached in the book and to discuss some of the implications. The chapter begins by summarizing the principal assumptions introduced in previous chapters. This summary serves as a basis for conclusions regarding the combinations of strategies and control systems that could be expected to facilitate the creation of competitive advantage. Since the matching of environment, strategies, and control systems may be assumed to be temporary, we also discuss the dynamics of fit and their probable effect on strategic congruence and integrated control. Thereafter, we present some practical managerial implications for those readers – managers, consultants, and other practitioners – whose work involves the creation of competitive firms. The necessary steps and common pitfalls in establishing strategic congruence and integrated control are treated in detail. The chapter ends with a section in which we consider some theoretical and methodological implications of the preceding discussion. In this section, we also relate our discussion to a number of previous studies. Moreover, since many important questions remain to be answered, we provide suggestions for further research in the area.

Summary and Conclusions

How to create and sustain competitive advantage is a subject that has received considerable attention from researchers in economics as well as business administration. The existing studies can roughly be classified into two groups according to the level of analysis: macro and micro. The former category relates to the competitive strength of entire nations; the latter, to the manner in which the individual firm creates competitive advantage on its own market. As noted in the introductory chapter, this book focuses on the micro level. Our purpose is to provide additional knowledge and understanding of the ways in which competitive advantage is created by the individual firm. Our principal areas of focus in this connection are strategic congruence and integrated control. The following two conditions – mutually consistent strategies and coherent strategic planning and follow-up – are regarded by us as prerequisites to being a strong competitor. It may be noted, however, that the two concepts of strategic congruence and integrated control for the most part have been treated separately and/or within a limited part of the firm. Few empirical studies have considered how strategies and control systems at the corporate, business, and functional level influence each other.[1] One probable explanation for this situation is that strategy, management control, and manufacturing control have been regarded as separate areas of research.

In our discussion on the ways in which strategies and control systems create competitive strength, contingency theory is an important point of departure. This means that competitiveness may be regarded as the result of a fit between the business environment, strategy, and internal structures (organization, control systems and processes) of the firm (*cf.* Lawrence and Lorsch, 1967).[2] Thus, the firm is viewed as an open system where one of the principal tasks of management is to choose a strategy that matches the internal structures of the organization with the environment – that is, to establish a so-called external fit. In Chapter 2, we show that in strategic management a number of different models have been developed for strategic analysis aimed at facilitating the achievement of an external fit. Although these models have been questioned, we believe that management can – and should – assume a significant responsibility for the development of the firm's strategy. This means that management must thoroughly understand both the environment in which the businesses of the corporation operate, and the ways in which the corporation should use its internal structures to position the product offering. In addition, management must ensure that the internal structures of the firm are well adapted to the chosen strategy – in other words, that there is a so-called internal fit. We have chosen to highlight the control systems in our analysis of internal fit since management control and manufacturing control are regarded as critical internal structures for the formulation and implementation of strategies (Simons, 1995; Hill, 2000; Anthony and Govindarajan, 2004).

In the normative literature, the formulation of competitive strategies is often described as a relatively non-problematic process (see, for example, Ansoff, 1965; Learned et al., 1965). The usual recommendation is to start with corporate goals and strategies and then to break these down to the business-unit and functional levels. This approach is intended to produce strategic congruence – in other words, corporate, business, and functional strategies that are mutually consistent and appropriate to the firm's competitive arena and overall strategic aims. In many cases, however, strategic co-ordination fails because of excessive dissimilarities between the corporate, business-unit, and functional subenvironments. These disparities are manifested primarily in the different degrees of uncertainty to which the organizational units are exposed (*cf.* Thompson, 1967). Thus, decisions are made more difficult in many vital areas – for example, the organization of manufacturing and the degree to which decisions can be decentralized. To avoid this type of problem, corporate management must limit their involvement to business units with similar competitive arenas and business strategies, units that would be closely related in regard to the nature of synergies and typical decision-making situations (Goold et al., 1994). From our review of the literature, it is apparent that a common business logic is one distinguishing feature of many competitive and financially successful firms. These firms have succeeded in choosing – for each organizational level – the environment where its internal resources can be used to best advantage.

Another distinguishing feature of a number of competitive firms is that they have begun to establish systems of integrated control (Nanni et al., 1992; Yoshikawa et al., 1994; Cooper, 1996). The purpose of integrated control is to facilitate the exchange of information between different organizational levels and decision-makers regarding strategic, tactical, and operative decisions. For example, the transparency of the planning and follow-up process can be enhanced through using similar concepts and principles in all of the firm's control systems (*cf.* Argyris, 1977). There will then be no need in management control to translate or reinterpret information from manufacturing control for use as a basis for decisions (*cf.* McNair et al., 1990). It should be noted, however, that we are not referring to systems integration in a strictly technical sense, but to the importance of a corporate-wide control model – in other words, guidelines for planning and follow-up for the corporation as a whole.[3] It will be easier to establish such guidelines if management has a clear conception of the kind of businesses on which the firm should focus and the way in which these businesses contribute to value creation. Just as an integrated system of control facilitates achievement of a high degree of strategic congruence, mutually consistent strategies favor the establishment of coherent planning and follow-up.

Despite research results suggesting that the competitive advantage of a firm is affected by strategic congruence and integrated control, there are few studies, as far as the authors are aware, in which these two areas are discussed in conjunction. Our analysis is therefore based on the variables and relationships presented in the tentative model described in Chapter 2 (see Figure 2.4) and further developed in Figure 6.1. One assumption is that management is in a position to choose a strategy appropriate to the environment. Another assumption is that in a longer-term perspective management can affect, at least to some extent, the degree to which the firm will operate in a turbulent or stable environment. In addition, we discuss the possibilities of achieving strategic congruence and integrated control on the basis of the conditions prevailing at the corporate, business-unit, and functional levels. As previously mentioned, we place emphasis on the subenvironment of the organizational unit and on the degree of uncertainty created in the interaction with various environmental elements.

In Chapter 3, where various strategic typologies are described, it is stressed that the matching between environment and strategy differs among the three organizational levels. Figure 6.1 shows that at the corporate level, synergy potential – that is, the potential for activity sharing by the business units – is a central dimension of corporate strategy. At the business-unit level, product uniqueness – that is, the degree of product differentiation – is significant in the choice of business strategy. Finally, technical flexibility – that is, the possibility of managing changes in the volume and mix of production – is of importance to strategy at the functional level. These three dimensions – synergy potential, product uniqueness, and technical flexibility – can be combined in a number of different ways, but only a few of them can be assumed to result in a substantial degree of strategic congruence. As previously emphasized, management often succeeds only in achieving a match between environment and strategy in a limited part of the firm. It is much harder to establish strategic congruence throughout an entire firm, that is, at the corporate, business-unit, and functional levels. To attain this goal, the firm must have a defined core business with the same critical success factors for the various operations.

We have emphasized that an external fit is not sufficient to achieve competitive strength and a good financial return. It is also important to match the firm's strategies with the design and use of its control systems – in other words, to establish an internal fit. This matching can be analyzed in a number of central dimensions of a firm's planning and follow-up. In Chapter 4 – and in Figure 6.1 – we show that it is appropriate to analyze management control in the following dimensions: intensity of monitoring (tight or loose), type of information used (monetary or non-monetary), and time perspective (short-term or long-term). As for manufacturing control, it can be analyzed in terms of type of information used (monetary or non-monetary), capacity and planning strategy (lag / level or lead / chase), cus-

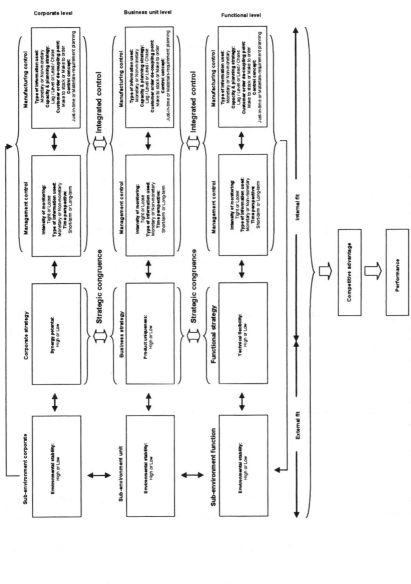

Fig. 6.1. Strategic congruence, integrated control and the creation of competitive advantage

tomer order de-coupling point (make-to-stock or make-to-order), and control concept (just-in-time or materials-requirement planning). To establish integrated control, the control systems must be similarly designed and used at the different organizational levels. This means, for example, that if monetary information is stressed in management control and manufacturing control, it is also important at the corporate, business-unit, and functional levels. As previously emphasized, this integration of control systems should be easier if there is already a high degree of strategic congruence. Another favorable condition is the presence of a clear and well-considered control model.

In Chapter 5 we analyze the possibilities of establishing a high degree of strategic congruence and integrated control in a total of ten different combinations of corporate, business-unit, and functional strategies. These combinations are based on a selection of various strategies, each of a single, unmixed type. In addition, the existence of different degrees of fit makes the number of possible combinations of strategies and control systems, with a reasonable degree of strategic congruence and integrated control, very large. We therefore make no claim that our analysis covers all possible combinations. Nor are the dimensions for analyzing strategies and control systems intended to present in detail the factors that determine whether strategic congruence and integrated control can be achieved. Our objective is to describe a number of tendencies, not hard-and-fast principles, concerning the fit between different strategic levels and the role of control systems in that respect. Since this analysis cannot be simply summarized, the reader interested in a more detailed discussion is referred to Chapter 5. However, we would like to present briefly our conclusions on two combinations where the prospects of achieving competitive strength – through strategic congruence and integrated control – may be considered especially favorable. Please observe that these two combinations, as well as the other tendencies in Chapter 5, are of a tentative nature and have to be thoroughly tested in future empirical studies.

1. The conditions for creating strategic congruence, as well as a high degree of integrated control, may be assumed to be favorable when (a) the corporate strategy is focused on portfolio management and combined with strategies of cost leadership and line / flow; (b) management control is tight and monetary, and reflects a short-term perspective; and (c) manufacturing control is based on a capacity and planning strategy combining lag and level, manufacturing is to the stock of finished-goods (MTS), and the control concept is based on just-in-time (JIT).

2. The conditions for creating strategic congruence, as well as a high degree of integrated control, may also be assumed to be favorable in the following circumstances: (a) a corporate strategy of activity sharing is combined with differentiation and job-shop / batch strategies; (b) management control is loose and non-monetary, and reflects a long-term perspective; and (c) manufacturing control is based on a capacity and planning strategy combining lead and chase, manufacturing is to customer order (MTO), and the control concept is based on materials-requirement planning (MRP).

As is shown in our analysis in chapter 5, other conceivable combinations do not seem to provide the same favorable conditions for achieving a high degree of strategic congruence and integrated control. Usually the reason is a poor fit between a least two strategic levels and / or a poor fit in regard to management control and the design and use of manufacturing control. In two of these cases (see Chapter 5, Figure 5.9), though, it should be possible to improve the possibilities of establishing integrated control by adapting corporate-wide management and manufacturing control to the needs at the business-unit level. As shown by the interrelationships between strategies and control systems in Figure 6.1, we may expect that such an adjustment will lead to a higher degree of strategic congruence.

The Dynamics of Fit

Up to this point the discussion of fit has had a relatively static emphasis. The matching between environment, strategies, and control systems has been analyzed primarily at a single point in time. In a longer-term perspective, however, it is reasonable to assume that the conditions for a fit are only temporary. Thus, one can expect that periods with a high degree of strategic congruence and integrated control will be followed by periods of instability and disequilibrium (*cf.* Bettis and Hitt, 1995; Fiegenbaum et al., 1996). Business dynamism – that is, changes in the environment of the firm – is frequently the reason why strategies and control systems may need to be reviewed. According to Zajac et al. (2000) examples of events or conditions that can lead to instability are changes in consumer preferences, actions of competitors, and shifts in technology. Another type of condition mentioned by the authors is organizational, such as when a lack of resources makes implementation of the selected strategy more difficult.

In many of the previous contingency-theory studies, it was assumed that changes in the environment directly affect the internal structures of the firm (see, for example, Burns and Stalker, 1961). The emphasis on a direct relationship between environment and structure – a form of structural contingency theory, according to Zajac et al. (2000) – still has many adherents. But with the emergence and importance of strategic management as an area of research, a firm's strategy is now regarded as a central contingency variable. As previously emphasized, it was frequently a basic assumption that strategy serves as a mediating variable between environment and structure (Archer and Otley, 1991). This means that strategy becomes an important instrument in the work of achieving a strong competitive position and a good financial return. Management must formulate a strategy well adapted to the environment (external fit), while also ensuring that the design and use of the control systems support successful implementation of the chosen strategy (internal fit).

Particularly after long periods of fit, when strategies and control systems have been the same for many years, sudden changes in the environment may make it necessary to modify the business. The literature on strategic management generally prescribes that this adjustment – for the purpose of re-establishing a fit – should start by aligning the unit with its competitive arena (Mintzberg et al., 1998). In Figure 6.2 we have chosen to designate this situation as Case 1. When there is a change in the subenvironment of a business unit, the aim is to adapt the unit's strategy to the new conditions (Learned et al., 1965). The modified strategy should be implemented, in turn, by changing the control systems so as to reflect the partially changed and new critical success factors (Anthony, 1965).

However, management may conclude that the management-control system[4] is a major asset and source of competitive strength. In such a case, where there is a misfit with an established and well-functioning internal structure, it is far from obvious that the strategy should be changed (Zajac et al., 2000). Thus, at least in the short run, tension arises between

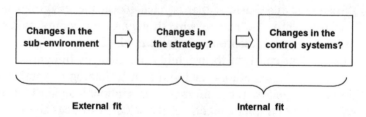

Fig. 6.2. Changes in environment, strategy, and control systems -- case 1

the demands of the environment, on the one hand, and the strategy and the internal structures of the unit, on the other. In that case, management must weigh the costs of this partial misfit against the benefits of maintaining a strategy and control systems more or less unchanged. In the longer run, management can attempt to influence the environment or to position the product offering in another competitive arena that is related.[5]

However, a need for adjustment does not always arise as a result of a change in the environment, but may also originate within the unit (*cf.* Case 2 in Figure 6.3). In the latter instance, for example, further development of the unit's control systems can result in the collection and processing of new information. Since the environment of the unit will then be regarded in a somewhat new light, management's view of the available alternatives for strategic action will be affected (Hall and Saias, 1980). Consequently, alternatives that were previously rejected may be reconsidered in view of new information and new methods of analysis (Simons, 1995). In such a case, management may consider changing strategy and may also seek to position the firm in a new competitive arena.

Whether a process of adjustment begins as in these two cases, with a change in the internal structure, or in the form of a change in the unit's environment, the firm's strategy is of central importance. As shown in Figures 6.2 and 6.3, strategy as a mediating variable is located in a stress field between the environment, on the one hand, and the control systems, on the other. Therefore, after a period of instability and disequilibrium, some form of strategic change is necessary to re-establish a fit and the firm's competitiveness. Zajac et al. (2000) noted the importance of strategic changes in their analysis of the dynamics of fit.[6] Based on extensive review of the literature, and an empirical study of 4000 U.S. savings and loan institutions, four scenarios were identified by the authors:

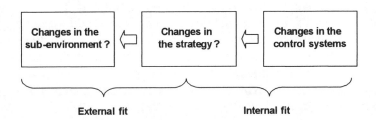

Fig. 6.3. Changes in environment, strategy, and control systems -- case 2

1. Beneficial Strategic Change: The firm must change (i.e. as defined by environmental or organizational contingencies)[7] and does so accordingly. A firm that responds in this manner will probably improve its chances of creating competitive advantage and thus of achieving good financial performance. In our model it is assumed that most companies will act in this fashion; in other words, they will constantly strive for a fit between the business environment, strategies, and control systems. However, this does not mean that these firms are highly active, i. e., changing even in the absence of environmental stimuli.

2. Insufficient Strategic Change: The firm must change but fails to do so; as a consequence, it becomes less competitive and shows unsatisfactory financial performance. In our model, this scenario is represented by the case where neither strategies nor control systems are changed even though they are obsolete or inappropriate in some other respect. Zajac et al. (2000) hold that a firm may be unwilling or unable to change strategies that have become entrenched.

3. Beneficial Inertia: The firm faces no need to change and does not do so, with a positive effect on performance as a result. In this scenario Zajac et al. (2000) refer to Selznick (1957), who maintains that firms which follow a particular strategy develop specific competencies capable of offsetting external pressures for change.[8] In addition, the authors discuss the importance of understanding both the potential and the limitations of the organization's capabilities. In this connection, strategic congruence and integrated control may lead to such effective decision-making that it suffices in itself to parry any threats from the external environment.

4. Excessive Change: The firm need not make changes but does so anyway, with a consequent decline in competitive strength and performance. Zajac et al. (2000) consider among other things cases where the change is made for the purpose of "empire building" or as "change for change's sake." In our model this scenario is present, for example, when changes in management control are made for reasons other than to achieve a good fit between strategy and control. Another example would be changes at one strategic level for the purpose of creating a fit with that particular subenvironment but without co-ordinating the change with other strategic levels.

The study by Zajac et al. (2000) identifies different types of strategic changes and also the forces that drive such changes. Although strategic changes are generally regarded as a continuous process, which is not fully reflected in the classification above, many interesting conclusions can be drawn from the findings of the study. One of these conclusions is that unnecessary change may be as harmful as not making any changes at all. Another conclusion is that management must ensure that changes in strategies and control systems at one organizational level are not counteracted by unfavorable conditions at another level. As for the driving forces behind changes, Zajac et al. offer a number of examples that make it easier to understand how a dynamic fit arises and can be preserved. It thus becomes clear that we have been referring to favorable combinations of strategies and control systems at a single point in time – although such a state of equilibrium can last rather long. Since strategic change and the forces driving it constitute a separate area of research, a more detailed discussion of these concepts is beyond the scope of this book. However, the analysis in Chapter 5, where we present the combinations of strategies and control systems that may be assumed to create a fit, should be of help in situations where the firm has entered a state of instability and disequilibrium.

Practical Business Implications

This book has implications both for business practice and for the development of theories and further research. As for practical business implications, it concerns a subject that has attracted much attention in the popular press: the creation of competitive advantage and ultimately shareholder value. One aspect of considerable interest is that of firm strategies and the question whether flaws in these strategies can explain the destruction of value that has afflicted previously well-managed firms. Conglomerates are a category of corporations that has received heavy criticism, with many analysts and journalists holding that the business concepts and strategies of these firms are unclear. These critics attribute the lack of clarity to the fact that conglomerates usually operate in a large number of unrelated industries. As a consequence, corporate management often lacks adequate knowledge of all the businesses of their firms and for this reason seldom participates actively in the development of unit businesses; instead, it assumes the role of "evaluator" of the strategies proposed by business-unit management. The critics maintain further that this passive participation in strategic planning creates no additional value, adding that the opportunities for value creation are severely limited by the low synergy potential of most conglomerates. With these arguments and the slogan of "back to basics," leading analysts have called for conglomerates to reduce the diversity of their business.

Even firms with a relatively clear scope of business and a potential for activity sharing have been regarded by the press as candidates for dismemberment. In cases of this kind, financial analysts have often reached a different conclusion than firm management concerning the actual extent of synergy benefits. Competitors may also be interested in certain parts of a corporation and be prepared to pay a price for these units that is attractive, at least in a short-term perspective. Finally, there is a category of company that despite considerable synergy potential is unable to remain competitive. The failures of these firms are the principal reason why commentators and journalists have begun to doubt the capacity of certain boards of directors and managements to craft value-creating strategies, as well as the appropriateness of the methods used. In some cases the criticism is misdirected, for example, when major unforeseeable changes in the environment rapidly deprive strategies and control systems of their relevance. In cases where the firm has been gradually losing its competitiveness over an extended period, on the other hand, it may be justifiable to question management and its way of planning and monitoring corporate businesses.

Another reason why increasing interest has been devoted to planning and follow-up is the debate in the late 1980's and early 1990's, in which management control was criticized for lack of relevance. Specifically, the principal criticism was that traditional control, with its monetary focus, bore little relationship to the firm's goals and strategies. With the emphasis on monetary information, the financial position and profits of the firm were the basis for virtually all planning and follow-up. The accounting system itself, and questions on matters like inventory valuation, became more important than using management control to help influence individuals to follow the chosen strategy. Johnson and Kaplan (1987) summarize their criticism in the following passage:

Many short-term measures are appropriate for motivating and evaluating managerial performance. It is unlikely, however, that monthly or quarterly profits, especially when based on the practices mandated and used for external constituencies, would be one of them. Today's management accounting systems provide a misleading target for managerial attention and fail to provide the relevant set of measures that appropriately reflect the technology, the products, the process, and the competitive environment in which the organization operates (Johnson and Kaplan, 1987, p. 3).

As previously mentioned, new models for planning and follow-up were developed in response to the sweeping condemnation of traditional management control.[9] Some of these models refined the traditional monetary measures in order to reflect more accurately the present value of long-term benefits (Nilsson and Olve, 2001). One example of these so-called value-based models is EVA[10] (Stewart, 1999), which is a further elaboration of residual income.[11] Another category of models – often called models for strategic management or strategic control – highlights the link between strategy and the focus of follow-up (see, for example, McNair et al., 1990; Epstein and Manzoni, 1998). Almost all models of the latter type are characteristically based on the assumption that strategy is to be translated into a number of monetary and nonmonetary measures. Through following up the business with the aid of these measures, it should be possible to obtain a continuous update on the degree to which the business is operating in accordance with strategy. As emphasized in previous chapters, perhaps the best-known model of this kind is the Balanced Scorecard, which was developed by Kaplan and Norton in the early 1990's (Kaplan and Norton, 1992, 1993). Despite the introduction of new control models, there are indications that many firms still use the planning and follow-up procedures criticized back in the early 1980's. This is probably one of the reasons why some firms were unable to formulate and implement value-creating strategies and consequently continued to become less competitive. On the front cover of their book *The Strategy-Focused Organization* (2001), Kaplan and Norton draw the following conclusion:

In today's business environment, strategy has never been more important. Yet research shows that most companies fail to execute strategy successfully. Behind the abysmal track record lies an undeniable fact: many companies continue to use management processes – top-down, financially driven, and tactical – that were designed to run yesterday's organizations (Kaplan and Norton, 2001, front cover).

Consequently, there is a pressing need to reconsider how strategies are formulated and implemented. In regard to strategic planning, our review of the literature shows that many of the methods used today originated with the normative models developed in the 1960's. At the corporate level, these analyses tend to focus on the question whether different types of businesses overlap or are complementary. At the business-unit level, the analysis is often directed at determining how the market and the product offering affect the competitiveness of the individual business unit. Our conclusions – summarized in Figure 6.1 – show that such a focused analysis does not offer sufficient guidance to firms seeking to create competitive advantage and to achieve a strong market position. For this purpose, the analysis must be broad enough to include all relevant strategic levels: corporate, business-unit, and functional.

When management has chosen its strategy, the next step is to ensure successful implementation. It is generally accepted among scholars in the field that the systems of control are important in this regard (Anthony and Govindarajan, 2004). Equipped with models like the Balanced Scorecard, practitioners have become more interested in the effect of strategies on the design and use of control systems. One consequence of the introduction of new models, however, has been that many business executives do not consider how other elements of the control system – the budget, investment control, etc. – should be adapted to the chosen strategy. According to our experience, it is much harder to explain why tight monetary control is appropriate for some strategies but not for others, or why the JIT control concept is especially suitable for a cost-leadership strategy. In addition, the need for integrated control will probably have to be discussed and debated further before being accepted by practitioners.

Our explanation for these tendencies is that the importance of the firm's systems of control in creating competitive advantage has clearly not been sufficiently recognized. Therefore, a brief list of some important areas to consider is provided below. These areas are then discussed sequentially, although a process of this kind has numerous iterative features:

1. Define the firm's core business

2. Define the firm's overall control model

3. Co-ordinate strategies and control systems

4. Choose IT support

5. Establish a culture based on the benefits of continuous improvement

Define the Firm's Core Business

We have emphasized that a clearly defined core business makes it easier to achieve strategic congruence and integrated control. A common basic assumption – both in the popular press and in scholarly publications – is that synergy potential should be the guiding consideration in formulating corporate goals and strategies. As is noted in the preceding section, this view has given rise to vehement criticism of conglomerates – that is, corporations with a portfolio-management strategy (see, for example, Porter, 1987). The essence of this criticism is that a corporation with little potential for synergy gains cannot create additional value since the costs of co-ordination will outweigh the benefits. Our review of the literature, however, indicates that this criticism is relatively overgeneralized and in some cases unjustified. For instance, empirical studies have shown that conglomerates, too, can deliver high returns (see, for example, Goold and Campbell, 1987a). In view of such evidence, we have chosen also to emphasize the importance of a common business logic for corporate operations. Corporate groups with a common business logic limit their holdings to business units with similar competitive arenas and business strategies, units that are closely related in regard to critical success indicators and typical decision-making situations.[12] To establish such a clear core business is easier if strategic planning follows a few "rules of thumb."

First, the strategic analysis should appropriately begin at the highest organizational level, i.e. the corporation. The aim is to establish clarity about the type of businesses that should be included in the firm. To achieve this objective, however, it is necessary to answer a number of important questions, some examples of which are listed below:

1. What is the corporate vision and business concept?
   - State the corporation's overall business goals.
   - Identify the corporation's most important stakeholders.

2. What are the specific financial goals of the corporation?
   - Indicate the required total-shareholder return.
   - Indicate the required return on investment.

3. What corporate strategy is appropriate for achieving these goals?
   - Describe the importance of synergies.
   - List the core competencies of the firm.

In the next step it is appropriate to begin analyzing what kinds of business units would be suitable for inclusion in the corporation. The answers to the questions on vision, goals, and corporate strategy will naturally provide guidance in this process. As previously emphasized, however, it is not possible simply to translate and break down these dimensions to the business-unit level. In order to establish a clear core business, one must seek to identify critical success factors and decision situations that are common to most of the business units. Figure 6.1 shows that such an analysis should start with the nature of the subenvironments at the corporate, business, and functional levels in order to determine the degree of environmental stability (i.e. high or low). As discussed in previous chapters, strategies typical of units operating on stable, mature markets differ from those of units on turbulent, emerging markets. Consequently, it is just as important to analyze the environment in detail and how the unit has adapted to it, as to determine the possibilities of knowledge transfer or activity sharing.

After the environments of the business units have been described, it is appropriate to examine how the degree of uncertainty has affected the choice of strategies. At the unit level, for example, it is interesting to establish whether the chosen business strategy is based on a high degree of product uniqueness or whether the focus is on standardized products. In this phase of the analysis, management sometimes underestimates the problems of incorporating a unit that deviates from other units in the firm. Not infrequently, it is believed that a management style with proven success in a certain kind of business can be applied to other – seemingly similar – businesses. This kind of situation, where a misfit unit is acquired, need not be a threat to the corporation's capacity to generate a good return.[13] However, since many corporate-wide decisions may disfavor the unit, there is a risk that its competitiveness will be gradually eroded.

A more serious situation at some large, well-established firms is that they seem not to have any deliberately chosen core business at all. At first glance, their business units may apparently have many features in common and considerable synergy potential, but the competitiveness of the business units and the financial return of the corporation tell a different story. In corporations of this type, it is vital to look for a reasonably large group of business units with a substantial degree of strategic congruence. This nucleus of business units should be the basis for restructuring the corporation. In the introductory phase of this work, the corporation should be subjected to a strategic analysis of the kind discussed in this section. When a clear core business has been identified, it will then be possible to decide definitely which units will form part of the future corporation. The strategic analysis may also lead to the acquisition of new business units to reinforce the firm's competitive power in its chosen core business.

Define the Firm's Overall Control Model

A clearly defined core business – that is, a high degree of strategic congruence – is not sufficient to achieve competitive strength and a good return. It is just as important that the control systems reflect the common business logic on which the choice of a core business is based. For this reason, management control and manufacturing control should be designed and used in accordance with the chosen strategies. As previously mentioned, an advantage of a high degree of strategic congruence is that critical success factors and typical decision-making situations converge at each organizational level. It is thus crucial to facilitate the establishment of strategic planning and follow-up that are coherent throughout the firm. The interdependence of strategic congruence and integrated control means, on the other hand, that it may be difficult to define the core business without a clear conception of the control model to be used. At some successful firms, the control model has even been the starting point for management's choice of the businesses to include in the corporation. For example, in view of the positive experience of other organizations, corporate management may prefer control models in which high cost effectiveness is the guiding criterion for all planning and follow-up. The introduction of a new control model can then be used as a driving force in the restructuring of the corporation, which will gradually divest units that would not do well under such a regime of tight, short-term control.

One important issue in the design of an overall control model is the role of corporate management in co-ordinating business-unit operations. The greater the opportunities for activity sharing, the more co-ordination is required to exploit synergy potential. A need for strong co-ordination means, in turn, that control systems will have to be much more highly integrated (*cf.* Jones, 1983). As emphasized in previous chapters, coherent and transparent planning and follow-up are essential if corporate management is to ensure that the business units are working toward the same goals. For example, the same strategic planning and budgeting routines for all business units and functions may be used to guarantee co-ordination of operations to exploit economies of scale. Integrated planning of manufacturing could then enable the firm to achieve long production runs, thus lowering unit costs. It is important in the design of the control model to ensure that the central dimensions of the management-control and manufacturing-control systems are mutually consistent. These dimensions were treated in detail in Chapter 4 and then, in Chapter 5, they were related to different combinations of corporate, business, and functional strategies. In our opinion, this discussion, which is summarized in several figures and analytical diagrams, should be a useful aid in defining an overall control model.

Co-ordinate Strategies and Control Systems

From the two preceding subsections, it is apparent that strategic congruence is difficult to establish without integrated control, and *vice versa*. Once the core business and the control model have been defined, the firm must decide how to proceed further in order to achieve a high degree of strategic congruence and integrated control. Of course, it is not possible to give a single clear answer to this question, for the unique situation of each corporation must determine what approach will be most appropriate. Despite numerous exceptions, however, a clearly defined core business is probably a natural starting point for further work. Particularly when the firm is facing major changes, such as focusing more narrowly and restructuring, it is essential to have chosen what course to follow. A clear conception of the kinds of business that the corporation will develop in the future will facilitate co-ordination of corporate, business, and functional strategies (*cf.* Figure 6.4). By contrast, vertical co-ordination without a defined core business may be quite complicated. The high proportion of failed acquisitions is clear evidence of the problems that can arise if the strategy of the acquired firm deviates from that of the acquirer (*cf.* Porter, 1987).

As for co-ordination of control systems, it is also simplified by a good fit between different strategic levels. A business unit with a strategy inconsistent with corporate strategy will make different demands on the unit's control systems than those we would expect to find at the corporate level. For co-ordination to be successful under such conditions, the control systems must meet the information needs of both corporate and business-unit levels (Nilsson, 2002). But even when there is a clear core business and a high degree of strategic congruence, integrated planning and follow-up will be difficult to achieve. We have found, though, that horizontal co-ordination of management control and manufacturing control provides certain benefits in the process of establishing integrated control. Above all, it will then be possible to ensure that both management and manufacturing control are adapted to the information needs at the organizational level concerned before the work of co-ordination proceeds to the next level (*cf.* Figure 6.4). In addition, it is an advantage to lead the integration of control systems from the top of the firm since the overall control model is based on the business of the entire corporation.

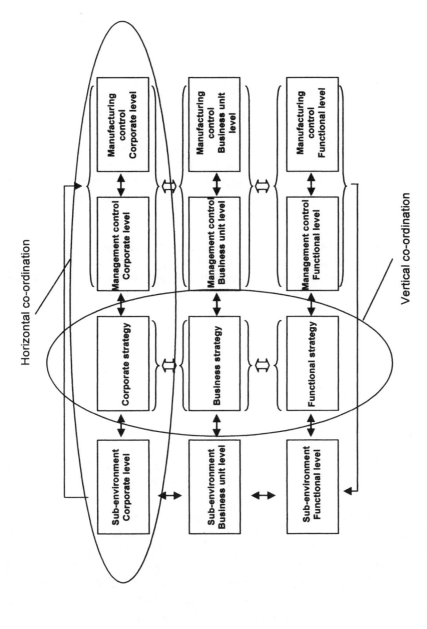

Fig. 6.4. Co-ordination of strategies and control systems

Choose IT Support

Considerable interest has been devoted in recent years to the advantages and disadvantages of integrated business-support systems, or as they are often called, Enterprise Resource Planning Systems (ERP-systems) (see, for example, Davenport, 2000; Hunton, 2002). One benefit of these systems is that they can handle large quantities of transactional data (i.e., accounting data) at relatively low cost. Another benefit is the possibility of achieving rapid integration of data. The full potential of the business-support system can be especially well utilized when it is expanded so that it can process tactical and strategic data. Granlund and Mouritsen (2003) summarize the opportunities presented by advances in the area of information technology:

> It has been suggested that new technologies such as ERP systems make it possible to model the details of the firm's operations in computer technology and make a highly integrated mode of management possible (Davenport, 1998). The prospect of an intense mapping of organizational processes in computer representations is there, and therefore the management of the firm can be made real time (ibid, p. 77).

> The recent interest in ERP systems has re-opened the issue of information technology because it promises to be a platform for the management of the whole business rather than merely about the management of certain parts of the business (ibid, p. 78).

One drawback that has been emphasized is the substantial cost of implementation often involved in systems of this kind. Because standardized systems are relatively inflexible, they require extensive, time-consuming changes in the firm's organization and control. Another – closely related – disadvantage is that the individual business unit may be forced to adapt to an established corporate standard that may be inconsistent with unit needs (Lindvall, 2001, p. 18). In corporations with little strategic congruence or integrated control, this kind of compulsory uniformity can lead to problems. The reason is that substantial differences in the strategies of business units entail equally large variations in information needs. It is apparent from the discussion in the two preceding sections that such a situation makes it more difficult to establish a clear corporate-wide control model. Granlund and Malmi (2002) made the following observation based on a field study of ten companies that had experience of ERP-systems in Finland.

There was one large organization (G) where every business unit was free to choose whatever ERPS they considered suitable. This is understandable, as the business logic between various parts of the organization varies quite a lot. As not all units use the same ERPS, budgets cannot be consolidated in a single ERP. Hence, it is reasonable to use the existing system for consolidation (ibid, 308).

In corporations where strategies and control systems are not mutually consistent, in principle only the transactional data can be assumed to be the same. This means that the benefits of an integrated business-support system cannot be fully exploited and that there will be additional costs. For example, certain special adaptations of the business system will probably be necessary since the requirement of total uniformity in tactical and strategic data will mean that the system will only meet the information needs of certain decision-makers. As previously emphasized, however, the information needs at the different organizational levels can be assumed to converge if there is a high degree of strategic congruence and integrated control. A high proportion of shared data permits uniform design and use of management control and manufacturing control. Of course, such uniformity does not ensure exact consistency with the wishes of all units and functions. However, it does provide favorable conditions for utilizing the many benefits of an integrated business-support system. Above all, the firm avoids the problem of numerous special adaptations that often still fail to meet the information needs of lower organizational levels.

Establish a Culture Based on the Benefits of Continual Improvement

An interesting question, touched on by Govindarajan (1988) and Hedberg and Jönsson (1978), among others, is whether there are any risks with a high degree of strategic congruence and integrated control. According to these scholars, a firm that has overadapted to its current strategy may have limited its capacity to devise and implement new strategies for value creation. Gary Hamel reasons along similar lines in his book *Leading the Revolution*, where he states that the structures of many firms rule out experimentation (Hamel, 2000). The difficulty is to find a reasonable balance between highly focused strategies and control systems, on the one hand, and continuous experimentation, on the other. Finally, Miller (1993) maintains that successful and focused companies risk being too "pure and simple." [14] According to the author, they have over time developed "too sharp an edge." Although such development may initially lead to considerable success, the risk – according to Miller – is that the firm may ultimately lose its competitiveness. [15] The quotation below summarizes Miller's view:

They amplify and extend a single strength or function while neglecting most others. Ultimately a rich and complex organization becomes excessively simple. It turns into a monolithic, narrowly focused version of its former self, converting a formula for success into a path toward failure (Miller, 1993, p. 116).

The thesis of this article is that in the long run, success will cause many organizations to become more "simple." Their rich strategic character will evolve into bland and truncated caricature. Culture, systems, processes, and world views will become too monolithic to allow organizations to embrace and adapt to complex currents of their settings.' And, ultimately, these developments will result in companies' reflecting the winds of change not with the responsiveness of sandy terrain but with the inertia of a field of boulders (ibid, p. 117).

It is easy to agree with these authors that overly rigid strategies and structures in themselves may in time risk weakening a firm's competitiveness. In the section headed "The Dynamics of Fit," we discuss the need for constant reassessment of the firm's focus and structure. However, there need not be a contradiction between a focused business and a business based on experimentation and development. On the contrary, the lack of a clear focus may be a reason why resources for development, rather than be concentrated sufficiently to have a useful effect, are spread too thinly to achieve results. In this connection, it may be noted that many of the world's leading firms in their industry seem to have a clear core business and a well-defined control model. Moreover, the management and employees of these firms appear to have a favorable view of change and continual improvement. Like many other researchers and analysts (for example, Kotter and Cohen, 2002), we believe that such an attitude is very important to the further development of strategies, control systems, and businesses. It is therefore crucial to establish a culture where the usefulness of continual improvement is a central theme. Creating such a culture is a demanding task that can be expected to claim considerable resources for many years. However, firms that are sufficiently persistent and ultimately succeed can probably expect a handsome return on their investment.

Implications for Future Research

This book is a contribution to the literature that treats competitive advantage on the basis of the match between the environment and internal structures. By focusing on co-ordination and integration of strategies and control systems, we seek to furnish an expansion of the literature in the area.

As a starting-point for future research, some of the theoretical and methodological issues involved are discussed in the following two sections.

Theoretical Issues

As for theoretical issues, we believe that three areas are particularly important to consider in future studies. First, the discussion in the section headed "The Dynamics of Fit" has demonstrated the importance of understanding how conditions of misfit can be managed through changing the environment, strategy, and control systems. Such periods of adjustment may even be necessary for restructuring the firm to ensure that it will be competitive in the long term. It may be noted, however, that models based on contingency theory are often criticized as static, i.e. for rarely dealing with the actual process of change (Otley, 1980; Hopwood, 1983). The criticism is directed particularly at large-scale questionnaire surveys where the matching between environment, strategies, and control systems is studied at a single point in time.[16] Above all, these studies have helped to enhance our understanding of the contingency factors that may explain why firms become strong competitors and earn a good return. One shortcoming is that the studies do not indicate how and why periods of instability and disequilibrium arise. Nor is it possible in most cases to draw any conclusions from these studies as to how the process of change should be managed.[17] On the other hand, case studies based on contingency theory provide some help in understanding the dynamics of fit (see, for example, Nilsson, 2002). As shown in the next section, these studies have the potential to shed some light on this critical process of change, but they are relatively few. Consequently, there is a pressing need for further in-depth case studies.

Second, future studies also need to take into account the process dimension. The literature contains many interesting analyses of process-oriented firms. Toyota is one such firm that is often cited as a case where a process-oriented organization can help to reduce lead times and improve quality (Olhager and Rapp, 1985). It may be noted, however, that in the majority of contingency-theory studies the choice has been to study strategies and control systems on the assumption that firms are organized and planned in a vertical dimension. Probably one reason why research has had this focus is that most strategic typologies apply to one of the traditional organizational levels: corporate, business, and functional. Another reason is that research in management control still has a relative strong vertical orientation. This situation makes it rather difficult to develop hypotheses on the relationship between process strategies and the design and use of horizontally focused control. Notwithstanding these obstacles, it is urgent that the process dimension be given more attention in the empirical studies with a clear focus on strategy and control. Future research can then help us to learn more about the relationship between process strategy and process control and, in turn, a strong competitive position.

Third, there is a need for in-depth studies of significant actors and their various roles in establishing strategic congruence and integrated control. Simons (1990) is an example of a qualitative approach that helped shed more light on management's use of control systems, especially the difference between interactive and diagnostic use. In studies based on contingency theory, relatively little interest is generally devoted to the actors involved. Future studies, particularly those with a contingency-theory focus, should therefore pay more attention to the interaction between management and employees in both the formulation and the implementation of the firm's strategy.

Methodological Issues

In regard to methodological problems, testing and further developing the model entails many challenges. First, it is important in our opinion that the variables included in the model be given an operational definition. The variables concerned may be identified on a general level as strategy (corporate, business, and manufacturing strategy), control systems (management control and manufacturing control), competitive advantage (strong market position) and performance (value created for principal stakeholders). Using standardized measuring instruments to capture these variables facilitates comparison with other studies as well as implementation of replica studies.[18, 19] Particularly the validity and reliability of future studies could probably be improved if this type of standardized measuring instrument were used as a complement to other data-collection methods, such as open-ended interviews (Yin, 1989; Abernethy et al., 1999).

At the same time, the complexity of the phenomenon under study might not be fully considered with such an approach. In the choice of measuring instruments, therefore, a balance should be found between the conflicting needs for comparability and descriptions of sufficient substance. Moreover, a comparative analysis of qualitative and quantitative data should be used to validate the measurement of constructs (Lillis, 1999). Converging data, for example, provide a much more reliable classification of the firm's strategy than when only one data source and one type of measuring instrument are used. A combined analysis also leads to a better understanding of the variables under study (Yin, 1989; Otley and Berry, 1994). In addition, qualitative data can be used to capture dimensions for which no standardized measuring instruments have yet been developed. Qualitative data are also appropriate in studying various actors and their roles in creating coherent strategies and control systems.

Second, and closely related to the previous challenge, is the importance of designing studies in which "rich data" are used. As indicated in the subsection headed "Theoretical Issues," there is a considerable need to study the dynamics of fit – that is, to consider strategy and control in regard to context and process. An interesting question, for example, is how strategic congruence and integrated control are affected over time by changes in political and economic conditions (*cf.* Hopwwod, 1983, 1989). A research design based on a longitudinal case study is probably most appropriate for such an investigation. As previously mentioned, case studies have proven to be particularly suited for following and analyzing change processes of this kind, and especially the dynamics between different contingency variables (*cf.* Hägg and Hedlund, 1979).

Notes

1. An organizational aspect that has received increased attention in recent years is the firm's processes. One common classification of these is into primary and supporting processes. The former can include activities like manufacturing and inbound logistics, while purchasing and human-resource management are examples of the latter type of process (*cf.* Porter's value chain, discussed in Chapter 2 in the section headed "Strategy, Structure, and Performance"). However, as shown in the review of the literature, research in the area of strategy and control has been dominated thus far by studies that consider the traditional organizational levels (corporate, business, and functional). In the section headed "Implications for Future Research," we discuss the consequences of this focus.

2. For readers desiring a thorough exposition and critical discussion of contingency theory, Lex Donaldson's book entitled *The Contingency Theory of Organizations* is highly recommended (Donaldson, 2001).

3. Integrated business-support systems – commonly referred to as Enterprise Resource Planning systems (ERP systems) – require a high degree of standardization in the format of information as well as the processes used for data collection. See also the section headed "Practical Business Implications."

4. Management control is only one example of what could be considered as the firm's internal capabilities and competencies. Another example is the firm's unique competence in the development of a certain type of products. For a discussion of core competencies, see Chapter 3, the subsection headed "The Prahalad and Hamel (1996) Typology of Corporate Strategy."

5. For a detailed discussion of management's possibilities of choosing the environment in which the firm will operate and the strategy that it will follow, see Chapter 1, the section headed "Matching Environment and Internal Structures."

6. Zajac et al. (2000) regard strategic fit as a dependent variable. Environmental and organizational contingences are independent variables. This means that fluctuations in those variables imply differences in the need for strategic change. In our model – summarized in Figure 6.1 –

we have assumed that there is interdependence among environment, strategy, and internal structures. See also Footnote 7.

7. According to Zajac et al. (2000), environmental contingencies refer to both general and local environments. Organizational contingencies refer to input resources, throughput competencies, overall competencies and current strategy.

8. According to Zajac et al. (2000), Selznick (1957) holds that there are many possible ways of becoming a strong competitor and that firm-specific resources can lessen the need for adaptation to environmental changes.

9. See the section headed "Management Control" in Chapter 4.

10. EVA is a registered trademark of Stern Stewart and Co. in the United States, the United Kingdom, and several other countries.

11. EVA (Economic Value Added) is basically residual income (RI = income minus an interest charge for invested capital). One difference between EVA and RI is that the former includes cost items like R&D (Young, 1997; Stewart, 1999).

12. Goold et al. (1994) has instead launched the concept of "Heartland Business"; see Chapter 1, Footnote 12 for a detailed discussion.

13. See also Chapter 1, Footnote 14.

14. One area of Miller's research is that of so-called configurations (see, for example, Miller, 1986, 1996). He regards a configuration as "a quality or property that varies among organizations." According to Miller (1996), one indication of high-level configuration is that strategy, structure, process and culture are based on a common goal or area of focus. Another example cited by Miller (1996) is that the power structure and the composition of the top-management team reflect the area of the firm's focus. This type of study can contribute to an enhanced understanding of what creates external and internal fit, respectively. One problem, however, may be that the number of organizational elements grows large. It is then difficult to understand in depth how one specific element affects the development of the company. There is also another problem, which is linked to the level of analysis. In an overview of a large number of studies on organizational configu-

rations and their relationship to performance, it can be seen that many of the studies were conducted at the business-unit level (Ketchen and Combs, 1997). Consequently, there is a danger that the link between corporate, business and functional strategies will be unclear.

15. In an article in *Business Horizons,* Miller and Whitney (1999) provides several examples where companies have succeeded in creating a configuration that helps make them highly competitive. Among other things, the article highlights control systems and ERP systems as central elements in the configurations of the companies cited. It should be noted, however, that in Miller's view configurations do not arise through rational planning. According to the author, they are more the result of taking chances, inspiration, etc.

16. For an overview of these studies, see the section "Strategy and Control" in Chapter 2.

17. Here we are referring to the studies reported in Chapter 2, the section "Strategy and Control." Zajac et al. (2000) is an example of a questionnaire study designed specifically to examine strategic changes. The study is described in Chapter 6, the section "The Dynamics of Fit."

18. For example, Rumelt (1974) has developed a measuring instrument, which can be used to operationalize Porter's (1987) typology of corporate strategy. Another example of a measuring instrument is the one developed by Govindarajan (1988). It was especially developed for the purpose of operationalizing Porter's (1980) typology of business strategy.

19. Measuring competitiveness and measuring performance are areas that usually entail major methodological challenges. As for the latter variable, a common and difficult problem is how performance should be measured and related to changes in other variables (Steers, 1975). For this reason, referring to Steers (ibid), Gupta and Govindarajan (1984) use a measuring instrument with both financial and non-financial criteria such as growth in sales, market share, market development, and R&D.

Epilogue

This book has described how competitive advantage can be created at the individual firm through strategic congruence and integrated control. The development of a tentative model has been facilitated by the "knowledge synergies" created through integration of selected portions of research in selected areas of strategy, management control, and manufacturing control. At the same time, we realize that competitiveness and strategic fit can be discussed from other perspectives than the ones presented here. Our purpose has been to discuss two concepts which have proven to be of importance in the creation of competitive advantage and which in our opinion have not received sufficient attention: strategic congruence and integrated control. It is our hope that this book will help students, practitioners and scholars to learn more about these two important concepts, particularly their effect on competitive advantage.

References

Abernethy MA, Chua WF, Luckett PF, Selto FH. 1999. Research in Managerial Accounting: Learning from Others' Experiences. *Accounting and Finance* **39**: 1-27.

Abernethy MA, Lillis AM. 1995. The Impact of Manufacturing Flexibility on Management Control System Design. *Accounting, Organizations and Society* **20**: 241-258.

Ansoff HI. 1965. *Corporate Strategy.* McGraw-Hill: New York.

Anthony RN. 1965. *Planning and Control Systems: A Framework for Analysis.* Graduate School of Business Administration, Harvard University: Boston.

Anthony RN, Dearden J, Bedford NM. 1989. *Management Control Systems. Sixth Edition.* Irwin: Homewood.

Anthony RN, Dearden J, Govindarajan V. 1992. *Management Control Systems. Seventh Edition.* Irwin: Homewood.

Anthony RN, Govindarajan V. 1995. *Management Control Systems. Eight Edition.* Irwin: Homewood.

Anthony RN, Govindarajan V. 2004. *Management Control Systems. Eleventh Edition.* Irwin: Homewood.

Archer S, Otley D. 1991. Strategy, Structure, Planning and Control Systems and Performance Evaluation – Rumenco Ltd. *Management Accounting Research* **2**: 263-303.

Argyris C. 1977. Organizational Learning and Management Information Systems. *Accounting, Organizations and Society* **2**: 113-123.

Askenäs L. 2000. *Affärssystemet: En studie om teknikens aktiva och passiva roll i en organization*, in Swedish (The Business System: a Study on the Active and Passive Role of Technology in an Organization). Linköping Studies in Science and Technology: Linköping.

Bartezzaghi E. 1999. The Evolution of Production Models: Is a New Paradigm Emerging? *International Journal of Operations and Production Management* **19**: 229-250.

Bengtsson L, Skärvad PH. 1988. *Företagsstrategiska perspektiv*, in Swedish (Business Strategy Perspectives). Studentlitteratur: Lund.

Berglund F. 2002. *Management Control and Strategy: A Case Study of Pharmaceutical Drug Development* (Lic. Thesis). Linköping Studies in Science and Technology: Linköping.

Berliner C, Brimson JA. 1988. *Cost Management for Today's Advanced Manufacturing: The CAM-1 Conceptual Design.* Harvard Business School Press: Boston.

Bettis RA, Hitt MA. 1995. The New Competitive Landscape. *Strategic Management Journal* **16**: 7-19.

Bhimani A. 1996. *Management Accounting: European Perspectives.* Oxford University Press: Oxford.

Bhimani A, Bromwich M. 1989. Advanced Manufacturing Technology and Strategic Perspectives in Management Accounting. *European Accounting News,* **January**: 21-31.

Biggadike R. 1979. The Risky Business of Diversification. *Harvard Business Review* **57**: 103-111.

Bozarth C, McDermott C. 1998. Configurations in Manufacturing Strategy: A Review and Directions for Future Research. *Journal of Operations Management* **16**: 427-439.

Bromwich M, Bhimani A. 1994. *Management Accounting Pathways to Progress.* CIMA: London.

Bruggeman W, Van der Stede W. 1993. Fitting Management Control Systems to Competitive Advantage. *British Journal of Management* **4**: 205-218.

Burns T, Stalker GM. 1961. *The Management of Innovation.* Tavistock: London.

Campbell A, Goold M, Marcus, A. 1995. Corporate Strategy: The Quest for Parenting Advantage. *Harvard Business Review* **73**: 120-132.

Campbell-Hunt C. 2000. What Have We Learned About Generic Competitive Strategy? A Meta-analysis. *Strategic Management Journal* **21**: 127-154.

Castells M. 1996. *The Rise of the Network Society. Volume 1 in The Information Age: Economy, Society and Culture.* Blackwell Publishers: Oxford.

Chandler AD. 1962. *Strategy and Structure: Chapters in the History of the Industrial Enterprise.* MIT Press: Cambridge, MA.

Channon D. 1973. *The Strategy and Structure of British Enterprise.* MacMillan and Co: London.

Chapman CS. 1997. Reflections on a Contingent View of Accounting. *Accounting, Organizations and Society* **22**: 189-205.

Chenhall RH. 1997. Reliance on Manufacturing Performance Measures, Total Quality Management and Organizational Performance. *Management Accounting Research* **8**: 187-206.

Child J. 1972. Organizational Structure, Environment and Performance: The Role of Strategic Choice. *Sociology* **6**: 1-22.

Collins F, Holzmann O, Mendoza R. 1997. Strategy, Budgeting, and Crisis in Latin America. *Accounting, Organizations and Society* **7**: 669-689.

Cooper R. 1996. Costing Techniques to Support Corporate Strategy: Evidence from Japan. *Management Accounting Research* **7**: 219-246.

Dagens Industri. 1999. Intervju med koncernchef Lars Ramqvist, in Swedish (Interview with CEO Lars Ramqvist). *Dagens Industri,* **12 August**.

Dangayach GS, Deshmukh SG. 2001. Manufacturing Strategy: Literature Review and Some Issues. *International Journal of Operations and Production Management* **21**: 884-932.

Daniel SJ, Reitsperger WD. 1991. Linking Quality Strategy with Management Control Systems: Empirical Evidence from Japanese Industry. *Accounting, Organizations and Society* **16**: 601-618.

Davenport TH. 1998. Putting the Enterprise into the Enterprise System. *Harvard Business Review* **76**: 121-131.

Davenport TH. 2000. *Mission Critical: Realizing the Promise of Enterprise Systems.* Harvard Business School Press: Boston.

Dent JF. 1996. Global Competition: Challenges for Management Accounting and Control. *Management Accounting Research* 7: 247-269.

Dixon JR, Nanni AJ, Wollmann TE. 1990. *The New Performance Challenge – Measuring Operations for World-Class Competition*. Irwin: Homewood.

Donaldson L. 2001. *The Contingency Theory of Organizations*. Sage Publications: Thousand Oaks.

Donovan J, Tully R, Wortman B. 1998. *The Value Enterprise. Strategies for Building a Value-Based Organization*. McGraw Hill: Toronto.

Epstein M, Manzoni J-F. 1998. Implementing Corporate Strategy: From Tableaux de Bord to Balanced Scorecard. *European Management Journal* 16: 190-203.

Espeland WN, Hirsch PM. 1990. Ownership Changes, Accounting Practice and the Redefinition of the Corporation. *Accounting, Organizations and Society* 15: 77-96.

Ewing P. 1995. The Balanced Scorecard at ABB Sweden – A Management System in a 'Lean Enterprise.' Unpublished working paper.

Fiegenbaum A, Hart S, Schendel D. 1996. Strategic Reference Point Theory. *Strategic Management Journal* 17: 219-235.

Ford RC, Armandi BR, Heaton CP. 1988. *Organization Theory: An Integrative Approach*. Harper & Row: New York.

Frenckner P. 1983. *Begrepp inom ekonomistyrning – en översikt*, in Swedish (Concepts in Management Control – an Overview). Studentlitteratur: Lund.

Frenckner P. 1991. *Kommentarer till ABC-kalkylen*, in Swedish (Comments on ABC Calculation). *Ekonomi & Styrning* no 1: 4-7.

Frenckner P, Olve NG. 1992. *Produktkalkylering*, in Swedish (Product Cost Calculation), in L. Samuelson (ed). *Controllerhandboken*, in Swedish (Handbook for Controllers). Förlags AB Industrilitteratur: Stockholm.

Fry LW, Smith DA. 1987. Congruence, Contingency and Theory Building. *Academy of Management Review* 12: 117-132.

Galbraith JR, Nathanson DA. 1978. *Strategy Implementation: The Role of Structure and Process*. West Publishing Co: St Paul.

Gilbert X, Strebel P. 1988. Strategies to Outpace the Competition. *The Journal of Business Strategies* 8: 28-36.

Goold M, Campbell A. 1987a. *Strategies and Styles: The Role of the Centre in Managing Diversified Corporations*. Basil Blackwell: Oxford.

Goold M, Campbell A. 1987b. Managing Diversity: Strategy and Control in Diversified British Companies. *Long Range Planning* 20: 42-52.

Goold M, Campbell A. 1987c. Many Best Ways to Make Strategy. *Harvard Business Review* 65: 70-76.

Goold M, Campbell A. 2000. Taking Stock of Synergies: A Framework for Assessing Linkages Between Businesses. *Long Range Planning* 33: 72-96.

Goold M, Campbell A. 2002a. Do You Have a Well-Designed Organization? *Harvard Business Review* 80: 5-11.

Goold M, Campbell A. 2002b. Parenting in Complex Structures. *Long Range Planning* 35: 219-243.

Goold M, Campbell A. 2003a. Structured Networks: Towards the Well-Designed Matrix. *Long Range Planning* 36: 427-439.

Goold M, Campbell A. 2003b. Making Matrix Structures Work: Creating Clarity on Unit Roles and Responsibility. *European Management Journal* 21: 351-363.

Goold M, Campbell A, Alexander M. 1994. *Corporate-Level Strategy: Creating Value in the Multibusiness Company.* John Wiley and Sons: New York.

Goold M, Campbell A, Luchs K. 1993a. Strategies and Styles Revisited: Strategic Planning and Financial Control. *Long Range Planning* 26: 49-60.

Goold M, Campbell A, Luchs K. 1993b. Strategies and Styles Revisited: "Strategic Control" – Is It Tenable? *Long Range Planning* 26: 54-61.

Govindarajan V. 1984, Appropriateness of Accounting Data in Performance Evaluation: An Empirical Examination of Environmental Uncertainty as an Intervening Variable. *Accounting, Organizations and Society* 9: 125-135.

Govindarajan V. 1988. A Contingency Approach to Strategy Implementation at the Business Unit Level: Integrating Administrative Mechanisms with Strategy. *Academy of Management Journal* 31: 828-853.

Govindarajan V, Gupta AK. 1985. Linking Control Systems to Business Unit Strategy: Impact on Performance. *Accounting, Organizations and Society* 10: 51-66.

Granlund M, Malmi T. 2002. Moderate Impact of ERPS on Management Accounting: a Lag or Permanent Outcome? *Management Accounting Research* 13: 299-321.

Granlund M, Mouritsen J. 2003. Introduction: Problematizing the Relationship Between Management Control and Information Technology. *European Accounting Review* 21: 77-83.

Gupta AK, Govindarajan V. 1984. Business Unit Strategy, Managerial Characteristics, and Business Unit Effectiveness at Strategy Implementation. *Academy of Management Journal* 27: 25-41.

Hall WK. 1980. Survival Strategies in a Hostile Environment. *Harvard Business Review* 58: 75-85

Hall DJ, Saias MA. 1980. Strategy Follows Structure! *Strategic Management Journal* 1: 149-163.

Hambrick DC. 1983. High Profit Strategies in Mature Capital Goods Industries: A Contingency Approach. *Academy of Management Journal* 26: 687-707.

Hamel G. 2000. *Leading the Revolution.* Harvard Business School Press: Boston.

Hansson L, Skärvad PH. 1992. Ekonomistyrning i divisionaliserade företag, in Swedish (Management Control in Divisionalized Firms), in LA. Samuelson (ed). *Controllerhandboken,* in Swedish (Handbook for Controllers). Förlags AB Industrilitteratur: Stockholm.

Hayes RH, Abernathy WJ. 1980. Managing Our Way to Economic Decline, *Harvard Business Review* 58: 67-77.

Hayes RH, Wheelwright SG. 1979a. Link Manufacturing Process and Product Life Cycles. *Harvard Business Review* 57: 133-140.

Hayes RH, Wheelwright SG. 1979b. The Dynamics of Process-Product Life Cycles. *Harvard Business Review* 57: 127-136.

Hayes RH, Wheelwright SG. 1984. *Restoring Our Competitive Edge. Competing Through Manufacturing.* John Wiley & Sons: New York.

Hedberg B, Jönsson S. 1978. Designing Semi-confusing Information Systems for Organizations in Changing Environments. *Accounting, Organizations and Society* **3**: 47-64.

Henderson BD. 1970. *Perspectives on the Product Portfolio*. Boston Consulting Group: Boston.

Henderson BD. 1972. *Perspective Experience*. Boston Consulting Group: Boston.

Hill T. 1989. *Manufacturing Strategy: Text and Cases. First Edition*. Irwin: Boston.

Hill T. 1991. *Production / Operations Management: Text and Cases. Second Edition*. Prentice Hall: New York.

Hill T. 2000. *Manufacturing Strategy: Text and Cases. Third Edition*. Irwin: Boston.

Hitt MA, Hoskisson RE, Johnson RA, Moesel DD. 1996. The Market for Corporate Control and Firm Innovation. *Academy of Management Journal* **39**: 1084-1119.

Hofer CW, Schendel DE. 1978. *Strategy Formulation: Analytical Concepts*. West Publishing: St Paul.

Hopwood AG. 1972. An Empirical Study of the Role of Accounting Data in Performance Evaluation. *Journal of Accounting Research* **10**: 156-182.

Hopwood AG. 1983. On Trying to Study Accounting in the Contexts in Which It Operates. *Accounting, Organizations and Society* **8**: 287-305.

Hopwood AG. 1989. Organizational Contingencies and Accounting Configurations. In B. Fridman and L. Östman (Eds.). *Accounting Development: Some Perspectives – A Book in Honor of Sven-Erik Johansson*. Economic Research Institute: Stockholm.

Howell RA, Soucy SR. 1987. Operating Controls in the New Manufacturing Environment. *Management Accounting (USA)*, **October**: 25-31.

Hrebiniak LG, Joyce WF, Snow CC. 1989. Strategy, Structure and Performance: Past and Future Research, in C. C. Snow (Ed). *Strategy, Organization Design and Human Resource Management*. Jai Press: Greenwich, Connecticut.

Hunton, JE. 2002. Blending Information and Communication Technology with Accounting Information. *Accounting Horizons* **16**: 55-67.

Hägg I, Hedlund G. 1979. Case Studies in Accounting Research. *Accounting, Organizations and Society* **4**: 135-143.

Ittner CD, Larcker DF. 1995. Total Quality Management and the Choice of Information and Reward Systems. *Journal of Accounting Research* **33**: 1-34.

Ittner CD, Larcker DF. 1997. Quality Strategy, Strategic Control Systems and Organizational Performance. *Accounting, Organizations and Society* **22**: 293-314.

Ittner CD, Larcker DF. 2001. Assessing Empirical Research in Managerial Accounting: A Value-based Management Perspective. *Journal of Accounting and Economics* **32**: 349-410.

Jansson Å, Nilsson F, Rapp B. 2000. Environmentally Driven Mode of Business Development: A Management Control Perspective. *Scandinavian Journal of Management* **16**, 305-333.

Jazayeri M, Hopper T. 1999. Management Accounting Within World Class Manufacturing: A Case Study. *Management Accounting Research* **10**: 263-301.

Johnson G, Thomas H. 1987. The Industry Context of Strategy, Structure and Performance: The UK Brewing Industry. *Strategic Management Journal* **8**: 343-361.

Johnson HT. 1992. *Relevance Regained: From Top-Down Control to Bottom-Up Empowerment.* The Free Press: New York.

Johnson HT, Kaplan RS. 1987. *Relevance Lost: The Rise and Fall of Management Accounting Systems.* Harvard Business School Press: Boston.

Jones CS. 1983. *The Control of Acquired Companies: A Study of the Role of Management Accounting Systems.* CIMA: London.

Jönsson S, Grönlund A. 1988. Life with a Sub-contractor: New Technology and Management Accounting. *Accounting, Organizations and Society* **13**: 512-532.

Kald M, Nilsson F. 2000. Performance Measurement at Nordic Companies. *European Management Journal* **18**: 113-127.

Kald M, Nilsson F, Rapp B. 2000. On Strategy and Management Control: The Importance of Classifying the Strategy of the Business. *British Journal of Management* **11**: 197-212.

Kaplan RS. 1986. Must CIM be Justified by Faith Alone? *Harvard Business Review* **64**: 87-95.

Kaplan RS, Norton DP. 1992. The Balanced Scorecard – Measures That Drive Performance. *Harvard Business Review* **70**: 71-79.

Kaplan RS, Norton DP. 1993. Putting the Balanced Scorecard to Work. *Harvard Business Review* **71**: 134-142.

Kaplan RS, Norton DP. 1996a. Using the Balanced Scorecard as a Strategic Management System. *Harvard Business Review* **74**: 75-85.

Kaplan RS, Norton DP. 1996b. *Translating Strategy into Action: The Balanced Scorecard.* Harvard Business School Press: Boston.

Kaplan RS, Norton DP. 2001. *The Strategy-Focused Organization: How Balanced Scorecard Companies Thrive in the New Business Environment.* Harvard Business School Press: Boston.

Kaplan RS, Norton DP. 2004. *Strategy Maps: Converting Intangible Assets into Tangible Outcomes.* Harvard Business School Press: Boston.

Kato Y. 1993. Target Costing Support Systems: Lessons from Leading Japanese Companies. *Management Accounting Research* **4**: 33-47.

Ketchen DJ, Combs JG. 1997. Organizational Configurations and Performance: A Meta-Analysis. *Academy of Management Journal* **40**: p. 223-240.

Kim Y, Lee J. 1993. Manufacturing Strategy and Production Systems: An Integrated Framework. *Journal of Operations Management* **11**: 3-15.

Kotha S. 1995. Mass Customization: Implementing the Emerging Paradigm for Competitive Advantage. *Strategic Management Journal* **16**: 21-42.

Kotha S, Orne D. 1989. Generic Manufacturing Strategies: A Conceptual Synthesis. *Strategic Management Journal* **10**: 211-231.

Kotter JP, Cohen DS. 2002. *The Heart of Change.* Harvard Business School Press: Boston.

Langfield-Smith K. 1997. Management Control Systems and Strategy: A Critical Review. *Accounting, Organizations and Society* **22**: 207-232.

Lawrence PR, Lorsch JW. 1967. *Organization and Environment: Managing Differentiation and Integration.* Division of Research, Graduate School of Business Administration, Harvard University: Boston.

Learned EP, Christensen CR, Andrews KR, Guth WD. 1965. *Business Policy: Text and Cases.* Irwin: Homewood.

Lebas M, Chiapello E. 1996. The "Tableau de Bord" a French Approach to Management Information. *Paper presented at the 19th Congress of the European Accounting Association, in Bergen.*

Lee B. 1996. The Justification and Monitoring of Advanced Manufacturing Technology: An Empirical Study of 21 Installations of Flexible Manufacturing Systems. *Management Accounting Research* **7**: 95-118.

Lillis AM. 1999. A Framework for the Analysis of Interview Data from Multiple Research Sites. *Accounting and Finance* **39**: 79-105.

Lindvall J. 2001. *Verksamhetsstyrning: Från traditionell ekonomistyrning till modern verksamhetsstyrning,* in Swedish (Strategic Control: From Traditional Management Control to Modern Strategic Control). Studentlitteratur: Lund.

Luft J, Shields MD. 2003. Mapping Management Accounting: Graphics and Guidelines for Theory-Consistent Empirical Research. *Accounting, Organizations and Society* **28**: 169-249.

MacMillan IC. 1982. Seizing Competitive Initiative. *The Journal of Business Strategy,* **Spring**: 43-57.

Madsen V. 1958. *Regnskabsvaesenets problemer og opgaver i ny belysning,* in Danish (Problems and Functions of Accounting in a New Light). Köpenhamn.

McDermott CM, Greis NP, Fischer WA. 1997. The Diminishing Utility of the Product / Process Matrix. *International Journal of Production* **17**: 65-84.

McNair CJ, Lynch RL, Cross KF. 1990. Do Financial and Non-financial Performance Measures Have to Agree? *Management Accounting,* **November**: 28-36.

Merchant KA. 1985. Organizational Controls and Discretionary Program Decision Making: A Field Study. *Accounting, Organizations and Society* **10**: 67-85.

Miles RE, Snow CC. 1978. *Organizational Strategy, Structure and Process.* McGraw-Hill: New York.

Miller D. 1986. Configurations of Strategy and Structure: Towards a Synthesis. *Strategic Management Journal* **7**: 233-249.

Miller D. 1987. The Structural and Environmental Correlates of Business Strategy. *Strategic Management Journal* **8**: 55-76.

Miller D. 1988. Relating Porter's Business Strategies to Environment and Structure: Analysis and Performance Implications. *Academy of Management Journal* **31**: 280-308.

Miller D. 1992. The Generic Strategy Trap. *The Journal of Business Strategy,* **January/February**: 37-41.

Miller D. 1993. The Architecture of Simplicity. *Academy of Management Journal* **18**: 116-138.

Miller D. 1996. Configurations Revisited. *Strategic Management Journal* **17**: 505-512.

Miller D, Friesen PH. 1986. Porter's (1980) Generic Strategies and Performance: An Empirical Examination with American Data. Part 1: Testing Porter. *Organization Studies* **7**: 37-55.

Miller D, Mintzberg H. 1988. The Case for Configuration, in J. B. Quinn, H. Mintzberg, R. M. James (Eds). *The Strategy Process.* Prentice-Hall: Englewood Cliffs.

Miller D, Whitney J. 1999. Beyond Strategy: Configurations as a Pillar of Competitive Advantage. *Business Horizons* **42**: 5-17.

Miller JG, Roth AV. 1994. A Taxonomy of Manufacturing Strategies. *Management Science* **40**: 285-304.

Mills J, Platts K, Gregory M. 1995. A Framework for the Design of Manufacturing Strategy Processes: A Contingency Approach. *International Journal of Operations and Production Management* **15**: 17-49.

Mintzberg H. 1990. The Design School: Reconsidering the Basic Premises of Strategic Management. *Strategic Management Journal* **11**: 171-195.

Mintzberg H, Ahlstrand B, Lampel J. 1998. *Strategy Safari: A Guided Tour Through the Wilds of Strategic Management.* The Free Press: New York.

Minztberg H, Waters JA. 1985. Of Strategies, Deliberate and Emergent. *Strategic Management Journal* **6**: 257-272.

Morgan G. 1986. *Images of Organization.* Sage Publications: London.

Nanni AJ, Dixon JR, Vollmann TE. 1992. Integrated Performance Measurement: Management Accounting to Support the New Manufacturing Realities. *Journal of Management Accounting Research* **4**: 1-19.

Nath D, Sudharshan D. 1994. Measuring Strategy Coherence Through Patterns of Strategic Choices. *Strategic Management Journal* **15**: 43-61.

Nayyar PR. 1993. On the Measurement of Competitive Strategy: Evidence from a Large Multiproduct U.S. Firm. *Academy of Management Review* **36**: 1652-1669.

Nilsson F. 1994. *Strategi och ekonomisk styrning: En studie av Sandviks förvärv av Bahco Verktyg,* in Swedish (Strategy and Management Control: a Study of Sandvik's Acquisition of the Bahco Tool Group [lic. thesis]). Linköping Studies in Science and Technology: Linköping.

Nilsson F. 1997. *Strategi och ekonomisk styrning: En studie av hur ekonomiska styrsystem utformas och används efter företagsförvärv,* in Swedish (Strategy and Management Control: a Study of the Design and Use of Management Control Systems Following Takeover [dissertation]). Linköping Studies in Science and Technology: Linköping.

Nilsson F. 2000. Parenting Styles and Value Creation: A Management Control Approach. *Management Accounting Research* **11**: 89-112.

Nilsson F. 2002. Strategy and Management Control Systems: A Study of the Design and Use of Management Control Systems Following Takeover. *Accounting and Finance* **42**: 41-71.

Nilsson F, Kald M. 2002. Recent Advances in Performance Management: The Nordic Case. *European Management Journal* **20**: 235-245.

Nilsson F, Olve N-G. 2001. Control Systems in Multibusiness Companies: From Performance Management to Strategic Management. *European Management Journal* 19: 344-358.

Nilsson F, Rapp B. 1999. Implementing Business Unit Strategies: The Role of Management Control Systems. *Scandinavian Journal of Management* 15: 65-88.

Olhager J, Rapp B. 1985. *Effektiv MPS: Referenssystem för datorbaserad material- och produktionsstyrning*, in Swedish (Efficient MPS: Reference Systems for Computer Based Materials and Manufacturing Control). Studentlitteratur: Lund.

Olhager J. Rapp B. 1995. Operations Research Techniques in Manufacturing Planning and Control Systems. *International Transactions in Operational Research* 2: 29-43.

Olhager J, Rapp B. 1996. On the Design of Computer-Aided Manufacturing Planning and Control Systems. *Working paper no. 238*. Department of Production Economics, Linköping Institute of Technology: Linköping.

Olhager J, Rudberg M, Wikner J. 2001. Long-term Capacity Management: Linking the Perspectives from Manufacturing Strategy and Sales and Operations Planning. *International Journal of Production Economics* 69: 215-225.

Olve NG, Roy J, Wetter M. 1999. *Performance Drivers: A Practical Guide to Using the Balanced Scorecard.* John Wiley and Sons: Chichester.

Olve NG, Petri CJ, Roy J, Roy S. 2003. *Making Scorecards Actionable: Balancing Strategy and Control.* John Wiley and Sons: Chichester.

Otley DT. 1978. Budget Use and Managerial Performance. *Journal of Accounting Research* 16: 122-149.

Otley DT. 1980. The Contingency Theory of Management Accounting: Achievement and Prognosis. *Accounting, Organizations and Society* 5: 413-428.

Otley DT. 1994. Management Control in Contemporary Organizations: Towards a Wider Perspective. *Management Accounting Research* 5: 289-299.

Otley DT. 1999. Performance Management: A Framework for Management Control Systems Research. *Management Accounting Research* 10: 363-382.

Otley DT, Berry AJ. 1994. Case Study Research in Management Accounting and Control. *Management Accounting Research* 5: 45-65.

Parthasarthy R, Sethi SP. 1992. The Impact of Flexible Automation on Business Strategy and Organizational Structure. *Academy of Management Review* 17: 86-111.

Pavan R. 1972. *Strategy and Structure in Italian Enterprise* (dissertation). Harvard Business School: Boston.

Perera S, Harrison G, Poole M. 1997. Customer-focused Manufacturing Strategy and the Use of Operations-based Non-financial Performance Measures: A Research Note. *Accounting, Organizations and Society* 22: 557-572.

Perrow C. 1986. *Complex Organizations: A Critical Essay.* McGraw-Hill: New York.

Peters TJ, Waterman RH. 1982. *In Search of Excellence.* The Free Press: New York.

Pettigrew AM, Whipp R. 1991. *Managing Change for Competitive Success.* Blackwell Publishers: Oxford.

Pooley-Dyas G. 1972. *Strategy and Structure of French Enterprise* (dissertation). Harvard Business School: Boston.

Porter ME. 1980. *Competitive Strategy.* The Free Press: New York.

Porter ME. 1985. *Competitive Advantage.* The Free Press: New York.

Porter ME. 1987. From Competitive Advantage to Corporate Strategy. *Harvard Business Review* **65**: 43-59.

Porter ME. 1996. *On Competition.* Harvard Business School Press: Boston.

Prahalad CK, Hamel G. 1996. The Core Competence of the Corporation, in M. Goold and KS. Luchs (Eds). *Managing the Multi-Business Company: Strategic Issues for Diversified Groups.* Routledge: London.

Rajagopalan N. 1996. Strategic Orientations, Incentive Plan Adoptions, and Firm Performance: Evidence from Electric Utility Firms. *Strategic Management Journal* **18**: 761-785.

Rapp B, Nilsson F, Askenäs L. 2000. Creating Competitive Advantage: The Importande of Strategic Congruence and Integrated Control. *Paper presented at the 17th European Conference on Operational Research in Budapest.*

Roberts J. 1990. Strategy and Accounting in a U.K. Conglomerate. *Accounting, Organizations and Society* **15**: 107-126.

Rudberg M. 2001. Linking Competitive Priorities and Manufacturing Networks: A Manufacturing Strategy Perspective. *Working paper no. 266.* Department of Production Economics, Linköping Institute of Technology: Linköping.

Rudberg M. 2002. *Manufacturing Strategy: Linking Competitive Priorities, Decision Categories and Manufacturing Networks* (dissertation). Production-Economic Research in Linköping: Linköping.

Rumelt RP. 1974. *Strategy, Structure and Economic Performance.* Harvard University Press: Cambridge, MA.

Rumelt RP, Schendel DE, Teece DJ. 1994. Fundamental Issues in Strategy, in R. P. Rumelt et al. (Eds). *Fundamental Issues in Strategy: A Research Agenda.* Harvard Business School Press: Boston.

Selznick P. 1957. *Leadership in Administration.* Harper & Row: New York.

Shank JK, Govindarajan V. 1993. *Strategic Cost Management: The New Tool for Competitive Advantage.* The Free Press: New York.

Sillince JAA, Sykes GMH. 1995. The Role of Accountants in Improving Manufacturing Technology. *Management Accounting Research* **6**: 103-124.

Simons R. 1987. Accounting Control Systems and Business Strategy: An Empirical Analysis. *Accounting, Organizations and Society* **12**: 357-374.

Simons R. 1990. The Role of Management Control Systems in Creating Competitive Advantage: New Perspectives. *Accounting, Organizations and Society* **15**: 127-143.

Simons R. 1991. Strategic Orientation and Top Management Attention to Control Systems. *Strategic Management Journal* **12**: 49-62.

Simons R. 1994. How New Top Managers Use Control Systems as Levers of Strategic Renewal. *Strategic Management Journal* **15**: 169-189.

Simons R. 1995. *Levers of Control: How Managers Use Innovative Control Systems to Drive Strategic Renewal*. Harvard Business School Press: Boston.

Skinner W. 1969. Manufacturing: Missing Link in Corporate Strategy. *Harvard Business Review* **47**: 136-145.

Skinner W. 1974. The Focused Factory. *Harvard Business Review* **52**: 113-121.

Steers RM. 1975. Problems in the Measurement of Organizational Effectiveness. *Administrative Science Quarterly* **20**: 546-558.

Stewart GB. 1999. *The Quest for Value*. Harper Business: New York.

Stobaugh R, Telesio P. 1983. Match Manufacturing Policies and Product Strategy. *Harvard Business Review* **61**: 113-120.

Thanheiser H. 1972. *Strategy and Structure of German Firms* (dissertation). Harvard Business School: Boston.

Thompson JD. 1967. *Organizations in Action*. McGraw-Hill: New York.

Törnqvist G. 1929. *Kostnadsanalys och prissättning i detaljaffärer*, in Swedish (Cost Analysis and Pricing in Retailing Businesses). Stockholm.

Venkatraman N, Camillus JC. 1984. Exploring the Concept of "Fit" in Strategic Management. *Academy of Management Review* **9**: 513-525.

Vollmann TE, Berry WL, Whybark DC. 1992. *Manufacturing Planning and Control Systems. Third Edition*. Irwin: Chicago.

Vollmann TE, Berry WL, Whybark DC. 1997. *Manufacturing Planning and Control Systems. Fourth Edition*. Irwin: Chicago.

Voss, CA. 1995. Alternative Paradigms for Manufacturing Strategy. *International Journal of Operations & Production Management* **15**: 5-16.

Ward PT, Bickford DJ, Leong KG. 1996. Configurations of Manufacturing Strategy, Business Strategy, Environment and Structure. *Journal of Management* **22**: 597-626.

Wheelwright SC. 1981. Japan – Where Operations Really Are Strategic. *Harvard Business Review* **59**: 67-74.

Wheelwright SC. 1984. Manufacturing Strategy: Defining the Missing Link. *Strategic Management Journal* **5**: 77-91.

Womack JP, Jones DT. 1994. From Lean Production to the Lean Enterprise. *Harvard Business Review* **72**: 93-103.

Womack JP, Jones DT, Roos D. 1990. *The Machine that Changed the World*. Rawson Associates: New York.

Wrigley L. 1970. *Divisional Autonomy and Diversification* (dissertation). Harvard Business School.

Yin RK. 1989. *Case Study Research: Design and Methods*. Sage Publications: London.

Yoshikawa T, Mitchell F, Moyes J. 1994. *A Review of Japanese Management Accounting Literature and Bibliography*. CIMA: London.

Young D. 1997. Economic Value Added: A Primer for European Managers. *European Management Journal* **15**: 335-343.

Young SM, Selto FH. 1991. New Manufacturing Practices and Cost Management: A Review of the Literature and Directions for Research. *Journal of Accounting Literature* **10**: 265-298.

Zajac EJ, Kraatz MS, Bresser RKF. 2000. Modeling the Dynamics of Strategic Fit: A Normative Approach to Strategic Change. *Strategic Management Journal* **21**: 429-453.

About the Authors

FREDRIK NILSSON is a professor of Economic Information Systems, at Linköping University and Institute of Technology. He is director of RAC (Research Programme for Auditors and Consultants) which is supported by the big four auditing firms in Sweden. He is also research leader of SES (Research Programme for Strategic Enterprise Systems). Professor Nilsson has published many articles in leading international scholarly journals. His research interests lie in issues relating to strategy and control systems – including both management and production control. Other areas of interest are financial accounting, mergers and acquisitions, and environmentally driven business development. For more than ten years he was employed part-time at Deloitte, in the final years as a Senior Manager.

BIRGER RAPP is a professor and holds a chair in Economic Information Systems at the Linköping University and Institute of Technology. He is chairman of the division of Information Systems and Management, and he is on the board of the Department of Computer and Information Sciences. Professor Rapp is director of the Swedish Research School "Management and IT" (MIT), a joint research school of eight Swedish universities. He has published several books as well as articles in leading international scholarly journals in the areas of investment theory, finance and accounting, environmentally driven business development, production planning and control, management and IT, Telework, applications of principal-and-agent theory, and strategy and control systems, and he has served as an expert in various Swedish government studies. He is a member of the advisory boards of the following journals: Omega, IJMDS, ITORS, JHRCA, and BJORS. He has been vice president at large of IFORS (International Federation of Operational Research Societies) and president of Euro (Association of European Research Societies within IFORS).

Printing: Strauss GmbH, Mörlenbach
Binding: Schäffer, Grünstadt